PSYCHEYE

PSYCHEYE

SELF-ANALYTIC CONSCIOUSNESS

AKHTER AHSEN, Ph.D.

A Basic Introduction To the Natural Self-analytic Images Of Consciousness
⊙ Eidetics ⊙

BRANDON HOUSE, INC., NEW YORK, NEW YORK

Copyright © 1977 by Akhter Ahsen, Ph.D. All Rights Reserved. No part of this book may be reproduced by any process whatsoever, without prior written permission of the copyright holder, except for brief passages included in an article or a review. For information address Akhter Ahsen, Ph.D., Eidetic Analysis Institute, 22 Edgecliff Terrace, Yonkers, New York 10705.

First Printing, 1977

Published by

BRANDON HOUSE, Inc.
555 Riverdale Station
New York, New York 10471

For orders write to P.O. Box 240
Bronx, New York 10471

International Standard Book Number: 0-913412-47-3
Library of Congress Catalog Card Number: 76-45271
Manufactured in the United States of America

Preface

When I began my research on the eidetic image in the early 1950's, it was being studied only in the experimental psychology field, as a vivid, lifelike image of astounding clarity, found among the gifted and in children. As my work unfolded, the image with these characteristics was consistently revealed in all normal people as an expression of positive life, and also connected with areas of emotional conflict, especially with parents. Following this finding, extensive evidence soon emerged showing eidetics to be a system of sensuous life in the psyche which makes the sensibilities of each individual readily available to him in consciousness. This indicated the presence of a vast and self-motivated therapeutic potential in the individual's own mind.

The central need in psychotherapy has been the development of a true language of emotions which breaks through artificial barriers, a language which is deep, authentic, and everyone can understand and share. The eidetic is this pictorial language of the mind which has been, in the literature, rightly called a new means of communication more subtle than verbalization of facts and associative thinking. This pictorial language is highly effective in presenting and elucidating mental issues.

During private practice, watching individuals growing and improving has convinced me that social prejudice, and programming through technical jargon, can result in frightening people away from attending mental issues with a sense of personal achievement. In the mental health field, a non-educational attitude persists in the form of a covert "priesthood" which continues to corrode the individual's faith in his own sensibilities, and his natural capacity to attend his own mind with self-educational benefits. Can a universal communication language be developed as a self-educational system which communicates and cures through a unitary idiom? Whatever the individual cannot know and achieve for himself with a sense of inner testimony is not truly his own and, therefore, represents a state of conflict, an enemy within. By not recognizing the need for a truly self-expressive idiom, the current psychological literature has been guilty of self-love and ambiguity, causing a fundamental weakness in the art of healing. Even if the individual must be helped by a therapist, why cannot the agent of healing be merely a guide in self-education, helping the individual to arrive at a self-communication center in himself from where spontaneous emotional help would always flow to him in the future? The center of creative and renewal activity in the individual is always his own self, and no high priest of any sort should be allowed to stand between him and that light. Eidetic Therapy insists on pursuing this course to its logical limit of providing freedom to the person who decides to investigate his emotional life.

It has been known that the need for dependence can achieve such monstrous proportions in psychotherapy that it can involve the therapist and patient in a relationship of mutual parasitism, complicating the issue of mental health to the point that no one knows who is the healer and who is the one to be healed. Dependence may even be encouraged to the point that it buries the individual deeper and farther in the original illness, which was composed of dependence and confusion from the beginning. Suffocated by the ever-growing vine of attachment, the individual's selfhood is contained and finally quashed. The blasé tradition of active-passive roles of "professional" and "patient" has covertly supported this dependence, with deadly disadvantage to both. By giving up dependence in favor of a demonstrative method of eidetics, both face the mental issue from an active angle of self-education, awareness, and freedom.

As a compilation of self-educational therapy methods through eidetics, this book has been written in terminology addressed to both professional and layman, with purposely blurred lines of demarcation to generate activity and hope in the setting of psychotherapy. Such suppression of distinction between "therapist" and "patient" follows the classic implications in the Greek approach to medicine. This approach is more explicitly presented here as a logical extension of the new social process discovered in the eidetic image.

The eidetic method of mental study and change presented in this book fosters change through self-discernment and self-direction, as the individual experiences the psychological material elicited by the imagery exercises both in a personal and social context. The book comprises a comprehensive network of imagery levels to be used as the primary vehicle for mental analysis and psychotherapeutic change. This precise tool of experience and treatment gives a detailed view of what really happens in the individual's mind and his interactions with people and the society he lives in. At a deep level, this experience through eidetics can be profoundly rewarding.

Seeing an image, deciphering its various aspects, developing the information, and experiencing change—as a consequence of these processes, one gradually grows out of the tyranny of memories, the control mechanisms which destroy the natural functions of the psyche. Even if a person does not view himself as suffering from problems, an expansion of consciousness and consequent enlightenment can be viewed as a virtue in itself. As the individual becomes free from fear, independent, and fulfilled, he comes to understand the sources of his nature, the roots of violence around him, and, especially, those networks of despair and passivity which contain and destroy.

The eidetic method is particularly suited to personal analysis, or collaborative work between two individuals, who induce analytic self-education material to each other. It is also suited to treatment of people in groups, in a leaderless setting or under a trained moderator. It can also be used by families or married couples to enhance understanding of each other.

In my own practice, I have found that professional treatment through eidetics helps an individual grow much faster, and enables a therapist to see five times as many patients as previously. Paraprofessionals can be usefully employed in the method because the procedure follows the lines of accountability. Each response is written down clearly and becomes a record of therapy which the therapist can safely guide from a distance. The meaning of the clinic expands considerably beyond the proverbial "couch" or the "lab." The individual can also do work at home on his mental exercises, and use his spare time to benefit from the technique.

Currently, psychotherapists spend a lifetime treating a small number of patients, using dependence-encouraging techniques, while at the same time the mental health field faces a dirth of trained professionals to administer psychotherapy to the vast numbers of individuals who desperately need it. This mental health crisis can be resolved by using active methods which make individuals independent, self-supportive, and even supportive of others who need encouragement back into the mainstream of life. The techniques presented in this book offer vast possibilities in this direction, and point to a geometric potential of health in the future, if the techniques are used to the maximum.

I would like to thank the many friends who have shown personal interest in my work and the many reviewers around the world who have written thoughtful and evaluative presentations of my techniques. I owe thanks to the various universities for arranging demonstrations and lectures on Eidetic Therapy. I am especially thankful to Michael Balint for a warm reception at London in 1966, and to Abraham Joshua Heschel for concerned and interested advice on presentation of my views and findings, at New York in 1970. I owe special thanks to Ralph A. Luce, M.D. for a caring intellectual hospitality when I was in Philadelphia. I feel compelled to say that I am grateful to Joseph Wolpe, M.D. for serving scientific interest in arranging a comparative study between the behavioral and eidetic treatment methods at Eastern Pennsylvania Psychiatric Institute, Temple University Medical School, Philadelphia. Later Arnold A. Lazarus and I wrote about this study in *Clinical Behavior Therapy*. I also recall with pleasure many elaborate discussions with Anees A. Sheikh, Ph.D., Director of the Child Development Laboratory, Marquette University, and Editor of the *Journal of Mental Imagery*, New York. I also recall and acknowledge many pleasant memories of discussions with many other behaviorists and psychoanalysts at Princeton and New York over the years.

My mind is especially preoccupied with the memory of a restful evening at Montreal overlooking the banks of a beautiful lake, sipping tea with Wilder Penfield. While we talked about Pavlov, he held a heavily scribbled over copy of my Invited Address, *Eidetics: A Visual Psychology*, given at the 81st Annual American Psychological Association Convention in 1973. I can still see his smiling face and hear his voice ringing clearly in my mind: "Don't lose your cool, my good friend, and stick to your science." As we discussed many things and took many pictures, including of a stone painting which he had done recently—composed of a Greek letter, spinal cord and brain—he repeatedly advised me to hold back on polemical involvement, and stick to the cold facts. At that moment I wondered about what the Greek idea of science really was. I was thinking (and still am) of what science really is, whether it is merely a cold body of facts or also represents a warm initiative to capture the spirit and glow of Nature.

I acknowledge my indebtedness to all these people and institutions.

New York   Akhter Ahsen

Contents

Preface   v

Introduction: A. T. Dolan, M. D.   15

   Eidetic Theory of Mental Change, *15*   Picture Process in the Mind, *16*   Eidetics as Stored Pictures, *16*   ISM, the New Method of Recall, *17*   Fixed Attention, *18*   Study of Conflict through Eidetics, *22*   Synthesizing Character of Eidetics, *24*   Difference from Other Schools, *25*   Idein, *26*   Mental Health as Ability to Distinguish between Various Forms of Imagery, *28*   Verbal Defense against Eidetic Imagery, *31*   Idein Longevity Theory, *32*   Psychosomatics, *33*   Consciousness-Imagery Gap, *33*   The Ego, *35*   Psychical Dialectics, *36*   Relationship with Pavlovian Psychology, *37*   Creative Thinking, *38*   Modern Semantic Man and His Dilemma, *39*   The True Man, *40*

1   Psycheye   44

   Concentration, *44*   The Eidetic Image, *46*   Reality and Illusion, *47*   Inner Light Hieroglyphs (Kirlian Photography), *48*   A Movie Cartridge (Penfield), *49*   Biolatency, *51*   Hemispheric Images, *53*   Early Images, *57*   Inversion Process, *61*   Early Anger and Pity Associated with the Mother Image, *61*   Images of Depressed Mother, *62*   Quarrelling Images of Parents, *63*   Mother: Communication Image, *65*   Double-Faced Emotions Concerning Father, *67*   Father: Communication Image, *67*   Positive Father, *68*   Father in the Evening, *69*   Eidetic Parents Test: Positive Images of Father, *70*   Father: Work Image, *71*   Father: Humor Image, *73*   Father: Man-Monkey, *74*   Helping

x CONTENTS

Father in His Problem, *75* Resolution of Identifications, *78* Parents as Mental Symbols, *79* Practical Experience of Good and Evil, *80*

2 High Fidelity Self-Images   82

Concentration or Memory, *82* Present Looks into the Past, *84* Experiment 1: Alternation of Consciousness between Pleasant and Painful, *86* Experiment 2: Influence of Selected Memory Scenes on Consciousness, *86* Personality Multiples, *87* Emanation Images, *89* Experiment 3: Self-Images That Leap out from Previous Images and Break Status Quo in Consciousness, *90* Parallel Projection, *91* Experiment 4: How Consciousness Becomes Similar to What Is Present in Consciousness, *91* The Magical Behavior of Images, *92* Bipolarity, *93* Experiment 5: Bipolar Seesaw Behavior of Two Opposite Images, *93* Experiment 6: How Consciousness Oscillates between Two Opposite States, Like a Pendulum, *94* Consciousness as an Oscillating Psychofeedback Field, *95* Experiment 7: How Pleasant or Unpleasant Objects Present Around a Person Change His Consciousness, *95* Experiment 8: How One Can Change Consciousness as One Wants by Attending a Previously Selected Image, *96* Experiment 9: Image Control of Memory through Selection, a Psychofeedback Control of the Past, *96* Experiment 10: Selection of Positive Objects and Scenes Connected with Parents, *97* Eidetic Images of Parents, *98* Symptom's Parallels to Parental Problems, *99* The Age Projection Test, *100* Self-Doubt, *102* Forgetting, Repression, and Unconscious, *103* Attachment to Parents, *104* Imitation of Parents, *105* Reaction to Parents, *105* Loss, *105* Identification, *106* Neurotic Projection, *107* Deeper Interaction with Parental Images, *107* Awareness of Symptoms, *107* Experiment 11: Awareness of Symptoms through Deep Rest and Concentration, *109* Symptoms in Parents, *109* Experiment 12: Deep Concentration on the Symptom and Associated States, *110*

3 The Frozen "I"–Image: How to Defreeze It   113

The Frozen "I"–Image, *113* A Map of Investigations, *114* Therapist's Self-Analytic Model, *116* Training in Projection of Images, *116* Therapist's Treatment of Images, *117* Suggested Homework for the Patient, *117* Therapy Process Model, *118* The Symptom, *118* Relationship with Parental Symptoms, *118* Reenacting the Problematic Experience, *119* Conscious Memory

Useless, *119* Initial Confusion, *120* Feeling of Contact with Target, *120* Target Recollection, *121* Target Amplification, *122* Like a Present Experience, *123* Original Situation, *123* Original Emotion, *124* Visualizer, A Part of the Situation, *124* Both Actor and Audience, *125* Fact = Fantasy, *125* Target Education, *127* Target Mediation into History, *128* General History Analysis, *128* Consciousness-Imagery Gap, *130* Image Gap, *131* Somatic Gap, *131* Meaning Gap, *132* Maternal Ground, *133* Eidetic Parents Test Interaction with Parental Images, *134* Deep Interaction with Father, *137*

4 Orientation Exercises — 138

Individual or Personal Analysis, *139* Basic Analysis Levels, *141* List of Orientation Exercises, *141* Analysis of a Problematic Event (List of Levels), *142* Analysis of Parental Ground (List of Levels), *142* Consciousness Friends, *142* Family and Marriage Counseling, *144* Group Therapy, *145* Professional's Analytic Guide, *146* Suggestions, *148* Routine, *149*

A Preliminary Note on Orientation Exercises, *153* Step 1: The Symptom, *154* Step 2: Awareness of the Symptom, *155* Step 3: Symptoms in Mother, *156* Step 4: Symptoms in Father, *157* Step 5: Integrating Information on Mother's Symptoms, *158* Step 6: Integrating Information on Father's Symptoms, *159* Step 7: Eidetic Parents Test Images, *160* Step 8: Analysis, Concentration, and Dialogue, *161* Step 9: Negative Images, *164* Concentration, *165* Step 10: Positive Images, *166* Concentration, *167* Step 11: Negative-Positive Alternation, *168* Training in Psychical Autonomy, *169* Step 12: Mother—Positive Body, *170* Step 13: Mother—Positive Objects, *171* Step 14: Father—Positive Body, *172* Step 15: Father—Positive Objects, *173* Step 16: Nature Images, *174* Concentration on Nature, *175* Step 17: Can You See an Eidetic?, *177* Eidetic Concentration on Objects, *178*

5 Eidetic Parents Test — 181

A Preliminary Note on Eidetic Parents Test, *180* Introduction, *181*
1. Image: House, *182* 2. Image: Left-Right Position of Parents, *184* 3. Image: Parents Separated or United, *186* 4. Image: Active-Passive Parents, *188* 5. Image: Running Faster, *190* 6. Image: Pattern of Running, *192* 7. Image: Freedom of Limbs, *194* 8. Image: Brilliance of Parents' Eyes, *196* 9. Image: Object

Orientation, *198*   10. Image: Story in the Eyes, *200*   11. Image: Loudness of Parents' Voices, *202*   12. Image: Meaningfulness of Voices, *204*   13. Image: Story in the Voices, *206*   14. Image: Hearing by Parents' Ears, *208*   15. Image: Understanding by Ears, *210*   16. Image: Parents Sniffing, *212*   17. Image: Warmth of Parents' Bodies, *214*   18. Image: Body Acceptance, *216*   19. Image: Health of Skin, *218*   20. Image: Arms Giving, *220*   21. Image: Arms Receiving, *222*   22. Image: Strength of Grasp, *224*   23. Image: Swallowing Food, *226*   24. Image: Drinking Fluid, *228*   25. Image: Jaw Pressure, *230*   26. Image: Parents' Brains, *232*   27. Image: Brain Efficiency, *234*   28. Image: Parents' Heartbeats, *236*   29. Image: Parents' Intestines, *238*   30. Image: Parents' Genitals, *240*

6 Positive Group: A Group Therapy Technique Against Mass Imagery 242

Mass-Image Society, *242*   Activation of Natural Foundation, *243*   Positive Group, *246*   First Session, *246*   Positive Group: Introductory Model, *247*   Empathy Responses to Bobby's Image, *248*   Second Session, *249*   Third and Subsequent Sessions, *249*   Visualization, *249*   Duplication, *250*   Pain and Sympathy, *250*   Action and Solution, *250*   Recording of Empathy, *251*   Communication of Empathy, *251*   Empathy Dialogue, *251*   For the Sake of the Other Person, or a New Reality, *254*   The Picture, *255*   A Report, *258*   New Member, *259*   Table of Empathy Pictures, *260*

7 More on Adjustment 263

A Guide for Further Study, *264*

Bibliography 268

Index 275

They first
Heard it
With the third ear
But they mixed it
With their own voices
And interpretations
Then they
Saw it
By the third eye
And this time
They believed it

Eidetic*

The Eidetic is a psychical visual image of unusual vividness. When this image is experienced in the mind, it is "seen" clearly like a movie image. This inner "seeing" is accompanied by pressure in the visual apparatus, and a definite change in consciousness.

The eidetic image has the quality of remaining very constant, so that there is a long-term access to an important experience. The individual, being more open in this state, readily learns new emotional perspectives.

*Pronounced eye-DET-ic, the word is etymologically connected and associated with the Greek words *eidos,* meaning "form," and *idein,* meaning "to see."

Introduction

"Dr. Ahsen is an astute and creative therapist who presents the fundamentals of eidetic therapy in a very definitive and concise step-by-step manner. Ahsen describes the basic unit of eidetic therapy as the ISM, a three-segment experience through the eidetic as an image (I), as a somatic feeling involving emotional and physiological states (S), and as meaning of a given experience (M). His emphasis on the eidetic experience as linked to both emotional and physiological states is bound to bring psychosomatics clearly into the field of psychiatry and might engender fruitful research projects.

"Another of Ahsen's significant concepts is the consciousness-imagery gap (CIG). This is a valuable concept in uncovering discrepancies between a patient's perception and his conscious evaluation of it. Awareness of such discrepancies leads the patient and the therapist directly into the understanding of defenses against concepts and feelings. Repeated projection of eidetic images progressively clarifies emotional perspectives through surfacing of further experiential detail. Since the patient is more open in eidetic awareness, the therapist can transmit his knowledge to the patient in a much more definitive manner"(10).
—*American Journal of Psychiatry*

The theory and practice of mental change through eidetics is now well known and intimately connected with the name of Akhter Ahsen at the contemporary psychotherapy scene. It is a method which uses the spontaneous and multipotential eidetic images instead of words for exposure to new life-related emotions and ideas.

The first major review of Ahsen's work appeared in *Existential Psychiatry* (Fall, 1967) in the following words: "American psychiatry is indeed fortunate to have the stimulation and enrichment of Ahsen's highly original and creative presence" (14). The famous British psychoanalyst Michael Balint wrote from London, "I must say your results are so remarkable that they are somewhat difficult to accept. . . . Having published one book will not be accepted as final proof of all your claims" (8). On publication of Ahsen's next book, the *American Journal of*

Psychiatry said, "The book represents a methodological advance" (10) and *Behavior Therapy* concluded, "It is possible that what Ahsen has achieved is a new means of communication, more subtle than verbalization of facts and associative thinking" (11).

The new eidetic method, which has been termed "an exciting and ingenious way of getting at conflict areas" (12) by *Contemporary Psychology* is best describable in the evaluative language of reviewers around the world who have given the approach a careful, scholarly examination. In this introductory presentation, excerpts from these reviews have been interwoven with critical discussion to present a collage of eidetic concepts and techniques and, through this, a valid picture of Eidetic Therapy for the reader.

Existential Psychiatry was the first to point out clearly that underlying Ahsen's contribution is the fundamental question: "Do we think more in words or in pictures? Are the two of relative importance or is there always a visual image associated with the word?" (14). The journal continued, "According to Freud, 'Thinking in pictures is only a very incomplete form of becoming conscious.' His belief in the supremacy of the rational, verbal or secondary process has had a profound effect on Western psychology. Ahsen disagrees and gives primary importance to visual imagery. The moguls of television, movies and photographic technique who bombard us continuously with pictures seem to feel similarly. Ahsen's contribution may be to re-establish the importance of imagery in the thought processes of Western psychology." However, the journal warned against a possible superficial understanding of Ahsen's approach, "The reader steeped in Aristotelian thinking, whether it be analytic philosophy or some related school, may have difficulty in appreciating the subtlety of Ahsen's method"; and it traced the roots of Ahsen's work in the diverse traditions of philosophy and science, saying, "Ahsen has evolved his theory of treatment from a thorough knowledge of both Western psychology and Eastern philosophy, mythology and religion. It is in the tradition of dynamic philosophy which began in the West with Heraclitus in 500 B.C." (14).

Ahsen's method, paradoxical at the surface and enigmatic to a casual reader, is systematic, phenomenological, and dialectical, and follows the human developmental process in personal memory, fantasy, and myth from birth to adulthood. Man is considered both determined and free, determined in the vicissitudes of development but free in internal perception potential. Ahsen stresses that learning experiences and traumata, along with original potentials, are stored mechanistically by the central nervous system in the form of vivid visual pictures, namely, the eidetics. He bases his method on the capacity in the eidetics to effect ready recall through instantaneous playback of any type of experience in the psyche. The method allows the individual a command on his consciousness and enables him to manipulate mental events in such a manner that he can evoke, study, and resolve a problematic experience at will.

Ahsen searches beyond the painful and laborious methods of recall which use months and years to retrieve and revive an important event for experience. This is the crux of his contribution, and there is no limit to its potential value for the development of fast moving, effective psychotherapy techniques. He shows a wasteful expenditure of time in the pursuit of memories to be unnecessary by demonstrating how the filing system in the psyche is naturally structured to revive an experience immediately, sometimes within a few seconds of the beginning of the procedure.

Ahsen conceives of the fast filing system in the psyche as eidetic, a system composed of visual units like a library of picture cards, each unit being a replica of an original experience. Each original experience is recorded in the form of a full-blown visual picture, or an ISM: i.e., *I* (*Image* portraying a situation), *S* (*Somatic state*, representing body feelings and emotions attached to the image), and *M* (*Meaning* of the image). The visual image, the somatic state, and its meaning component represent a single unified recorded experience.

The primary triangular ISM quality of the experience never goes unrecorded. During each significant emotional encounter, whatever is important in the conscious field of the person is spontaneously preserved in detail for later reference and use and stored in the brain in such a manner that, long afterwards, it is capable of being played back. The unity of the ISM is built around the centrality of the visual image. In its final recorded form, the original ISM is led by a more condensed ISM, in which the visual image plays the central role. Here, pure visuality dominates the experience, serving as an astonishingly efficient filing system which can retrieve and enact an experience in a split second. Neither words nor pure sound serve as an equally efficient mechanism of condensation and filing, since innumerable condensed sound indicators simultaneously appearing in the brain would make too much garbled noise, generate low audibility, and cause painful distraction. Light, on the other hand, is fast and silent, and innumerable photographs, composed of light, can be efficiently condensed without confusion or loss of detail, as happens in aerial photography. When reduced to extremely small points, these distinct yet merged points of light can still be differentiated, and also serve as a background of light like a silvery screen, a ready neutral ground to a new foreground image which is brilliantly differentiated in color and detail. When a condensed small point, an implicit photograph, is selected out of this neutral silvery screen, the experience is immediately retrieved in a living, vivid form, as an eidetic. According to Ahsen, the demonstration of the existence of such condensed images that represent and belong to various levels of developmental consciousness and can be retrieved through attention and concentration, is one of the first steps toward a psychology of the mind. He explains, "When attention is applied to an eidetic area, it will produce a visual picture. The picture is usually static as well as moving. After a number of repetitions it changes, according to how it was originally recorded. It follows the originally observed or imagined events, and tends to progress toward new evolvement" (4).

In ordinary day-to-day mental experience, one starts from the static dimension of a neutral consciousness or a consciously remembered mental picture and allows the recall effect to emerge. However, Ahsen cautions that this in itself does not retrieve an authentic experience, but only a corrupted variation of it: "When a patient does not repeatedly capture the picture in its original form, he may hurriedly superimpose his imagination over it and thereby generate a false movement not contained in the original picture" (4). According to the revealed clinical evidence, "it is in the static and moving aspects of the eidetic where practical use of the phenomenon lies. Each evocation has to be captured authentically in both dimensions in order to comprehend the experience completely" (4). From his clinical and experimental work Ahsen concluded an important distinction between the memory image and the eidetic, and he theorized that corruption in memory stems from hurried recall of the original impression. An individual, during such recall, has ample opportunity to change and corrupt the impression as he wishes. Repeated activity of the original eidetic image, however, generates a spontaneous concentration process, bringing about a refreshing encounter with the original content of the experience. Demonstrating behavior of repeated and fixed attention on the eidetic picture, Ahsen reported: "Mr. Newman said: 'When I paid attention to the eidetic, the eidetic presented itself in the same way over and over again. That a picture could be so fixed in my mind was astonishing to me'" (4). When fixed attention is further aided by repeated concentration on an eidetic, the picture repeats itself mechanistically and this presents a rare opportunity to the person to evaluate an experience from all angles without losing it. Ahsen's report continued, "Mr. Newman said: 'Fixed attention, no doubt, helps me bring the image into my consciousness. However, when I concentrate, the experience becomes detailed and strong'" (4). Ahsen carried this discussion regarding false memory effects and how to avoid them into the relationship of attention and concentration with eidetics as follows:

> "The relationship of a stimulating electrode applied to the memory cortex appears to be the same as the relationship of fixed attention applied to an eidetic area; attention thus acts as an exact equivalent of the stimulating electrode. Because attention can be fleeting or fixed, it therefore always contains some element of concentration, and the duration and intensity of electrical stimulation, as a result, can be considered an equivalent of concentration. . . . It is probable that the fixed attention or concentration increases the normal voltage available at the selected point in the eidetic area, thereby causing a response to emerge. The stimulating electrode, attention, and concentration thus are equivalents in some sense. The eidetic image can always be forced upon a patient through attention and/or concentration, and the psychical experience produced in this manner stops when attention and/or concentration is withdrawn and

repeats itself when the attention and/or concentration is reapplied. In some cases, however, a powerful eidetic will appear on its own in consciousness, and, later on, even force itself upon consciousness although the patient does not want to attend it. The tendency on the part of the eidetic to appear on its own originates from the eidetic content, in which a visual cue has a specific ability to attract attention in an almost magnetic manner. This visual cue in the eidetic is another variant of the stimulating electrode, like fixed attention and concentration. When a patient attends the visual cue, the eidetic will almost 'leap' into consciousness with accompanying body feelings and meanings. As a result, some patients keep a deliberate distance from an eidetic, fearing the experience contained in it, and maintain fleeting attention instead" (4).

The special relationship with fixed attention and concentration distinguishes eidetics from imagination, hypnagogic images, daydream and dream images in an important way. According to Ahsen, the special characteristics of eidetics differentiate them from dreams in a significant way. Psychoanalytic tradition has long considered that dreams pose "enormously complex problems" in psychotherapy, being dissociated in a highly specific manner from the conscious personality. Dreams, due to their characteristics of "elusiveness" and "subtlety," contain limitations of recall and understanding and reflect upon the conscious processes in the personality in an obstructive manner. The therapeutic attempt to reach mental content through the dream process falls prey to a vicious circle in which an obstacle is raised to circumvent it and an unceasing struggle ensues to avoid what is inherent in the technique, namely, defense, censorship, and rationalization. Psychoanalysis had always hoped for a different psychological tool which would bypass the elaborate paraphernalia of defense and rationalizations associated with the dream process, one which would show how to come directly to the experience itself. Ahsen's eidetic evocation of the experience fits the description of such a tool. It clearly shows how one can deal directly with the mental processes in their gut expression.

Ahsen's eidetic approach gives us an experiential tool for psychotherapy decisively more effective than conscious learning, free association, or words. His technical formulations demonstrate a psychological tool which bypasses the elaborate network of dream mechanisms and shows how to come directly to the experience itself. A psychotherapist, when in pursuit of experience through the eidetic process, answers squarely the important question of how to evoke an original experience without evoking the defense structures at the same time. He succeeds in creating an entirely new experience.

While evaluating Ahsen's work and its significance for psychotherapy systems, the *Glasgow Journal of Psychology* took up the issue of experiential distinction afresh. "The first problem to clarify for those who are not well informed about research and development in this area, is what he [Ahsen] meant by 'eidetic.' In most instances, eidetic imagery has usually been thought of as photographic memory, that is, the ability to reproduce in detail some perception. . . . The individual reports that he 'sees' in some sort of literal way the reported experience. In a sense it is like re-examining the original sensory perception. It also differs from normal memory images, not only in its vividness but also in its reproducibility and in that the same vividness of the recalled perception does not diminish with passing time. Perhaps one of the most important points to be made is that it is the total experience which is recalled and perceived in this particular way. It is not simply a visual experience and Ahsen would want to emphasize the emotional nature which accompanies many eidetics" (15). The journal underlined the totality of the eidetic experience, and its universality: "Ahsen has also shown that the eidetic is a truly universal phenomenon; it is not restricted to people having a particular gift or talent in the perceptual area, and it is possible for each person to have experiences which can be reproduced in this eidetic way" (15). Through his enormous clinical evidence Ahsen has successfully disproved the old opinion that the eidetic disposition or experience represented a special gift and showed that nature has endowed every person with a reproducible basis of total experience in the eidetic. This total reproducibility of the original experience through the eidetic answers key questions regarding the nature of human experience and its relationship with developmental conflict.

"Perhaps one of the key factors in Ahsen's system is the idea of reproducibility," said the *Glasgow Journal of Psychology*. "For Ahsen, eidetics can be reproduced in detail, the experience in total can be reproduced or recreated. Insofar as the exact internal stimuli can be reproduced time and time again, we have a situation where internal stimulation can be manipulated in a way which is outside the realms of normal psychological techniques"(15). The eidetic perceptual system is structured to deal centrally with the reproduction and treatment of stored problematic experiences. It is fashioned to store and repeat experiences in order to readjust the relationship of conflicting elements with the normal flow and activity of consciousness in the current units of awareness. Systematic studies have revealed the technical efficacy of tripartite repetition of the I (image), S (somatic state), and M (meaning), to help stage parts of the experience for resolution. During tripartite reproduction of the experience, the ISM unity represented in the original situation is advanced to the point of new development of consciousness units. How does the eidetic maneuver really work? The Indian psychological journal, *Manas,* answered, "In the course of his empirical investigation and clinical work, Ahsen discovered that eidetics are a series of inner links with a specific visual part of the eidetic setting up a causal movement generating other eidetics. In Ahsen's language, 'when an eidetic is located and repeatedly projected, other eidetics grow from it, like a new shoot growing from a parent branch of a tree.' Through such repetitive and organized procedures the experimenter can bring out hidden materials pertaining to various stages of development and this ultimately offers insight into the subject's history as well as symbols"(25). This tendency toward spontaneous progression is maintained by an autonomous tendency in the eidetic to regenerate experience through unchanged images and push them forward toward reenactment of conflict and resolution. Reflecting on this, the journal *Manas* referred to the eidetic data from Indian Ss: "In the course of our use of the test with the Indian adult *Ss*, we have seen that the eidetic images convey to the tester vital clues to the tested subject's conflict through relatively unchanged images with somatic qualities and indications. The eidetics change only when the problems are removed and the conflicts are resolved"(25). How does this really happen?

Putting across the relationship of the unified eidetic process to symptom formation, the *Journal of Learning Disabilities* described Ahsen's position involving the ISM in the following words: "If an emotionally upsetting event is not brought to a resolution, this structure can break down. A situation comes about in which you may have stored in isolation either the image, the somatic state, or the 'meaning.' This set-up determines how symptoms are manifested, e.g., psychosomatic, phobic, obsessional, etc. Reuniting the eidetic is part of the therapeutic process"(20). Unless the underlying conflict is resolved through the reuniting thrust of the eidetic, the original positive state of the organism is not restored.

According to Ahsen, the unification of conflictual elements in the experience, and the generation of entirely new purposeful experience, are the main creative qualities of the eidetic image; and precisely these attributes differentiate the eidetic from all other psychical phenomena. The main thrust of the eidetic experience is not toward breakdown but enactment, unification, and resolution, which generate repetitive behavior in the original elements, causing them to recur again and again for the individual's consideration. This repetitive tendency toward unification Ahsen links with purposive biological behavior. He distinguishes death-oriented repetition from life-oriented repetition, the former being a symptom-based, non-resolutory fixation, the latter a repetition which progresses life. The positive, educative, and progressive nature of the eidetic process, Ahsen finally traces to the function of parents to sustain growth of the human organism by a supportive, repetitive activity. He considers that human parental images provide a basic biological support to the repetitive behavior of positive images in man because (1) they coexist with the child's protracted learning period, which is characterized by the tendency toward repetition, and (2) as teaching agents, they show a special potential for support of repetitive, demonstrative structures. Regarding the eidetic imagery of parents, Ahsen stated: "A critical finding, however, was the discovery that eidetics not only spontaneously emerge at points where conflict in the mind is present, but particularly center around the parents' images, a finding furthest removed from the Marburg school's perspectives, which put less emphasis on parents' personality and influence. The eidetic images of the parents were found to be intimately linked with developmental problems, and to appear in the mind as carriers and resolvers of conflict"(4). Ahsen concluded that for proper unified experience, one must involve a parent's image in some manner in a situation of conflict, whether or not the parent was present in the original situation.

A fundamental in Ahsen's concept of the psyche concerns the importance of the parents and the role and function of their eidetic images in the psyche. Ahsen posits a phylogenetic link between the individual's personal ego and the parental images. The purposeful biological link between the processes in the individual and the parental images is concluded from the biological fact that human parents have reared their children from the beginning of time. He considers that the encoded memory of this link is now a dynamic part of the brain function itself. Ahsen's therapeutic emphasis on parents' imagery departs radically from the current emphasis on the individual's own resources resulting from technological isolation, which undercuts parents' important role in the psyche.

Ahsen's concept of parents describes them as foundation images playing a central role as psychical instigators in the development, not only during childhood but also in later life. All pleasure or conflict originates from pleasure or conflict with or between the parents, and the individual receives only the end result of this healthy or disruptive mode of biological functioning. According to Ahsen, the parental images function at the very core of the mind stuff. Eidetic images of parents bring out this fact convincingly. The journal, *Manas*, put this in simple terms, emphasizing the clinical relevance of eidetics: "It is Ahsen's discovery that eidetics particularly appear at points underlying psychic conflicts but centre around the parents' images since parents usually form the basis of individuals' life and development in our societies. Thus, the images of the parents appearing in the eidetics in most cases offer clues to the developmental problems being linked with them and needless to mention here that such images differ in quality from ordinary images of the parents"(25).

The *Glasgow Journal of Psychology* linked together conflict, parental eidetics, and Ahsen's Eidetic Parents Test to show the therapeutic necessity for a valid experience of the developmental area which generates exposure to the biological foundation and initiates healing in the original context: "Another discovery of Ahsen's was that the eidetic images related to conflict seemed to be principally associated with the parents of the individual and therefore the method of investigation is concerned with getting the subject to reproduce eidetics of the parents in various postures and situations. We can now see the origin of the idea of an eidetic parents' test"(15). The *Pakistan Journal of Psychology* added detail about the affect laden eidetics in the above-mentioned test: "The parental images are seen in situations involving the various physical and social interactions of the patient with them in different settings. It involves the patient experimentally in the personality of each parent through pictorial representation of the internal attitudes he directs towards them or the developmental influences they extend towards him"(26). *Behavior Therapy* pointed to the realistic and symbolic significance of the test items in this direction: "For the purposes of this initial search for affect-laden eidetic imagery, Ahsen presents a hierarchy of 30 test items. Beginning with eidetic tasks that are relatively straightforward, such as the imaging of the parents' whereabouts in the patient's childhood home, they become progressively more abstruse, eliciting imagery which may be virtually surrealistic"(11).

The "item-phenomenology" of the Eidetic Parents Test was described in detail by the *Journal of Learning Disabilities* as follows: "The test consists of 30 situations which the subject is requested to image. During the first exposure, the patient is not pushed, nor is the resulting material explored. These are the situations the patients are asked to explore visually: How and where the parents appear in the house in which the patient was raised; the left-right position of the parental figures in front of the patient; whether the parents look separated or united as a couple in the mental picture; the feeling of whether the relationship between the two figures is active or passive; which parent seems to run faster; the pattern and purpose of the parents running; freedom of the parental limbs while running; comparative brilliance of the parental eyes; object orientation of the parental eyes; the feelings and 'story' told by the parental eyes; the comparative loudness of the parental voices; the meaningfulness of the voices and the story they tell; the degree of hearing by the parental ears in the picture; the degree of understanding by the parental ears when they hear the patient speaking to them; the parents sniffing the home sensing whether they like it or dislike it; the feeling of personal warmth imparted by the parental bodies; the feeling of acceptance or rejection felt in respect to the parent's skin; how healthy the skin feels. Others have to do with: the extent to which the parents extend their arms; the strength of their hand grasps; the way they swallow food; the pressure in their jaws while biting; the beating of the parents' hearts seen through imaginary windows in their chests; the appearance of the parental intestines visualized in the abdomen; and last of all, what would appear to some to be a controversial item—the temperature and appearance of the parents' genitals and their reaction to the patient's touching them"(20). The journal continued: "Ahsen gives very complete instructions on how these stimuli situations should be presented and recorded. He lists a number of defenses likely to be encountered in using the test, and suggests ways to deal with them. Ahsen explains it this way: '(The subject) should be instructed to look at the images as if he were looking at a movie, without trying to create an image or to force any movement. He should allow the image to flow of its own accord, and use words only to describe what he sees.' Ahsen does not want any imagery scene to turn into an extended fantasy. He wants piecemeal projections. Fantasies which persist over a period of time are to be stopped. He identifies the *first response*, which is the manner in which the patient initially responds. This may be defensive in nature. The *primary response* is the image that seems to dominate the ensuing proceedings, the one that appears repeatedly regardless of how the instructions for any particular situation are varied. The *secondary response* is material associated with the primary response in some superficial way. It may contain elements of routine daydreams, rationalizations, etc. It can throw light on the patient's defensive structure. The *interjected response* is verbal or fantasy creations given along with the primary material. What he calls the *underlying primary response* may be summarized as the unconscious direction in which the response is moving. For example, a neutral image may turn into an anger image. The *overt behavior* is the behavior the patient manifests while responding, for example, indifference or boredom"(20). The nature of the response itself provides the guidelines for handling the revealed experience, along with the emotions and events presented in it.

Contemporary Psychology, which described the Eidetic Parents Test in a similarly detailed manner, but with emphasis on its practical clinical implications and self-analytic orientation, said: "As an initial diagnostic instrument, it [the test] can be administered either by the therapist or a tester in its minimum essential form in about an hour. If desired, it can also be used for a comprehensive analysis or an integral part of the therapy by returning to the original images any number of times, and having them elaborated or made part of an associative chain of images that can unravel important themes. It can be used with both child and adult patients, and can also be used for self-analysis"(12). This review emphasized the "unique" nature of the Test and said, "The close relationship of test responses to the subsequent therapy should be a strong point in its favor among those who have discarded diagnostic instruments on the grounds of their irrelevance for treatment"(12).

In fact, the Eidetic Parents Test is the only test in the psychology field which can claim both diagnostic and therapeutic relevance. It can give eventful descriptions of mental life in such a vivid manner that abstruse corners of the psyche stand out quickly and sharply to the observer's eye. The experience in the present is creatively interlocked with the remote events in the past.

Early reviewers had noted the new creative thrust of Ahsen's work and its synthesizing character. For them, the orientation of his work had revealed a fuller meaning of perception; how it is registered, stored, and reproduced, and the complex yet understandable ramifications of systems in the area of conflict and resolution. These scientific ideas embodied a breakthrough in psychotherapy diametrically opposed to the currently accepted principles of psychology, which described perception as merely a one-dimensional, impotent mental event subject to conscious thought and manipulation. By revealing new vital aspects of perception in self-kinetic forms, Ahsen brought to clinical light hitherto unrecognized aspects of human development and mental functioning and moved the perception theory in the direction of a long overdue synthesis. Recent reviews throughout the world have reiterated this position. For instance, *Contemporary Psychology*, commenting on the concentric aspect of this system between various schools of psychotherapy, said, "The test is reported to link psychoanalysis and behaviorism,"(12) suggesting psychoanalysts as well as behaviorists are forced to deal with internal images as part of their therapy, and their points of view naturally converge on Ahsen's theoretical framework. The reviews pointed out the existence of imagery procedures, albeit in amorphous form, in all the current schools such as Jungian, Adlerian, Hypnotherapist, Existentialist, and others, and the urgent need to synthesize the procedures of these schools with Ahsen's work. For instance, the *Journal of Projective Techniques and Personality Assessment* said, "Suggestive of Angyal's principle of universal ambiguity is Ahsen's claim that every symptom has a bipolar character. The therapist uses imagery to get the patient to enliven and strengthen the *positive* pole, which is always the *weaker* one. The patient is taught voluntarily to shift his attention between the positive and negative eidetic aspects of these critical incidents, and to enliven the positive pole"(21). And, the *Pakistan Times Book Review* said, "Sometimes Akhter Ahsen's technique reminds one of Rosen's direct analysis. But Rosen has anchored his method in Freud's theory of personality. At other times, especially when he isolates eidetics, his method seems more akin to the behavior therapy of Andrew Salter and Wolpe's reciprocal inhibition. But these therapies are based upon Pavlov's theory of conditioned reflex. It appears that Akhter Ahsen is concerned with a new meaning of personality as a whole"(27). Arnold A. Lazarus, in his book, *Clinical Behavior Therapy* (1972), said, "While the psychoanalytic undertones reflect Ahsen's orientation, it should be understood that his *active* use of imagery departs radically from the passive and indirect stance of psychoanalytic therapy. Upon reading this chapter, one may not be aware that Ahsen is, in fact, very directive in selecting images, identifying their polarities, exploring them with the patient, and in assigning 'homework' for the patient in the form of rehearsed images and fantasies"(7). In his later book, *Multimodal Behavior Therapy* (1976), Lazarus attempted to establish a closer relationship between Ahsen's work and behavior therapy (23). Wolpe had similarly attempted this prior to Lazarus (7, 35). Earlier, the journal of the Pavlov Institute, India, *Manab Mon,* had dealt with the issue of synthesis between the schools in the words, "Dr. Ahsen has done a commendable service by contributing a lot to our present stock of knowledge in the field. . . . The two principal contending schools of psychotherapy have found a common platform in E.P.T. for resolving disputes and a common technique for a quicker and better approach to understanding the area of conflict"(24). The journal observed, "Free-association and dreams have been found to be of little use in many cases of psychoanalytic therapy, where Ahsen's method may be of great help, though the classical analysts may not feel happy over it. The accusation levelled at behaviourism for treating man as a soulless machine may be mitigated to a certain extent, if it accepts E.P.T. as a therapeutic procedure. Both the schools should remain grateful to Ahsen for his test procedure based on a more rational basis of body-mind relationship, which may bridge the gulf between the attitudes of these two schools" (24).

The distinction between the eidetic and other imagery processes appearing in various schools is of central importance in Ahsen's work, since the repeatable perceptual quality of the eidetic image is pivotal in his therapeutic procedures. Ahsen's clinical studies have brought the central core of the therapeutic process under a magnifying glass. An evaluative article on Eidetic Therapy published in

The International Journal of Social Psychiatry gave the following brief introduction on the eidetic image as it appears in Ahsen's work:

> "Ahsen's Eidetic imagery can be distinguished from other common forms of mental imagery. It is not the Jaensch type (Jaensch, 1930) of eidetic imagery which is a property of the chosen few. It is not an imagery generally associated with daydreaming. It is neither an imagery arbitrarily imposed upon the patient by the therapist. Nor is it the imagery commonly studied by those primarily interested in verbal learning. Ahsen talks about developmentally determined images that pertain to key memories and fantasies associated with basic growth and conflict situations and are arranged in a predetermined sequence. They are a composite imagery phenomenon with a visual nucleus to which are attached somatic and affective components, the whole of which is said to display certain lawful tendencies toward change. The behaviour of the Eidetics, spontaneous or manipulative, is purported by Ahsen to have specific meaningful relations to psychological processes"(28).

The specific meaning of the eidetic as it emerges in Ahsen's work centers around the meaning of an idea, as implied in his concept of the ISM. The term "ideomotor" in current psychological dictionaries means the nervous discharge connected with an idea. The term "ideomotor," however, appears in Ahsen's work in the classical sense, as originally presented in most scientific manuals around the first two decades of this century—the nervous discharge connected with an image. For instance, *A Dictionary of Scientific Terms* by Henderson and Henderson, published in 1920, defined "ideomotor" as "[Gk. *idein*, to see; L. *movere*, to move.] *Pert.* unwilled movement in response to a mental image" (17). Unfortunately, it is not widely known that in the twenties the biological scientific systems linked motor enervations on a one-to-one basis with the mental image. In fact, biological science did not restrict the relationship of *idein* merely to muscular motor activity, but recognized its relationship with other biological activations, such as vascular and glandular changes. For instance, the same dictionary next defined "ideovascular" as "[Gk. *idein*, to see; L. *vasculum*, small vessel.] *Pert.* circulatory changes induced by a mental image" and the word "ideoglandular" as "[Gk. *idein*, to see; L. *glandula*, small acorn.] *Pert.* glandular activity induced by a mental image"(17). The combination of *idein* with its related motor aspect was thus stated in a highly specific manner, and it dealt specifically with the fact of a single mental *image* generating a single *specific somatic response*.

In later decades the original clarity of the image-motor link was given up in favor of a more corrupted definition of the term "ideomotor," which now came to mean not something specific, but something fuzzy and vague. For instance, the *Dictionary of Psychology* by Howard C. Warren published in 1934 defined "ideomotor" as "the sequence of movements upon ideas" and "ideomotor activity" as "responses which follow upon thought processes, even though of a fleeting character"(33). Two decades later, *A Comprehensive Dictionary of Psychological and Psychoanalytical Terms* by English and English (1958) described "ideomotor" similarly—"characterizing a sequence in which a motor response is elicited by an idea"; and it further elaborated in the words, "The ideomotor theory held that there is an inherent tendency in each idea to result in corresponding action, and especially that the idea or thought of a movement tends to bring it about"(13). It appears that, although the word "idea" originated from the Greek *idein*, "to see," the confused connotation of idea as a thought ripple entered the definition and succeeded in corrupting the original scientific clarity. Following this lead, the general dictionaries (such as *Webster's Seventh*) have to date defined "ideomotor" as "resulting from the impingement of ideas on the system"(34). What is exactly meant by the word "idea" and what these thought ripples or "impingement" exactly mean in the strict scientific sense is left totally vague. Although *Webster's Seventh* traces the root of the word "idea" to *idein*, it refers to the related definitions as obsolete. Then it describes the new corrupted tradition concerning "idea" as, "a formulated thought or opinion," or "whatever is known or supposed regarding an object"(34). In fact, the extreme imprecision of the word "idea" as a scientific term has revealed an infinite capacity to generate confusion, as stated in *A Comprehensive Dictionary of Psychological and Psychoanalytical Terms*: "Nothing less than the complete *Oxford English Dictionary* can give any idea of the many uses of idea. Such a term has no place in science, but this one is difficult to avoid since no substitutes have been generally agreed upon"(13).

Historically, the current meaning of the word "idea" can be traced to a slow emergence in power of Locke's philosophical libertinism, which defined "idea" as "whatever is the object of understanding when a man thinks"(13). Emphasis on the value of conscious thinking processes came about through the growing Victorian odyssey of the modern political man, which transformed the primary mental roots of the ancient man into an active will process, a manifestation of man's conscious process. This position was well enunciated through the famous statement of Descartes, "Ipso ergo sum," "I think, therefore I am." In the new world it was no longer acceptable to state, "I image, therefore I am," but instead one said, "My body states do not result from my image states, but through the force of my conscious thought." As the odyssey further proceeded toward its current statement, expressed in total self-manipulation and manipulation of others, man came to be recognized through what he consciously thought and did, and was closely identified with what he posed to others as to what he was. This brought history to the ethos of man as stated by psychoanalysts and behaviorists, a faithless man beyond self-dignity. Thus, "idea" and "man" were both finally conceived in the Lockean tradition of a political view of thought, and how it could be manipulated.

Ahsen's statement of the eidetic theory in terms of the *idein*-motor structure suggests not only a return to the original proper position concerning thought, but also a building of distinctions within imagery formations on the basis of the visualization process, a return to the original endowment of man. Ahsen often makes such statements as "*idein* must be analyzed," meaning "what a person sees visually must be examined in terms of structures"(6). He uses the word *idein* in the more general sense of the existence process, which he equates with the visualization process itself.

To understand Ahsen's theory of distinctions in relationship to the *idein*-process, one needs to refer to an old perception issue investigated by philosophers and psychologists which addressed itself to the criteria for distinctions. The classical discussion maintained that various types of imagery not only resemble each other, in that they are all images, but also distinctively differ from each other, each being in some manner an independent individual phenomenon. The argument followed the line that if there were no criteria for distinctions, man would be exposed to danger in his daily life. For instance, if we imagine a person driving his car on a road, we see that he experiences and responds to various types of imagery through automatic recourse to the criteria of distinctions, and, by virtue of this, is able to drive safely to his destination. He, for instance, never mistakes an actual blinking signal for a dream image. Or if he remembers a daydream in which he was once travelling in his car on an imaginary scenic road, he does not treat that recollection as a current reality; he knows that he is travelling on a real road, which is different from the one in the daydream. Similarly, he is able to distinguish a sudden illusion on the road from a passing thought in his mind, and so forth. Due to this automatic recourse to the criteria for distinctions, he is able to act appropriately and in time. On the other hand, if a person cannot or will not resort to spontaneous use of the criteria for distinctions, he will mix various levels of imagery and treat an actual blinking caution signal for a previous memory, a dream image, or an illusion, thus causing a fatal accident.

According to Ahsen, Psychology as a discipline attempts to establish distinctions similar to those spontaneously applied by the person driving his car. However, he points out that careless research in imagery comes to treat various levels of imagery as though various forms of imagery were nonspecific effects. As various schools attempt to explain image phenomena from their own specific standpoint, they eliminate distinctions. Ahsen considers that such researchers behave like the motorist in the above analogy who shows an unfortunate confusion which, in turn, leads to insidious consequences.

Ahsen builds his theory of neurosis on the fact that in neurosis suppression of the criteria for distinctions occurs spontaneously either in a limited area or on a large scale. A person who is afraid of experiencing the imagery affects of his consciousness is not really afraid of the imagery per se, but of the distinctions within the experience to which it leads. When one sees an image clearly or acts appropriately concerning it, he observes an imagery distinction. The disturbed individual, on the other hand, resorts to suppression of these distinctions, thereby reducing the impact of the experience itself. Such a person "successfully" confuses his experience by equating one level of imagery with another and dulling the various imagery manifestations to the point where they all look alike. In this manner he removes himself to a safe distance from the truth. After he has dulled the imagery levels of the experience, he can easily replace a real memory with an imaginary event; or, he can divert affect belonging to one image manifestation to another image manifestation, and so forth. Suppression of the criteria for distinctions, i.e., diffusion, confusion, superimposition, replacement, and displacement, are the steps which this person takes when he reacts inappropriately to a threatening experience. Recovery from neurosis means facing truth, i.e., undoing all these complex attempts against the criteria for distinctions.

Ahsen considers that eidetic images, being the unitary, original, and first manifestation of the imagery phenomena, contain the beginning of the criteria for distinctions. He shows this in the nature of the eidetic image, i.e., when the eidetic is seen clearly, and repeated slowly and definitively, it spontaneously reveals the criteria for distinctions, revealing to the experiencer which parts of the experience represent what, which parts are original, where one has imposed his own imagination, and where one has diverted the affect and how. For Ahsen, absence or presence of the criteria for distinctions becomes the definition of neurosis, or the core of the health nucleus. The troubled individual must be retrained to experience his imagery states in the threatened areas in a vivid manner, so that all distinctions are recovered without ambiguity or confusion.

Thus, Eidetic Therapy works through the presented experiential structures in a spontaneous, self-analytic fashion. The technique requires the individual to explore his eidetic following the general principle of elucidating the picture aspects, the feeling aspects, and the meaning aspects. This self-initiated exposure to distinctions differs from active recall. As the experience is slowly repeated, the presenting visible structure of the eidetic becomes the moving vehicle of self-correction. The experience first coincides completely with the presented picture; then begins the course of differentiation, which leads to the growth of the original details without censor or pressure from conscious beliefs. Each separate aspect of presentation is carefully repeated and its features are evolved without interference from memory. As the core of the eidetic presentation is repeated carefully and systematically, the person is encouraged into relating to the experience without panic. This new experiential ability is made possible because of the technique of systematic presentation and the eidetic's own tendency to allow criteria for distinctions to emerge from an undifferentiated unity.

The theory that the eidetic is the undifferentiated unity of all mental levels is combined with the criteria for distinctions by Ahsen to provide us the distinctive approach he offers. Ahsen clinically established the use of this combination by showing how the disrupted mental experience starts anew from an eidetic, in which elements of the original experience lie undifferentiated. Ahsen's clinical work is supported by the neurological proof in Wilder Penfield's experiments, that in pictorial evocations elicited through application of an electrode critical images travel toward the center of consciousness without meeting any resistance or imposition from conscious thought, belief, or memory. These pictures also proved the undifferentiated unity of the initial evocation and its later tendency toward progression and diversification from a source other than the conscious process of recall.

Earlier, some doubt had been thrown on the Marburg school's theory that the eidetic is the undifferentiated unity of all mental levels, and that between the after-image, the eidetic, and the memory image, the eidetic image is more primary and both the after-image and the memory image arise out of it. Some writers had found the position unacceptable, because proof and practical use of the concept were lacking. According to G. Allport, for instance, to consider memory an ontogenetic development out of the eidetic was not to recognize memory as a function, and to confuse the memory image with the eidetic amounted to disavowal of the criteria for distinctions, for which there was neither experimental evidence nor any necessity. According to Allport, "If memory-images were nothing more than copies of impressions our mental life would be inextricable chaos of photographically accurate records. Such a state would not facilitate the organizing, fusing, abridging, and interchanging which enable the individual to vary his reaction; an image too closely bound to a specific previous situation would tend inevitably to stereotype his modes of response"(9). However, Ahsen argues, this is not true. The memory image, which feeds upon the eidetic image, as a rule performs a different function from the eidetic, which aims to preserve and elaborate the original situation in such a way as to enhance the unifying aspect of experience. The eidetic intensifies for the individual the original situation and enables him to repeat and perfect anew his adaptive responses to it according to original endowment rather than according to mere conscious memory, which brings about an inferior level of synthesis prone to many corruptions. It is in this dialectical rather than pure memory function that the use of a mutual action and the criteria for distinctions between the eidetic and memory lies.

Since the eidetics share points of resemblance and distinction with all other types of imagery and, especially, since they feed material into the memory image, eidetics can show how an original adaptive response has been developed through the memory function and thereby disclose how an error in memory can be corrected. The memory function being essentially a rehashing process, its adaptive response cannot easily restore the original synthesis, because when the original experience is examined for possible error in the adaptive response, the adaptive response again plays a part in the "discovery process," successfully corrupting the result. Finally, this process does not generate the original material, but that which has now been rehashed twice through the same corruptive memory adaptive response.

Investigations on children have long established the existence of a normal eidetic phase, said to be preceded by the unitary phase. In laboratories in many countries, the accumulation of data has pointed in the same direction, except where the studies had been rather carelessly conducted through a theoretical framework which disregarded the covert eidetic processes and treated only the manifest processes as properly eidetic. These studies have resulted in generating confusion regarding both methodology and results. It is well known that some of the covert or latent eidetic processes can be so strong when manifested through proper methods that the individual experiencing them appears visibly moved. The popular standard methods used during the experimental study of eidetics generally fail to induce eidetic imagery for obvious reasons. Unless these techniques are carefully used for the detection of "latent eidetic imagery," the results cannot be called representative. E. Gottheil, who studied 18 non-eidetic pupils, ages 12 to 17½, showed that most individuals of this age manifested behavior involving latent eidetic imagery(16). Henning reported that many individuals in whom the application of Jaensch's standard method had failed to discover any trace of eidetics, in fact, had such vivid spontaneous eidetics that they would even call out for help(22). A comprehensive study should involve manifest as well as latent eidetic phenomena, and must use proper methods and conditions. Ahsen agrees with Henning, and argues that Jaensch and his methodology, which addressed itself to the study of externally and recently induced eidetic effects, in fact, backfired and helped to underestimate the prevalence of eidetic imagery.

The eidetics not only respond differently to control and spontaneity at the manifest and latent levels, but also appear to relate to the varied cultures of nations and their educational disciplines. For instance, technological cultures and business oriented educational disciplines, which emphasize figures and abstractions, tend to isolate and suppress the eidetic ability, replacing it with an abstracted body of knowledge. This unnecessary defense against eidetic imagery is not restricted to technological orientation; it even seeps into the artistic pursuits, since many artists due to loss of flexibility relate to their art materials with overemphasis on technique and control. It is well known that at one time piano teachers considered eidetics even evil because in the form of "daydreams" they interfered in the rigid administration of the teaching discipline. They found that under the influence of the eidetic, some of their pupils invariably tended to wander off into another world.

Since the emergence of hostility and a temporary lull in eidetic research around the Second World War, the current educational disciplines have encouraged abstraction to the point that the individual no longer has any use for his natural eidetic ability. The spontaneous part of the individual lies dead. Once the individual rises again from the level of mere abstraction to the level of natural imagery process, he can learn to unlock his inborn abilities from the conflictual pockets. In the process, he can learn to trust the natural flow of his nature again. Release of the eidetic ability in this manner becomes a growing spiral of a true life which taps and resolves conflicts in a self-correcting, spontaneous fashion. Such a process involves the techniques which capture the original *idein* of the biological structures. In the general flow of the natural imagery process, the original gift is located and developed to the point where the original emotive perspective of life is made explicit. In Ahsen's method of eidetic analysis, the *idein* process appears in its full form, with clinical proof and clarity of technique.

In Ahsen's ISM concept of the *idein* one experiences not only a refreshing return to the classical view of medicine, but also a new visionary horizon concerning the nature of man. One comes to understand and appreciate the scientific conceptions involved in such terms as "ideomotor," "ideovascular," and "ideoglandular." One clearly sees how a healthful change in the individual can be brought about at the mental as well as physiological levels. Ahsen's conception that mental and somatic states can be controlled positively by original mental images which supervise the natural functions of the affected areas is a fascinating one. Following his argument, the eidetic approach can not only remove neurotic symptoms but also psychosomatic problems of the resistant type by strengthening the body functions through release of the original visual images and evocation of the natural positive motor response attached to them in their original genetic encoding. This aspect of Ahsen's contribution shows the application of his theory from mere treatment of an existent ailment to the strengthening of the genetic potential itself by releasing the original genetic link relevant to a specific organ. Ahsen states that just as there is a decay of the human body due to neurotic interference, there is also the capacity to bring about an enhanced effectivity of the organs through positive genetic images. Calling his theory of longevity the "*Idein* Longevity Theory," he argues, "If Neurosis can kill, *Idein* can generate long life, health, and pleasure" (6). He conceives of Neurosis and *Idein* as two extreme ends of the body processes, and in the middle of these two extremes lies the human body as we know it in the anatomy books. Through a clever use of *Idein* we can repair functionally destroyed organs and strengthen the weak ones through positive genetic codes. Man's ability to consciously evoke positive genetic images is a superior potential with vast horizons.

Ahsen examines man's mental imagery in the contemporary context of a verbal and abstract civilization which has developed resistant and inappropriate life styles and become trapped in conscious thought processes and abiological goals. Recognizing this, most journals had emphasized that Ahsen examines the behavior of eidetics to show what light the image can throw on the nature of Man's experience. Through his experiments he brings out the fact that the use of eidetics circumvents the patient's prevalent intellectual resistances inherent in verbal, western psychotherapies. The *American Journal of Psychiatry* said, "The technique enables patients to attack or circumvent resistances, undergo an experience deeper than conscious recall of memories concerning their parents, and develop spontaneous insights into family interactions and symbols. As consciously held views concerning the parents are corrected, perplexing sources of anxiety are explained. The meaning-building process released through eidetic visualization retrieves, reconstructs, and corrects consciousness"(10).

The *American Journal of Psychiatry* described the psychosomatic underpinnings of Ahsen's approach in the mechanistic structure of the eidetic, saying, "Ahsen describes the basic unit of eidetic therapy as the ISM, a three-segment experience through the eidetic as an image (I), as a somatic feeling involving emotional and physiological states (S), and as meaning of a given experience (M)," and predicted that "His emphasis on the eidetic experience as linked to both emotional and physiological states is bound to bring psychosomatics clearly into the field of psychiatry and might engender fruitful research projects"(10).

Ahsen's approach emphasizes the unity of mind and body. "But what does this emphasis practically mean?" asked the *Pakistan Times Book Review*. "Practically, it may mean treatment of psychosomatic disorders. It may also mean that all character disorders originate from the disruption of the primal unity of Psyche and Soma, in which the ego tends to become a mind-ego and discards the soma as a superfluous accretion of the mind. Wouldn't the eidetic for such a disorder lie way back in early infancy? Akhter Ahsen has not only discovered its importance in the aetiology of psychosomatic ailments but has also devised an approach to therapy on its basis. The technique, as I understand it, consists in making the disturbing eidetic conscious and reinforcing its agreeable aspects by bringing them again and again into consciousness"(27).

As becomes clear, Ahsen has artfully exploited the scientific structure of the eidetic by showing how it elucidates the mental issues and how this elucidation can be used to progress health. He points out the natural coexistence of two levels of information whenever an eidetic is brought into the focus of consciousness, one pertaining to the neurosis, the other to the health. The conscious thought of the individual bounces off the eidetic and measures its own conceptual distance from the presented truth. This potential in the eidetic leads to an especially advantageous position in which not only the conscious views are corrected, but completely new and nourishing information is brought to awareness from sources outside of the conscious thought processes. This biological feature in the eidetic truly is a major clinical discovery in its own right. The discovery also benefits both the patient and the therapist in creating a bridge for the transmission of appropriate information. Elucidating this feature, the *American Journal of Psychiatry* said, "Another of Ahsen's significant concepts is the consciousness-imagery gap (CIG). This is a valuable concept in uncovering discrepancies between a patient's perception and his conscious evaluation of it. Awareness of such discrepancies leads the patient and the therapist directly into the understanding of defenses against concepts and feelings. Repeated projection of eidetic images progressively clarifies emotional perspectives through surfacing of further experiential detail. Since the patient is more open in eidetic awareness, the therapist can transmit his knowledge to the patient in a much more definitive manner"(10).

Ahsen's approach takes the patient through the shortest route and presses him to begin unfolding his problems and avenues of health in the very first stages of the encounter; that is its most distinctive feature. *Existential Psychiatry* said, "The directness of the method enables conflict material to be evoked within the first few minutes of the initial interview"(14). Ahsen, however, prefers to initiate the process slowly, starting from the surface consciousness. Said the *Indian Journal of Psychiatry*: "His method is to start the exploration by getting the eidetic responses which are easily available to the patient. Ahsen then cautiously and carefully manipulates the patient into the areas of greatest resistance uncovering the repressions caused by emotions like rage, pity, death-wish, fear and many others. Once uncovered, he uses the same images for therapy"(18).

Eidetic Therapy is a fast moving, positive therapy which is self-directive in approach. The issuance of positive imagery potential depends entirely on the individual's own encounter with a self-kinetic imagery process at the level of appearances. All imagery presentations suggestive of a context are filled in by personal experience, thereby countering suggestion. *Existential Psychiatry* said: "The techniques of eidetic psychotherapy are directive. . . . Yet the method employed is phenomenological. The content of the images and the sequence is unique to each patient. There is a seeming paradox here which is best explained in terms of the dynamics of opposites. We are both determined and free, and, as long as all images are the patient's images, he remains free to reject any suggestion by the therapist"(14). In the words of *Behavior Therapy*, Ahsen "presents a technique by which the therapist can tap this vast reservoir of percepts, and, by drawing them into the patient's verbalization, permit a cognitive approach to come into play as part of the treatment procedure. The patient thus contributes a critical role by assisting in his own therapy. What Arnheim concluded about eidetics, Ahsen has independently applied in the service of therapy"(11).

Eidetic images, in fact, behave like natural sensations, not like conscious products of the mind; and they serve as material for reconstruction of emotion and thought correction. The reviews have shown a keen interest in this phenomenological potency of the eidetic, welcoming it as an ingenious way of getting at conflict areas and providing a positive and exciting source of material for therapeutic sessions. The reviews converge upon the position that eidetics provide a relief from triviality of measurement and that the eidetic process provides a deeper, demonstrable, and therapeutic insight into the personality. By demonstrating to the individual his own internal states and internal-to-internal causation, the individual is led into a state of self-generated cure. *Psychologica Belgica* gave a psychometrician's view in the words: "Although we, as psychodiagnosticians and psychometricians, are entering into someone else's territory here, we see the plausibility of this technique, above all, from the material that it can elicit, either for pre-therapy (especially when using the short application) or as therapy itself when applied in its extensive form"(30). The East German *Zeitschrift Für Psychologie* said, "Akhter Ahsen's method, which uses the liveliness and verbally unattainable emotional directness of the eidetic image as a probe for the relationship of the patient to his parents is, in fact, a very original and very promising approach. It is certainly to the merit of the author to have shown the possibility of gaining insight into the almost unreachable aspects of the relationship of the individual to his parents by means of the eidetic developmental images"(36). Confirming this, the *Swiss Archives for Neurology, Neurosurgery and Psychiatry* added, "Without doubt, the method offers possibilities for a rapid and deep investigation probe"(31). Ahsen's exceptional conception of the psyche gives the therapeutic process a transparency, determinism, freedom, and potency which is not available in any other known psychological model.

Ahsen considers the ego as basically a pleasure-seeking manipulatory complex which depends for experiences on the areas of the psyche outside of itself and comes to develop its special structures gradually in the face of known pleasures or frustrations. As the ego disengages itself from its early positive base in the psyche, it becomes fixated on negative experiences and manipulatory functions. Large portions of conscious manipulatory life, therefore, belong to these fixations and do not, in any sense, comprise the ego's true freedom. In fact, these fixations limit the ego's true biological scope. When released, the encoded early experiential basis gives the ego a sense of existence, of being in contact with life, of being a source of pleasure in itself. These early experiential potentials provide a spontaneous life base on which the ego should build itself. However, during a slow and tortuous disengagement from the foundations of life emerges a separate superstructure of artificial life, and finally the compulsive manipulatory function, the obsessive control impulse, comes to represent the individual himself. In this role of illusory manipulatory freedom the individual is chased internally by true encoded life and externally by a flow of memory-based reality. The manipulatory ego is faced with imaginary grave dangers from the early eidetic experience and is now free only in its isolationist and not its life aspects. The ego defensively develops further false perspectives, seeking transitory modes of pleasure and externalizing the more permanent basis of life which it considers painful. As a result, it builds within itself self-centered structures which reject and deny life.

A healthy choice for the ego is a choice in favor of discovery of the original relationship with the positive early potential, a recovery of the original foundation of life. If it fails in seeking this relationship, the manipulatory ego will be trampled by a self-destructive life style and die alienated from the foundations of life. The decision of an alienated, fearful, and exhausted ego to work at this point with the "rational" instead of the experiential enables it to accept the minimum help rather than the maximum, which is life itself. The ego must be provided with power in a true living form. In Ahsen's words, in the ultimate analysis, "This power is provided by the Eidetic"(1).

Ahsen calls the varied noneidetic systems of psychology basically superficial ego-psychologies, systems which examine ego functions to generate defensive reorientations in the individual. Ahsen considers that these approaches culminate in blind procedures of control. He rejects all control-oriented methods and recommends that the individual be taken directly to the life process itself, manifested in the eidetic. The mechanisms within the eidetic should be explored and harnessed to free the individual through a direct vision of life. In this attempt the dialectical potential present in the bipolarity of the eidetic structure becomes the main method of manipulation of defense structures and retrieval of life processes into the open. Ahsen recommends that the old one-dimensional and dichotomous procedures be given up in favor of a psychical dialectical confrontation between the ego and the general psychical ideation potential. He indicates that control-oriented operations repeat the negative fixations in the personality ad infinitum. He points out that the conscious personality of the individual is, at best, a partial and erroneous view of the total potential and the individual should be helped to outgrow his limited boundaries. Ahsen said, "As the individual gets an introduction to the life fountains in his past, this spontaneously changes his personality patterns. He is reorientated without persuasion, or unnecessary analysis carried out through subtle argument. He is not confused into a seemingly new life, he is directly landed into its experience"(1).

The term "dialectics" historically means the science which treats of the rules by which the mind, in its search after truth, may judge rightly and proceed correctly. Many branches and departments of learning have devoted themselves to such a systematic search, the department of logic being one of them. As such, dialectics have seen many other developments apart from logic. Ahsen appears to be interested in the application of dialectics at the mental level, namely, the consequence of bipolar interactions between the stimulations of the external world and the first principles of the psychical organism. He calls this study "Psychical Dialectics." He considers that the space-time structure of the world is a dialectical manifestation between the original endowment of the organism and the pressures of a progressively more complex historical environment. In the past, theoreticians of material dialectics have searched for various possible frameworks to interpret the organism's relationship with the external world, and their attempts to integrate these frameworks with the dialectical material system have included the two extremes of Freud and Pavlov. Ahsen shows that the gap between Freud and Pavlov is real, based on two irreconcilable theoretical frameworks and their respective orientations. He suggests that psychical dialectics are not an artificial and forced union between two essentially irreconcilable elements, but a body of experimental knowledge which shows how bipolarities function in the experience in a manner that a clearly dialectical process can be seen at work at the psychical plane. He points out that the eidetic is the only known function in the psyche which, when concentrated upon, changes the conscious processes (containing environmental condition), and, as it changes them, it changes too (progression of the eidetic), resulting in a new synthesis which is more inclusive and adaptive. Without in any way minimizing the original endowment or the value of the new environment, the eidetic brings about a more effective response to the presented environment.

The specific issues involved in Ahsen's dialectical concept of the psyche were discussed in the language of "dialectic materialism" by *Manab Mon*, the journal of the Pavlov Institute, from the specific angle of Pavlovian psychology. Since another critical review of various mental imagery techniques published in the *Journal of Perceptual and Motor Skills* evaluated Ahsen's description of association around the eidetic as "in Pavlovian rather than psychoanalytic fashion"(32), it shows that there is, in fact, nothing contradictory between Ahsen's concept of psychical dialectics as an eidetic psychical process and Pavlov's theory of the two signalling systems. Concerning whether Ahsen had successfully achieved a monistic statement of the mental process, *Manab Mon* said, "But this reviewer is of the opinion that Pavlovians will not accept that Cartesian dualism has been properly challenged by the author. They will hold that so long as the reflex nature of psychic activity is not properly understood, Cartesian dichotomy will hold its sway. The reflex theory must be taken to be a special form of expression of the dialectical materialist principle of determinism. Psychology, according to Pavlovians, is a science dealing with the nature of man, and this nature is the product of history. Human mind may be affected by infantile and childhood traumas; but to think that the effect of the trauma remains unaffected and the memory of the conflict situation remains detached and retained in a cache of the mind in the form of eidetics long after the occurrence, is to deny the Pavlovian concept of learning through development of new reflexes formed under the influence of new stimuli of the changing environment of the man passing through life"(24). Following this, the review hinted at the possible point of agreement between Pavlov and Ahsen: "In conclusion, this reviewer would like to state that all images including eidetics, according to Pavlov, belong to the first signalling system, but while developing they became inseparably connected with the second signalling system. Though it cannot be denied that images and perceptions are mostly word-oriented, yet it should be remembered that in the second signalling system the entire content of the images are not adequately reflected. It follows that the study of imagery through verbal accounts cannot be fruitful. Those sensations and conceptions, which cannot be adequately described verbally; or in other words, what the first signalling system has not been able to pass on to the second signalling system is considered unconscious by Pavlovians. All healthy mental activities and processes are results of interaction and integration of the two signalling systems. In cases of mental disorders, as well as in certain types of brain, this integration may not take place and the dialectical unity may break"(24). After pointing this out, the journal congratulated Ahsen "for this outstanding publication which is really a 'break-through' and is of a distinctive flavour" and brought the question of a subject's self-observation into the center of the discussion by quoting Pavlov's phrase about man as a "self observing animal organism"(24). Pavlov's positive attitude toward eidetics is not very widely known. For an interested reader a single quote from his work, *Conditioned Reflexes and Psychiatry*, should suffice. In this quote Pavlov clearly and without reservation recognized the synthesizing and integrating nature of the eidetic, implying that it forges together the two signalling systems by bringing a force from the first signalling system to exert upon the second signalling system, and that this corrective thrust from the eidetic heals the division generated by thought and the verbal process. He wrote: there are "two categories of people—artists and thinkers. Between them there is a marked difference. The artists . . . comprehend reality as a whole, as a continuity, a complete living reality, without any divisions, without any separations. The other group, the thinkers, pull it apart, kill it. . . . This difference is especially prominent in the so-called eidetic imagery of children. . . . Such a whole creation of reality cannot be completely attained by a thinker"(29). Pavlov further stated that in the average person the two processes are expected to be found together rather than apart.

Ahsen developed his psychical dialectic theory of the eidetic process both at the individual and societal level, explaining how eidetic ideation starts as an harmonious process of psychical differentiation and then enters into a blocked or conflictual state due to historical conflict. He calls the original differentiation process the ground process on which the history process builds its own manifestations. However, the two processes coalesce to generate the visible structures as we know them. In other words, natural endowment is followed by the conflictual state in history, which is followed in turn by still another phase of synthesis in which the original biological endowment is fulfilled in a true historical context.

Ahsen considers the eidetic a special psychical dialectic process in which endowment, conflict, and resolution appear simultaneously; and what precedes the conflict (i.e., endowment), the conflict (i.e., interlocking of endowment and environment) and what follows the conflict (i.e., resolution) appear as three intertwined segments. His time analysis of the psychological process involves a continuum of three segments—past, present, and future—in the form of a spiral. He treats the present as the moment in which the conflict pertaining to dialectics is manifested and the future as the moment in which the three segments of time are found unified. In his article, "Anna O.—Patient or Therapist?", Ahsen described how relentless control over the natural, spontaneous dialectical movement results in the birth of a man who is obsessed with the verbal process because it gives him a temporary control over the dialectics of experience. Man likes the word because through this he can manipulate, misrepresent, and twist the natural endowment to fit his preconceived models of control. The birth of this verbal man symbolizes the pinnacle of control obsession. This is the man of "ideas" and "semantics" playing brinkmanship with his own self. Explaining intervention by the eidetic, Ahsen said: "The new life made of this condensed imagery tends to superimpose itself over the mistakes of the Age, and in this superimposition the dead habit coalesces with intense, outward moving imagery"(5). He further stated: "What Pavlov said about the individual also holds true about society. There comes a period in human history when thinking assumes a negative posture and needs to be redeemed by the artistic process. It is possible that a whole era of Man can think itself into a trap, and spin without resolving anything, instead creating new problems. When an age decays and uses words as a manipulative weapon to perpetuate what has already lost relevance, the eidetic becomes the symbol of much-needed fresh experience. In this sense eidetics not only serve an important function in the psyche of the individual, they also represent a sociological mode for the progress of civilization"(5).

Since Ahsen does not treat what lies outside of the conscious ego merely as a cache of retained conflictual memories, but also as solutions spontaneously designed by the brain activity outside of the narrow ego activity, the general brain activity outside of the ego appears to be futuristic rather than a manifestation of primordial chaos. What lies outside of the ego is positive and involves an emotive interplay between various parts of the mind.

Ahsen's concept of the eidetic is dynamic and involves a complex interaction between various layers of the psyche. Experiences from many levels exert upon the ego, lifting it from a mere manipulatory function into a social nucleus. The eidetic represents a movement beyond the corrupting influence of a disintegrating life style and encourages the individual to avoid abstraction. The psyche should be treated not as a mere flux of ideas, but as a configuration which can exert a meaningful change and force the past, present, and future into a unity of purposeful development. Through the eidetic this basic movement is brought to fruition.

As we all know, the current image of psychotherapy describes it as a dealer in vague, esoteric goods, and as a rigid and narrow system which confines the mind. There is nothing known definitely and clearly, and there is a credibility gap concerning the system which plunges concepts into the patient like a cold surgical knife. The system demands complete acceptance from the individual, ranging from submission to neotechnical concepts to styles of life. There is reason for the state of growing impatience with psychotherapy, and a general distrust of its authoritarian operations which now threaten the very institution of healing itself.

In this contemporary world of confusion, misrepresentation, and conceptual assaults, everyone seems to need a clarification of the mental issues involved. In a world where even the healer appears to have been infected by the self-brain-washing, the disturbed individual is only one in the hierarchy of a long list of disturbed people who are distributing the deadly virus which causes dysfunctions of the mind. The natural and spontaneous functioning of the mind is brought to a halt to satisfy the need to induce ideas from outside. This manufactured individual is no longer real. Once disconnected from his internal spontaneous ideation, nothing seems to hold together. After having lost the natural glue, the individual then enters into a state of self-splitting ad infinitum, the well known progressive disorganization technically called schizophrenia. This process is now known to be so common that some theorists, such as R.D. Laing, have called it normal, even desirable, and have written extensively to support its manifestation in the individual as a pseudomystical way of living.

How do the weak threads of mind hang together for the unfortunate contemporary man who has been thus beguiled and misled? Fortunately, the internal basis of sanity is not totally destroyed in him, and its beginnings appear to be traceable inside of his mind in the form of spontaneous imagery of the eidetic type. This is where the issues in his mind can again be clarified by developing the experience and referring it to itself for renewed self-correction and evolvement of the healthy beginnings of consciousness.

Briefly, the essence of the renewal is the reinstatement of the mental structures in their original form. Through projection and re-experience of the eidetic images in the vital areas of human issues, consciousness is regenerated in its original form. By repeated regeneration of these experiences, the individual is led to health and vitality, a rediscovery of the original natural gift in him. This approach, by showing progress, negates the assertion that the psyche suffers from a natural fault or it is born crude and needs reeducation. The psyche, like anything else of the natural order, is born harmonious and if conceptual assaults do not mislead it, it naturally matures and blooms. The application of this new method has now been heralded by the keen reviewers across the world as revolutionary.

The approach offered through Ahsen's work should strengthen hope in those who have been discouraged by emergence of a negative emphasis in most traditional systems of mental change. The analysis approach presented here generates change by using a precision tool which identifies experiences in a clear, yet personal, manner. By providing a personal view of the mental content in the most lucid manner, this new method allows freedom of choice, self-direction, and self-change to take place in the spirit of self-testimony. The sketches of this method presented in Ahsen's three main published works (1,2,3) have now been reviewed across the world in the most favorable terms. His work is a practical and systematic presentation of a method for the individual's enlightenment. The reader, with his intuitive feel for his own reality, grasps the structures spontaneously and without effort. The reader soon settles down with relief that mental change can be a knowable process, a process which can be conveyed without unnecessary confusion of meaning or blind, relentless control.

This synthesizing direction of Ahsen's work has been welcomed by many journals around the world. The *Glasgow Journal of Psychology* called it "one of the most significant developments yet to emerge in psychotherapy since Freud's psychoanalysis"(15). *Behavior Therapy* referred to it as "a new means of communication, more subtle than verbalization of facts and associative thinking"(11). And, the *International Journal of Clinical and Experimental Hypnosis*, reviewing

Eidetic Parents Test and Analysis, enthusiastically interpreted the trend in the words: "Akhter Ahsen has written an original work which does full credit to Isadore Chien's thesis that philosophy and science can and should be amalgamated to create a systematic view of reality. For that part of the psychological reality with which he deals, Ahsen has given a theoretical framework and a methodology which is one example of how one can unite a metaphysical position with a physical system and put the Cartesian dichotomy aright. In his work he has, albeit in a small existential area, reunited body and soul and given us an approach which enables the patient to cut through the mind/body problem and deal with the essential unity which is himself as a human being"(19).

A. T. Dolan, M. D.

Chief of Psychiatry
Yonkers General Hospital
Yonkers, New York

REFERENCES

1. Ahsen, A. *Eidetic psychotherapy: A short introduction.* New York: Brandon House, 1965.
2. Ahsen, A. *Basic concepts in eidetic psychotherapy.* New York: Brandon House, 1968.
3. Ahsen, A. *Eidetic Parents Test and analysis.* New York: Brandon House, 1972.
4. Ahsen, A. Eidetics: A visual psychology. Invited Address, presented at the 81st annual convention of the American Psychological Association, Montreal, August 1973.
5. Ahsen, A. Anna O.—Patient or therapist? An eidetic view. In V. Franks and V. Burtle (Eds.), *Women in therapy,* 263. New York: Brunner/Mazel, 1974.
6. Ahsen, A. Idein: The real meaning of ideomotor. Paper presented at the Eidetic Analysis Institute, Yonkers, New York, 1975.
7. Ahsen, A. and Lazarus, A. A. Eidetics: An internal behavior approach. In A. A. Lazarus (Ed.), *Clinical behavior therapy,* 87. New York: Brunner/Mazel, 1972.
8. Ahsen, A. Letters and communications, Volume 1: 1952–1975. References and Records Library, Eidetic Analysis Institute, Yonkers, New York.
9. Allport, G. W. Eidetic imagery. *British Journal of Psychology,* 1924, *15,* 99.
10. *American Journal of Psychiatry,* Book Review, *Eidetic Parents Test and analysis,* 1975, *132,* 314.
11. *Behavior Therapy,* Book Review, *Eidetic Parents Test and analysis,* 1973, *4,* 607.
12. *Contemporary Psychology,* Book Review, *Eidetic Parents Test and analysis,* 1974, *19,* 655.
13. English, H. B. and English, A. C. *A comprehensive dictionary of psychological and psychoanalytical terms.* New York: Longmans, Green and Co., 1958.
14. *Existential Psychiatry,* Book Review, *Eidetic psychotherapy: A short introduction,* 1967, *6,* 386.
15. *Glasgow Journal of Psychology,* Book Review, *Eidetic Parents Test and analysis,* 1974, *12,* 16.
16. Gottheil, E. Über das latente Sinnengedachtnis der Jungendlichen und seine Aufdeckung. *Ztsch. f. Psychol.,* 1921, *87,* 73.
17. Henderson, I.F. and Henderson, W.D. *A dictionary of scientific terms.* Princeton: D. Van Nostrand Co., 1920. *Seventh edition* by J. H. Kenneth, 1960.
18. *Indian Journal of Psychiatry,* Book Review, *Eidetic Parents Test and analysis,* 1975, *17,* 154.
19. *International Journal of Clinical and Experimental Hypnosis,* Book Review, *Eidetic Parents Test and analysis,* 1975, *23,* 211.
20. *Journal of Learning Disabilities,* Book Review, *Eidetic Parents Test and analysis,* 1975, *8,* 65.

21. *Journal of Projective Techniques and Personality Assessment,* Book Review, *Eidetic psychotherapy: A short introduction,* 1968, *32,* 96.

22. Klüver, H. Studies on the eidetic type and on eidetic imagery. *Psychological Bulletin,* 1928, *25,* 69.

23. Lazarus, A. A. *Multimodal behavior therapy.* New York: Springer Publishing Co., 1976.

24. *Manab Mon, Human Mind* (Calcutta), Book Review, *Eidetic Parents Test and analysis,* 1975, *3,* 84.

25. *Manas, A Journal of Scientific Psychology* (Delhi), Book Review, *Eidetic Parents Test and analysis,* 1975, *22,* 67.

26. *Pakistan Journal of Psychology,* Book Review, *Eidetic Parents Test and analysis,* 1974, *7,* 61.

27. *Pakistan Times,* Book Review, *Eidetic psychotherapy: A short introduction,* April 10, 1966.

28. Panagiotou, N. and Sheikh, A. A. Eidetic psychotherapy: Introduction and evaluation. *The International Journal of Social Psychiatry,* 1974, *20,* 231.

29. Pavlov, I. P. *Conditioned reflexes and psychiatry.* Trans. and ed. by E. Horsley Gantt. New York: International Publishers Co., 1941.

30. *Psychologica Belgica,* Book Review, *Eidetic Parents Test and analysis,* 1975, *15,* 178.

31. *Schweizer Archiv für Neurologie Neurochirurgie und Psychiatrie (Swiss Archives for Neurology, Neurosurgery and Psychiatry),* Book Review, *Eidetic Parents Test and analysis,* 1976, *118,* 191.

32. Sheikh, A. A. and Panagiotou, N. Use of mental imagery in psychotherapy: A critical review. *Perceptual and Motor Skills,* 1975, *41,* 555.

33. Warren, H. C. (Ed.) *Dictionary of psychology.* Boston: Houghton Mifflin Co., 1934.

34. *Webster's seventh new collegiate dictionary.* Springfield, Mass.: G. & C. Merriam Co., 1971.

35. Wolpe, J. *The practice of behavior therapy.* New York: Pergamon Press, 1969.

36. *Zeitschrift für Psychologie,* Book Review, *Eidetic Parents Test and analysis,* 1975, *183, 128.*

1 ⋅ Psycheye

I

Plotinus said that the eye would not be able to see the sun, if in a manner it were not itself a sun. The sun is the source of light; and light signifies intelligence and activations of the psyche. The process of seeing is also a process of understanding. The circle of the iris, with the pupil at its center, feeds the fire of the psyche in man, but his third mental eye represents the penetrating vision of a unifying consciousness. It is in this mental eye that union, destruction, and regeneration take place. This light in the eye is the manifestation of action, morality, and virtue, a creative force which dialectically breaks, unites, breaks again, and then reunites for revelation of experiential content.

Most approaches to mind ignore this and center on the echoing laments of the conscious ego and its laborious processes, believing in the futile rational analyses that tear at the wound rather than heal it. The counterpoint of healing through visualization has emerged in psychological circles as the most hopeful standpoint. Careful studies continue to document proof that proper regulation of mental functions can be achieved through deep visualization or concentration techniques. The more precise technique of concentration on imagery manifestations represents a signpost halfway between God and secularism. This new approach promises scientific salvation from the tensions that split the mind and from the dread of the unknown death states spreading fast and free between true internal feelings and the conscious thought processes as we know them.

Concentration

What is concentration? It is an ideation process which is fundamentally different from forced thinking. When forced thinking is made to give up its agitated, anxious behavior and allowed to become a restful process, another mental process develops in its place, which is ideation through concentration. A relaxed mind generates its own ideas, and the distinguishing feature of such ideas is that they are invariably energizing and potent. Popularly, concentration has been considered merely a blank state of consciousness. In fact, the blank state of consciousness is only an intermediate stage between forced thinking and true ideation through concentration. The passing blank moment has no virtue of its own except emptiness, in which the person becomes completely empty of forced thought. At the next moment true ideation begins in the form of a spontaneous release of pleasurable images. Therefore, if concentration does not spontaneously burst out in the form of these deep images, in the end it cannot be considered true concentration. In this process of deep centeredness and visualization, the mind unfolds itself and thought generates on its own. As the mind ideates from its own true ground, a breakdown of negative structures occurs, and through this breakdown new, fresh interactive structures are achieved in which the original nature of mind reasserts itself. During this state one translates an original element of nature into a new, living, effective unit of thought.

In the past, popularized concentration techniques often taught concentration on a mere dot or a candle, or they taught one to look at mere nothingness and experience the great Void itself. More recently, mental concentration has been introduced through the individual's mental tracking of inner signals through instrumentation, as in biofeedback. But evidence has disclosed that the practitioners of these techniques soon return to their ordinary troubled consciousness in a predictable way. At the deeper layer of mental response, mechanistic control of thought eventually comes to face a formidable challenge from problematic images which recurrently show up and disturb the artificial peace.

If mental activities can be regulated by a mechanical device or a mere magic formula, why should we involve ourselves in laborious dissection of problematic image states? Fortunately or unfortunately, mental blueprints, like any map, are a complex web of representations deserving very careful study. Proper awareness is born of disciplined concentration on meaningful mental content; it is not born of dissipated and chaotic states of consciousness represented by control or panic.

The idea that the process of seeing in some way represents an act of understanding is central to the concentration theory, which treats the functions of the eye as a miniature brain mechanism within the larger brain. This little brain, the watching eye, organizes the activity of the larger brain. For instance, examine the German word, "Einfühlung," meaning, "to feel within," which refers to the ability in a person to know what another person is experiencing through the latter's eyes. Various theories in the clinical and experimental field, whether a role playing theory, an inference theory, or a theory searching for a clinical dialogue between a therapist and his client, all center on the interpretation of psychical behaviors through some kind of "watching." To know, in brief, means to "watch," and to "watch" means to "see." To think, therefore, really means to see in a profound sense, a state of ideation in which true thought spontaneously flows, without any force or coercion on the part of the visualizer.

Concentration as a meaningful mental activity culminating in restful mental functioning has been discussed very often in literature but has not been understood. We often look at objects through colored glasses of bias, habit, and suspicion. Familiar ideas and prejudices provide known modes of security to us in the cold expansiveness of the world. But these modes have conceptual limitations and often cannot be of much use, and in the end, they imbue our minds with feelings of negative attachment, sorrow, and excruciating pain. On the other hand, we cannot help but prostrate ourselves before these useless, frozen ideas. The rhythm of our forced thinking helplessly marches on through compulsive worship of these little gods of clay, while our deeper side yearns for the lost expression of life.

It is argued that few in the contemporary world are able to invest the time and energy required to attune themselves to their inner selves. In addition to the attitude of suspicion concerning mind and insistence on body functions, modern man shuns the silent place immune to the pressures of immediate anxiety, given as he is to machine technology. For most people, the necessity to keep functioning at the "optimum level" demanded by technological standards completely rules out the possibility of finding time for the mind. The seemingly unanswerable question arises: How can we join the historical reality represented by modern man's time-space limitations with his need for expanded consciousness? The answer lies in the use of a specific type of image which does not limit and bind the individual to a restricted ritualistic space for concentration, but elucidates and frees his mentation through its own ongoing dynamics—the eidetic image.

The Eidetic Image

The central question in psychological literature concerns the true nature of our mental being. Studies have attempted to establish whether what the mind knows is merely learned or whether the mind is creative and free in nature, and whether we think in abstract words or in living pictures. Experimentalists in mnemonics and imagery processes, such as G.H. Betts, B.R. Bugelski, A. Paivio, J.C. Yuille, and P.W. Sheehan, have progressively emphasized that mind is, in fact, more free than controlled, and dependent on imagery processes. For instance, they have recognized a central role for the imagery process and have ruled out the contending hypotheses which consider motivational factors as the basis of the effectiveness of imagery mnemonics or emphasize verbal processes. Experiments have shown that measures of verbal meaning are, in fact, clearly weaker and inconsistent in their effects than concrete imagery processes.

The eidetic, which is most representative of these unique and central attributes of imagery, is proverbially noted for its perceptual qualities, persistence, and clarity of detail. It provides optimum concreteness to the visualizer because it can be evoked and experienced over and over again in a vivid manner and can be scanned. Clearly differentiated from all other imagery processes of mind, such as memory, dream, daydream, guided fantasy image, free association image, or imagination, eidetic images affirm the most central qualities of imagery. According to T.A. Ribot, R. Arnheim, A. Richardson, L.W. Doob, J. Kamiya, and others, eidetic images reveal a level of psychological life more concrete than what can be conceptualized in words. These mobile pictures represent photographic records of objects, interactions, and impressions of the external environment and mirror our participation in them in a living manner. When concentrated upon, these activated points of light in consciousness magnify the mind material and scan its various layers like a radar beam. They register, elaborate, and decipher our experiences so that we can relive our past in the wholeness of the deeper mind. The fact that these images draw percepts into the stream of verbalization provides an interesting clue to their therapeutic function. Eidetic images at the internal plane behave like the projections of stimuli and serve as new material *for* thought.

Reality and Illusion

The nature of mental content has been a study of some magnitude—imageless thought, imagistic thought, types and varieties of imagery, reasoning processes, etc. We also talk about conscious and unconscious, and about dream analysis, free association, hypnosis, archetypal analysis, conditioning, encounter, "consciousness raising," "psychedelic," etc. As opposed to the Western, the Eastern sources treat the consciousness elements essentially at the functional level as: stable or unstable; clear or obscure; and centered on a single point or completely chaotic. Through the process of concentration the individual seeks to destroy the latter units of the three paired manifestations. The related techniques categorize the subject matter into three distinct groups: errors and illusions, which includes dreams, hallucinations, misconceptions, confusions, and the like; the normal flux of psychological experience, including everything felt, perceived, or thought of; and the unification of experience brought on by the specific technique of mental concentration. The basic mental tool explicitly consists in the unity of concentration, which dwells on mental content and attempts to absorb it. It is well documented that through such a procedure one achieves suppression of agitated thought processes and arrives at the calm flow of the mind. The mind passes beyond error, confusion, and anxietyful change of forms into its own original endowment and condition. We who have recognized the need for such a definitive method have, however, abandoned understanding the psychic structures in favor of the pseudo-mystical aberrations. The eidetic is an instrument which combines the best of Eastern and Western traditions. It deals with conflict through a technique that illuminates the psyche.

There has been a lot of debate about what it means to "see," when it deals with something at the inner plane of the mind. Does it mean that a person experiencing such a "sight" actually witnesses a "vision," or that he "sees" an object that is psychically there, but cannot really be touched? Linguistically, to perceive means "to gain knowledge through one of the senses such as by seeing or hearing," or "to apprehend with the mind's eye." This common definition is not much different from the old *Upanishad* definition of the eye in *Brhad-āranyaka Upanishad* (S. Radhakrishnan's translation): "The seven imperishable ones stand near him (to serve). Thus, there are these red streaks in the eye and by them Rudra is united with him. Then there is the water in the eye, by it Parjanya (is united with him). There is the pupil of the eye, by it Aditya (the sun is united with him). By the black (of the eye), fire (is united with him), by the white (of the eye), Indra (is united with him), by the lower eyelash earth is united with him, by the upper eyelash the heaven (is united with him). He who knows this, his food does not diminish" (p. 191). The thinking that directly proceeds from the act of seeing in such a profound manner is probably the most true thought. It obviates agitated, confused reasoning processes and brings about true awareness. By releasing the original perceptions through the visualization process, one suddenly comes to know that what he was thinking at the conscious level was mere confusion.

Perception through such an *eidetic experience* cuts through the layers of confusion and arrives at a single point of consciousness through which it releases the experience afresh. At that point, one has an experience which is neither error nor illusion, nor is it a mere sum total of memory experience; one instead reaches that pure awareness state which relates to the fundamentals of mind. In a perfectly dark room a mirror cannot reflect the man who stands before it, but when a light is brought in, the mirror immediately reflects the man. In the mind, the light which illuminates consciousness is the eidetic image.

Inner Light Hieroglyphs

Light performs for human beings in a way no other phenomenon does. It spontaneously achieves clarity of consciousness, remanifests the total experience, and creates a feelingful reliving of it. Light in this sense is not only a physical but symbolic entity in our minds. "In living things, we see the signals of the inner state of the organism reflected in the brightness, dimness and color of the flares," said Semyon and Valentina Kirlian, referring to the phenomenon of Kirlian photography. "The inner life activities of the human beings are written in these 'light' hieroglyphs" (*The Sciences,* January/February, 1974).

The widely known Kirlian process startled the scientific community by producing a "phantom" or "ghost" image of the absent part of a leaf on film. Under the red glow of a darkroom light, a partly severed fresh leaf was placed on a 4" × 5" piece of black and white film set in a film-holder. On top of this a glass weight was placed for uniform pressure. A small, disc-shaped metal electrode was then put on the glass weight and a timing device activated for a 0.05-second exposure. At this point, through a cable, the film-holder, the film, the leaf, the glass, and the electrode flowed a pulsed, high-frequency field from the power source. The result was a bright electrical discharge from the main body of the leaf. It produced an aura which comprised an image of the entire leaf, cut portion included. The photograph successfully produced the image of the missing part of the leaf.

Just as the only physical evidence of the missing leaf is the implicit or latent electrical pattern reproducible on the film arrangement designed to respond to its cues, the implicit or latent eidetic cues in the mental space are the only reminders of what we have experienced in our lives but may have forgotten. Rephrasing the Kirlians' statement, the eidetic represents the complete, though latent, life activity and involvement of the organism at a specific moment preserved in an inner light hieroglyph. When our eye photographs an experience, our mind retains it for a while as a total unity without mutilation—an image, a body state, and a meaning attached to the experience. For instance, if you visualize an event selected from yesterday, it will be composed of all three features, for it is recent and fresh, but, as time passes, gradually the somatic and meaning responses are dropped, and the event is mutilated by conscious memory. However, in spite of these suppressions and mutilations, the experience is still present in the mind in the original form. As in Kirlian photography, the event which has been filed in the mind can be reproduced again in totality through the eidetic. The key is fixed attention, or concentration, which adds the desired electrical potential to the original pattern, making it accessible. When attention is fixed on the inner image event (the available severed leaf), the "ghost" image of the severed part appears, giving original details of the experience, image, body response, and meaning. This entity, now visible and experientiable in consciousness, is the whole experience, the record of which includes all those things present in the focus or periphery of our attention at the time the experience actually occurred.

A Movie Cartridge

In the neurological laboratory, Wilder Penfield, the neurosurgeon from Montreal, discovered a similar phenomenon, what he called a tape recorder in the brain. Through thousands of experiments with patients, he found that human experience does not integrate by conditioned reflex or by words, but by the image process, which shows striking characteristics of original retention. During gentle electrical stimulation on a point in the interpretive cortex, the patients, who were under local anesthesia and thus conscious at all times, reported pictures which progressed in time and unfolded more details with repeated application of the electrode. Stages in continuous progression were demonstrated by Penfield in the case of S.B.:

"Stimulation at point 19 in the first convolution of the right temporal lobe caused him to say: 'There was a piano there and someone playing. I could hear the song, you know.' When the point was stimulated again without warning, he said: 'Someone speaking to another, and he mentioned a name, but I could not understand it. . . . It was just like a dream.' The point was stimulated a third time, also without warning. He then observed spontaneously, 'Yes, 'Oh Marie, Oh Marie!'—Someone is singing it.' When the point was stimulated a fourth time, he heard the same song and explained that it was the theme song of a certain radio program" (Penfield, *Memory Mechanisms*).

These pictures, which progressed during repeated stimulation, also contained other participating sense impressions, such as feelings and thoughts. Patients reported that they were not merely remembering but actually reliving the event of the past as a current experience, while as observers, they were also simultaneously aware of the present. They termed these experiences "flashbacks," likening them to the motion picture technique of presenting again a scene from the earlier history of a character in the play. The experiments revealed that the flashbacks were completely experiential, included original events and the patient's interpretation of them, and during experience of them, the patient felt the attendant emotions and understood the meaning of the experience.

Penfield referred to these imagery evocations as "experiential responses" or "strips of time." He argued that without conscious knowledge or effort such strips are being recorded constantly by our eye, taking close up and distant shots and focusing on the most pertinent experiential features of an event while cueing in important emotional and intellectual responses. These high fidelity single image frames, as in a cinematographic film, catch every nuance in split-second miniatures and preserve them for later recall. When released again in consciousness, these frames reenact the whole experience to the most minute detail for the consideration of the individual.

A life experience, when remembered through the more "economical" voluntary recall, no longer represents authentic experience since the process of conscious recollection is completely different from the experiential one. Conscious recollection involves conscious, forced, selective, and corrupted remembering rather than total experiential recall. The eidetic, as shown in Penfield's experiment, catches the total experience in all its original authenticity. Contrary to William James' famous statement that "Consciousness is never quite the same in successive moments of time. It is a stream forever flowing, forever changing," and Heraclitus' comment, "We never descend twice into the same stream," through the eidetic we can experience the same moment all over again and can do so repeatedly. The stream of experience does leave a remarkable and repeatable record in the living cells of the brain.

The brain has been called the most complex machine, and some have asserted that, indeed, there are "ghosts" in this machine, referring to the abstruse phenomena of images, feelings, and ideas. The brain is both a subjective experiencer and an objective perceiver of "reality." This orthodox definition of the brain functions can no longer be upheld in the face of increasing psychological and neurological evidence. The overlap between imagination and reality cannot be rationally delineated by an observer and his external standards, but by the experiencer himself, and only through his internal witness. In the contemporary world of machines and external control, the manipulative word is utilized as the "diagnostic key" to reveal the "problems" of the individual. Herein lies an inherent defect, for what really bothers a person is not even known to the observer, or it may be only "hypothetically" connected to what the observer believes to be the problem. The ordinary frames of reference and their related question-answer methods will not arrive at the fact of experience. Only in psychology and psychiatry do we rely on preconceived notions and conclusions as to what is bothering the individual; in other medical disciplines, we go directly to factual information for verification. The new facts in psycho-neurology issue a clear warning to psychology and psychiatry about preconceived frames of reference and authoritarian control of the individual's mental processes. The seekers after truth of the mind must honor the pristine qualities of the experiential response itself.

Biolatency

This takes us to a further simplified concept of the mental process which we call "bio-latency," i.e., the encoded descriptions of positive life impressions in the organism gifted through genetic endowment. The organism appears to preserve a strong encoded picture of the life process in the brain cells, so that, when a life activity has been traumatically mutilated, its original is still available whole and complete in the encoded cell in the form of an arrested picture. This picture can be rejuvenated. The successful photography by the Kirlians of the ghost image implicitly contains the concept of biolatency.

When we apply the lesson of the Kirlian experiment to the mental process, we can say that while dealing with a memory, we might get a premanufactured notion or even a reaction notion at the ordinary level, but if we search deeply, we can sidestep the whole conspiratorial brain, the volitional side of consciousness, and hit right at the core of what the mutilated experience is setting off in the person, namely, the ghost image of truth. In dealing with this process, one is dealing with the life process at the latent level. The core of the finding is that in the nucleus of the latent experience, one finds the exact biosituation and the reassertion of life which had been suppressed. Even if that individual had recalled that experience through memory, he would have slanted it.

During the eidetic experience the person or his mind "thinks" at the biolatent level. The experience generates the ghost image of truth. When Kirlian photography evoked the missing image, the original patterns belonging to the absent image were recreated again, an event that would not have happened with the ordinary crude photography; similarly, in psychology the person can bypass the usual rationalizations and verbalizations and go right into the "gut" structure of the experience. The eidetic brings out not only the details of a specific experience, but a whole assertion of the life process itself. This is manyfold better than volitional thinking, which is circular; the eidetic process is fundamental, precise, and progressive.

The instrument of volitional thinking is words, but the instrument of the life process is the eidetic, which appears in consciousness to educate and transform the individual. The biolatency of the eidetic process changes the very thought processes of the individual. The ego in its best ordinary states is able to have only fleeting moments of life intermixed with inevitable feelings of limitation. However, when the ego opens itself to the nonconscious biolatency process to what lies beyond its limiting horizon, it experiences a luminous opening. Parts of the mind outside of the ego enter the ego and break its limitations and containment, initiating a nourishing orientation to life.

This concept of biolatency should be differentiated from the Freudian unconscious and Jung's archetype. In terms of the Kirlian finding that an electrical presence of the missing part is projected by the available part of the leaf, the eidetic projection is a reproduction of the positive latent biological potential. The Freudian unconscious does not deal with a positive latent biological potential projected by an arrested life condition in the form of a clear image. The Freudian unconscious does not contain detailed biostructures, and recovery of the presumed negative structures is effected through examination of the censoring process and the use of free association. Yet, in the development of the biolatent image along the lines of the Kirlian approach, it is not censoring and free association but enactment, repetition, and concentration which generate the undeveloped ghost image. Next, following the Kirlian approach, the imagery phenomena is not outside of known consciousness, like Mars is outside of the Earth's sphere; it is the process of traumatized life searching for its own missing part with which it wants to unite. The Jungian archetype, on the other hand, is concerned with an image nucleus external to the nucleus which is searching for it; it is not concerned with the ego state dealing with a mutilated part of life which was once a continuous part of it and evolving its missing ghost image through a nucleus which resides in it. The biolatent process deals with an interaction in which the life process was arrested and from where it can be re-initiated.

What happens at the level of plant life happens in the human brain too. This function in the biological world, captured by Kirlian photography, was not known before or at least not captured in such a convincing fashion. The discovery proved that there were actual electrical discharges in the empty space which were associated with the leaf space, one discharge being an existent pattern and the other a projection. The relationship between the existent and the projective was harmonious and derived from the genetic memory within the part of the leaf which was still present. This part biolatently knew the part which was now absent. The knowledge was not hypothetical but real in the form of a projection into the empty space of a real electrical pattern which could be photographed.

The Kirlian experiment showed us that even plant life is "cue-loaded," "prophetic," and "imaginative," that in some way it knows what is absent and if nature had been allowed its own course, it should have been there. We who believe in the restricted consciousness of the individual do not see that the image experience can, in fact, speak for itself and can "imagine" and "see" what is missing. The image can project a complete vision of reality for the individual to see and profit by. Such a concept of the experiential vision has vast potential for psychotherapy techniques.

There is a vast world of experience within us not governed by words or even recognized by them, a world of memory traces or eidetics encoded apart from speech. Recent experiments on the brain have shown that the stored experiences can be divided into two halves: the abstract thought originates primarily from the left, the analytic hemisphere, and the images originate from our right, artistic side. The abstract obviously depends for its facts on the concrete world of images; language and thought are ultimately based on prior concrete experience.

Recent interest in the different worlds of abstract and concrete in the two hemispheres has centered around the work of Roger Sperry, Philip Vogel, Joseph Bogen, Michael Gazzaniga, and others. In 1961, Vogel and Bogen cut through the corpus callosum of a 48-year-old veteran whose head had been hit by bomb fragments during World War II. After the operation, W.J.'s personality appeared unchanged, and he seemed perfectly normal. However, when Michael Gazzaniga, with Bogen and Sperry, later performed a number of tests on W.J., many interesting facts came to light. W.J. could carry out verbal commands, but only with the right side of his body. The right hemisphere, which controls the left side of the body, apparently did not understand language. Blindfolded, W.J. could not tell what part of his body was being touched when it was touched on the left side. It appeared that W.J.'s left hand did things the right hand did not like: while pulling his pants down with one hand, he would pull them up with the other; when threatening his wife with the left hand, his right hand tried to come to her aid. Only the left half-brain could speak, and with the right forever mute, it was as if the right hemisphere was blind, unable to do any tasks requiring judgment or interpretation based on language. But one day W.J., pencil in left hand, was shown the outline of a Greek cross, which he quickly copied, drawing the entire figure with one continuous line. The right hand, however, could not do it, made disconnected lines, and was unable to finish the pattern.

Later, Gazzaniga carried out a landmark experiment on two patients who were being examined for brain tumors and were about to undergo angiograms, X-rays of the blood vessels of the brain made visible with a special dye. While a needle was in place in their left carotid artery in the neck, to prepare them for the injection of dye, small doses of Amytal were injected into their left hemisphere to anesthetize it. This put it briefly to sleep. Twenty seconds after the drug went in, the right hand of the patients sank down. Gazzaniga described the events as they happened: "he's completely paralyzed on the right side, though the other side of his brain remains awake, for a minute and a half. This is our testing time. We put an object, say a cigarette, in his left hand. He feels it. His right hemisphere, which controls that hand, is wide-awake. We remove the cigarette. Then the effects of the Amytal wear off and the left hemisphere wakes up. We ask the patient how he feels. 'Fine,' he replies. 'What did I put in your hand?' I ask. 'I don't know,' says the patient. 'Are you sure?' 'Yes,' he says. Then we show him a series of objects—a pencil, a pad of paper, a comb, a cigarette—and ask him, 'Which one was it?' In spite of everything he has said, his left hand immediately points to the cigarette" (*The New York Times Magazine,* September 9, 1973). The cigarette was a picture encoded in his right hemisphere. While the picture could be expressed nonverbally, the verbal side of the patient's brain did not have access to it. While setting out to show which side the speech center was on, the results of this experiment took on a new significance for the unearthing of mental life, dramatically proving that there may be something which is in a person's brain and that influences his behavior but that in a conscious manner he cannot get at.

During clinical work conducted through eidetics, evidence similar to Gazzaniga's emerged when H.B., age 34, was asked to see his parents standing directly in front of him in the form of images. He initially reported his mother on the left and his father on the right in the psychical space in front of him. He was then asked to switch the positions around. He said, "I find it very difficult to switch the positions and they return spontaneously to their original positions." He was asked to comment on his conscious feelings concerning these images. He said, "In the spontaneous position where my mother is on the left and my father on the right I feel comfortable and warm toward my mother in the image. I see father the way I saw him always, not in direct communication with me, busy with his papers, etc." Next, H.B. was asked to switch his parents' position in front of him with conscious force. He reported, "When I switch my parents and see my father on the left, I see him standing alone and my mother completely disappears. She does not appear on the right. The image fades. I feel that the father does not belong there, to the left side. When I see him on the left side, I get feelings of annoyance and I say, 'You do not belong there; get away!' It bothers me if he is on the left side. I become aware of a certain negativism in me concerning my father. I consider him weak. I start thinking that he did not assert himself in his relationship with the mother or in his own desire to do things. The whole image now has faded out. I see neither my mother, nor my father." Next, H.B. was asked to switch the parents' positions (again, see mother on the right and father on the left) and maintain the projection by forced concentration on it. Through concentration he was able to keep the parents' images in the new position for a long period of time. During concentration he said, "But mother's image is still somewhat vague in this position. She tends to fade away temporarily and then comes back. As I look at her, she appears shrivelled up. It is like the witch who has been splashed with water." At this point H.B. was asked to keep looking at mother's visual image through concentration, and try to hear mother's voice. He said, "As I try to hear her voice, I see her calling my name. As I concentrate on her, I respond by just looking at her. She is just talking. She is not yelling. She is not smiling." With father's new visual position on the left, H.B. was asked to hear the father's voice. He said, "I experience my father's voice. He is talking directly to me, in general, with my mother there. I have no feeling. I am listening. There is talking of my coming down to his hardware store on Saturday." At this point H.B. was asked to hear his mother's voice again as he saw her on the right side (father on left—mother on right position), and he reported a sudden change in the picture. Mother's picture brightened up visually and became spontaneously stable. He no longer needed forced concentration to keep her image on the right side. At the same time as this change took place, the content of mother's image became full of powerful negative material. H.B. reported, "In the image I now see her berating my father, and she is the instigator. The picture is spontaneous and she appears clear and bright. She does not fade away." He was asked to continue his concentration on mother's image and report whether he experienced any further change. He said, "In the image she is all over the place, and it is nonsense what she is talking. She is disturbed about something, and it is a sad picture. She looks very upset. She is creating this unnecessarily. It is coming out of her own anxieties. She is pouring it out. I used to feel justification for her. Now I see that this is her self-imposed, self-created unhappiness. I look at her in the image with pity. There is no justification for it. I see it very clear. It is painful to see that your parent is not well, especially when you have taken an opposite view all your life" (Ahsen, 1975).

What was left vague in Gazzaniga's report of conflicting behavior of the two hemispheres became clear in the case of H.B. In all probability, two conflicting experiences are, as a routine, registered in the two hemispheres separately in order to keep the two experiences clearly differentiated. Similar extensive experimentation has revealed that individuals, as a rule, see their parents' images standing in front of them in fixed left-right positions. Since these positions are usually difficult to change, it indicates the neurological significance of these images. When parents are forced to switch positions, two different levels of imagery appear in consciousness, one conflicting with the other. We can also clearly conclude that there are at least two levels at which developmental experience is registered or reproduced: left hemisphere and right hemisphere. The character of experience is not revealed to be the same at these two levels. Since conflictual experiences are represented in these two levels, access to the identity of an event depends on whether access to the original level where the experience was originally encoded has been achieved.

What would be the meeting ground between the conflictual levels of experiences and the observer himself, and how could it be reached in its original identity? It was originally believed by the associationist school that the mind works by "thought associations," and, therefore, if one would allow the mind to move spontaneously from one thought to another through free association, it would arrive at the original experience through its own natural channels. Penfield, commenting on the voluntary process, said, "What a man remembers when he makes a voluntary effort is apt to be a generalization" (Penfield, *The Interpretive Cortex*). Similarly, Kirlian photography noted that the ghost image of the cutoff part of the leaf was not perceivable except through a systematic process, although that absent leaf section was still actually there. Confirming these two findings, eidetic experiments in the clinical setting showed that even if an experience was totally suppressed, or not even formed, it can be made accessible to consciousness by mental concentration on the area where it is present as a "ghost" image.

Seeing and repeating the eidetic with concentration and absorption generates contact with the original mental content. The eidetic experience pulls out the mental content from its original level within the center of attention in a spontaneous manner. It represents an unbroken flow of new thought and feeling to and from the presented image, in which the true nature of the experience emerges undisturbed by the conscious mind of the individual. This creates a genuine tendency toward resolution of problematic history and conflict through the underlying biolatent process. The solution, which is already contained in the image itself, binds the conflict and the resolution in the activated eidetic state.

The eidetic demonstrates beyond doubt that an object which exists in the psychical world has a very real existence in the physical world, and that this counterpart exerts an influence over our thoughts in a way which defies the rational process. Eidetics represent the mind's own internal control on its content, the way it thinks, feels, and acts. For example, if in an eidetic experience we kick a stone that we kicked in fact in the past, the eidetic of the stone will create in us the same physiological feelings we experienced at the time of the actual kick. If we were traumatized when we kicked it, we will feel the same trauma again when we see the eidetic. And if we thought at that time that the stone should not have been there, we will think of the same idea again as we go through the eidetic experience and the mind will, in fact, attempt a solution along these lines. But if we do not see the original eidetic and its presented solution in the mind, our toe will continue to feel the pain, but we will not know why; and we may kick angrily or avoid every stone we see in our way for some vague compelling reason, and never know why. When an image pertains to a more intense life relationship, the original conflict which continues to affect us in vague and haunting ways can be thrust forward into full view and realized in complete, minute detail through the eidetic. The picture which represents it carries the feelings and meanings as we felt and thought them at the original time, and as we focus on the image details, we relive and progress that event.

Reality is what some people call the external world which remains unchanged by our transitory thoughts and emotions, the material object which is out there and can be touched, felt, and held, and which remains fundamentally the same in all passage of time. Yet, in a fast changing world where the psyche has been proved to have many levels, reality is no longer what we have called or thought it; reality is what we know to be true in the deepest layers of our minds.

II

The unfolding of mental life is a gradual process proceeding out of the monoconsciousness of the newborn. In his first days, the child breathes, feels, and touches everything, and he is a part of nature. Light and shades of color blend with objects in the atmosphere; he lives in all objects, and all objects live in him. No lines divide what is in here from out there; he is a container, as are all objects containers. He is fluid, as are they; he is content, as are they; he is form, as are they. He is each object, and each object is him. Although in the beginning nothing really contrasts, and confluence rules in a primary way, the emergence of an object satisfies a primary need of the infant. The object experience is a fascinating one for the child, leading to his personal growth.

"An acute observation," said Jean Piaget in *The Origins of Intelligence in Children* (p. 72), ". . . surpasses all statistics." He found that the infant tends to preserve the perception of light, gropes to rediscover it when it vanishes, and smiles when he finds it. He commented on the intrinsic qualities of an object experience in connection with the child's emotional expression: the smile. "As for us," he said, "examining our three children has left us no doubt concerning the fact that the smile is primarily a reaction to familiar images, to what has already been seen, inasmuch as familiar objects reappear suddenly and release emotion, or again inasmuch as a certain spectacle gives rise to immediate repetition." (Piaget, *The Origins of Intelligence in Children*, p. 72).

As the infant gradually emerges out of these states, the parents play a crucial role for him, having the ability either to expand or inhibit the spectrum of interactions to clarify or confound the infant's internal life, and to place him in harmony or conflict with his natural states. Piaget recorded the overt manifestations of this psychic relationship with parents as follows:

> "When one leans over him, as when dressing him, he explores the face section by section: hair, eyes, nose, mouth, everything is food for his visual curiosity. At 0;1(10) he alternately looks at his nurse and at me and, in examining me, his eyes oscillate between my hair and face. . . . At 0;1(25) he looks in turn at his nurse, his mother, and myself with a change of attitude when confronted by each new face and an abrupt and spontaneous moving of his glance from one face to the other.

"But, quickly enough, his interest in faces is no longer a purely visual one. Through coordination with the schemata of hearing in particular and with the global situations of eating, dressing, etc., the familiar faces become fraught with meaning" (Piaget, *The Origins of Intelligence in Children,* pp. 68, 69).

Such recognition of parents in the infant, which starts with the image of parents, physical exploration, and meaning, goes deeper than mere perceptual discrimination. It entails a whole panorama of psychic responses involving "needs" or "drives" centering around the fulfillment of body and personality functions. In diverse studies on the subject, the most notable spokesman for the evidence in favor of such "attachment behavior" is the British researcher, John Bowlby, who wrote:

"There is good evidence that in a family setting most infants of about four months are already responding differently to mother as compared with other people. When he sees his mother an infant of this age will smile and vocalise more readily and follow her with his eyes for longer than he does when he sees anyone else. . . . Although attachment behaviour was shown by these children also towards other familiar adults, towards mother it was nearly always shown earlier, more strongly, and more consistently."

And—

"That visual contact is of great importance is further supported by the fact that, during routine caretaking, a mother tends to hold her infant in such a way that face-to-face contact occurs only rarely; whereas when she is feeling sociable she habitually holds him facing towards herself (Watson, 1965). This observation is in accord with the finding that an infant becomes attached to figures who initiate interaction with him rather than with figures who do little more than attend to his bodily requirements" (Bowlby, *Attachment,* pp. 199–201; 319).

In order to mediate attachment behavior, the infant uses signalling patterns, i.e., crying, smiling, babbling, and, later, calling—to bring the mother to him, and approach behavior which includes seeking and following to bring himself to the mother as soon as he is mobile. The patterns observed in attachment have been reported to generally follow certain lines at approximately the ages noted in parentheses below:

The infant vocalizes more frequently in interaction with the mother and more readily (5-6 weeks); the baby continues to cry when held by anyone other than the mother (9 weeks); the baby smiles more frequently, more readily, and more fully at the sight of the mother (10 weeks); the baby cries promptly when the mother, though not anyone else, leaves the room (15 weeks); the baby keeps his eyes on the mother even when held by another (18 weeks); after absence, the infant greets the mother with a combination of smiling, vocalizing, and general body excitement including the lifting of arms (21 weeks, possibly earlier); the infant climbs over the mother, exploring and playing with her face, hair, clothes (22 weeks); the child cries and follows only the mother when she leaves the room, even as soon as he can crawl (24 weeks); the baby crawls toward mother rather than anyone else in the room (28 weeks); the child buries his face in the mother's lap or elsewhere on her person, and never with anyone else (28 weeks); the child makes exploratory excursions away from her with occasional returns (28 weeks); the child returns to the mother when alarmed (8 months); the child follows the mother without crying (9 months); the child shows differential clinging to the mother, especially when alarmed, tired, hungry, or unwell (final quarter of first year) (Bowlby, *Attachment*, pp. 300-303).

It is generally the mother who is the first experiential object in the child's life. As such, she is the primary container of object experience. As she is loving and gratifying and responds sensitively and promptly to the child's calls, he grows accordingly in strength. If she is cold, unloving, agitating, and gives double signals, she thwarts the interactive life functions, and the child responds with spontaneous discord, exhibiting emotional difficulties.

The mother is the first known object and the child the first knower. As she imparts impressions, he receives them, and in biological purity he responds to her affection or lack of it. As she gives out signals, he receives them and in delight or anxiety responds to the unfolding of the relationship. The child's existence represents two poles of this psychical seesaw on which feelings given off and received by two living organisms are conserved as a living mental blueprint for future experience.

Out of this nest of euphoria or conflict, the child moves out to know the father. Here he is exposed to a truly outside partner in life who is not related to the womb directly and intimately, and is active and contending in the world. He starts a new phase of development with the father, who has the capacity to nurture or thwart the child's further awakening through a life-giving or a life-denying relationship. The child moves into this relationship with the father ready to learn new ways of expressing himself. Naturally, the relationship shows some shades of distrust from the side of the child, who earlier relied on the mother's nourishing love completely. Father is a powerful figure whose love nudges the child into actively relating with others; he represents the child's first awareness that the world outside of the mother can be warmly interactive and challenging. In his study on the play of children, Piaget treated the relevance of father's relationship in the words:

> "On the same day I knocked against J's hands with a rake and made her cry. I said how sorry I was, and blamed my clumsiness. At first she didn't believe me, and went on being angry as though I had done it deliberately. Then she suddenly said, half appeased: *'You're Jacqueline and I'm daddy. There!* (she hit my fingers). *Now say: You've hurt me.*—(I said it.) *I'm sorry, darling. I didn't do it on*

purpose. You know how clumsy I am,' etc. In short, she merely reversed the parts and repeated my exact words.

"At 4;7 (2) we were walking close to some nettles and I told her to be careful. She then pretended to be a little girl who had been stung. The same day she played at scything with a thin, pointed stick. She then said to me of her own accord: *'Daddy, say: You won't cut yourself, Jacqueline, will you?'* Then she told a story similar to the preceding one.

"At 5;8(5), being for the moment on bad terms with her father, X. charged one of her imaginary characters with the task of avenging her: *'Zoutab cut off her daddy's head. But she has some very strong glue and partly stuck it on again. But it's not very firm now'*" (Piaget, *Play, Dreams and Imitation in Childhood,* pp. 133–134; 134–135; 174).

The presence of an interactive father has a deep positive effect on the child, and his absence has a profoundly negative one. For instance, a four-year-old whose father had just deserted the family three months earlier now always wanted to be cuddled, whereas before she used to dress herself and be self-reliant in other ways. "She's continually clinging round me," said the mother. "She keeps saying, 'Do you love me? You won't leave me, Mummy, will you?' . . . she's afraid of being left on her own, I mean, if I go to the toilet, I have to take her with me, she won't even stay in the room then on her own'" (Bowlby, *Separation,* p. 214).

The impact of an unsettling relationship with the father may also have very subtle, long-range results. The father being the child's first meaningful link with the world outside of mother, his lack of attention may be profoundly debilitating. In a study by McCord and his colleagues regarding 255 overdependent boys between the ages of nine and seventeen from a high-density industrial area, mainly the working class, the statistics were revealing: "Nearly twice as many of the dependent boys as of the controls were rated as being rejected by father (51 per cent compared with 28 per cent) and/or by mother (39.5 per cent and 20 per cent)" (McCord, quoted by Bowlby, *Separation,* pp. 241–242).

Piaget observed that when the child was feeling rebellious, he would frequently play at being an orphan, but it was much more rare to find even a pretence of decapitation of the mother, as rebellion against her was more disturbing than against the father. He denoted the father as "the object of ambivalent feelings: he is loved, but he is often a nuisance and his removal is not too serious a matter. . . . It is interesting to note how . . . frequently in play the attitude to the father varies according as the parents are together or the father is alone" (Piaget, *Play, Dreams and Imitation in Childhood,* pp. 175–176).

Bowlby remarks in his account of loss that quarrels between the parents have a deep effect and that children hear more than parents would like to believe. Rather than placing the onus of the child's emotional problems on the child alone, he comments, "When after much patience the facts become known, it is usually far less difficult to understand how a child has come to be disturbed and why he fears whatever he does" (Bowlby, *Separation,* p. 235).

Inversion Process

A systematic analysis of most case histories reveals a consistent feature: in the very beginning of surfacing the information, individuals blame their fathers for many of their problems. Further analysis, however, reveals the blame to be usually (though not always) due to an inversion process, i.e., defects which are usually ascribed to the father at the upper level turn out to be really the defects of the mother. Due to a failing in the maternal process, the primary nature of her defect not only makes it inaccessible to ordinary consciousness, but also necessitates that it be seen through inverted projection. The inversion process thus succeeds in generating a portrait of the father which blames him in such a way that the original source of frustration in the mother can be kept hidden in the most subtle fashion. Following this line of inverted imagery structure, a careful investigator who is alert to early signs of inversion in the images can retrieve the true phase of imagery when it emerges. This would involve looking for a clear primary defect in the maternal process while elaborating imagery pertaining to the negative portrait of the father, and seeking evidence in the actual historical events to prove or disprove the negative behavior of the father. If then the negative portrait of father is not borne out convincingly through historical events, it can be safely concluded that the related primary defect in the maternal process needs to be investigated.

The sections of imagery analysis which follow next describe the content and behavior of the parents' imagery involving problems in interaction or symbolism of development. These presentations are expected to serve as suggested imagery exercises in the area of difficulty and in management of the general analysis process. The empty spaces are meant for writing responses. However, to find out exactly when these individual exercises should be brought into analysis, the reader should consult the chapter, "Orientation Exercises."

Early Anger and Pity Associated with the Mother Image

When the ground perceptions pertaining to the maternal process reveal the mother to be insufficiently gratifying and supportive, the individual relates to her image with feelings of isolation, pity, and anger, which usually turn out to be very severe or traumatic. The early relationships and their associated images need to be surfaced in their original form, along with the traumatic expressions associated with them. After authentic recall and enactment, the individual needs to develop in the direction of more gratifying relationships and emotions.

Every child experiences a difficulty with the mother due to some serious limitation in her. For instance, she may have unreasonable anger, or she may be unresponsive or depressed. The child cannot help but receive these impressions, which force an unnatural congestion in his otherwise responsive constitution. If he had been an adult, he would have handled the situations of maternal limitation well, with cleverness and flexibility. Since he was not an adult but a child, he was transformed by these emotionally restrictive events; now that he is an adult, he can reverse this by picking up the same unresolved points and relating to the mother with active initiative and flexibility. By re-experiencing and re-doing the negative situation images, he can release the trapped growth potential and become aware of a new basis of life and action within himself which is full of initiative and resourcefulness.

The following images, which effect retrieval, projection, and progression in this vital area, can build new cause and effect structures, giving a new structured expression to emotional life. Naturally, these images start with a rudimentary attempt to build a communication bridge with the mother in an area of some early difficulty and become progressively more complex.

Images of Depressed Mother

If the ground perceptions reveal the mother to be actively negative toward the child, the content of the mother images can be considered negative in an active way. However, if the mother image appears to be merely withdrawn and pathetic, it indicates a need on the part of the mother to express herself. In the latter case, analysis demands that an imagery process be set up in which she is seen wishing, longing, energetic, and active. The imagery of maternal release through this wishing activity gives expression to her self. Such imagery expresses her imagination and its propensity toward formulation of mental objects. This fundamental imagization process feeds into the usual perceptions of environmental objects, which get activated in return and respond with more energy and effectiveness. The following steps for imagery projection have been found useful in this direction. When the individual's attention has been directed toward the formulation of these images, a change in consciousness occurs.

1. See your mother depressed in the image.

2. Talk to her in the image, asking questions as to why she is depressed.

3. If she is depressed and withdrawn, like a statue, mildly pound at her body with your fists to get a reaction.

4. Express anxiety and profusely cry in front of her, wishing that she would respond in some manner.

5. Become aware of her needs. Carefully write down each need in the form of a list.

6. Concentrate on her needs one by one. Know these needs one by one, and concentrate on them as an expression of her biological self.

7. See images of mother wishing and wanting things, things of mind and matter.

8. See her wanting things with an endless feeling of desire. See her imagination freely flowing.

9. See her wanting and longing, even becoming somewhat angry.

10. See that people do not understand her and condemn her when she wishes and wants.

11. See her banging pots and pans and slamming the doors in the house.

12. See yourself wishing and wanting with her, banging the pots and pans and slamming the doors with her.

13. See mother, yourself, and her other children wishing, longing, and banging the pots and pans and slamming the doors.

14. See your father first becoming slightly apprehensive and then smiling, becoming aware that it is only the process of wishing and wanting that is being released in these images.

15. See that your father understands this imagery process of wishing, wanting, banging the pots and pans, and slamming the doors in front of him.

16. See that all of you, including father, finally smile, showing understanding.

Quarrelling Images of Parents

The conflict between parents' images (see chapter entitled "Eidetic Parents Test") at various levels represents a state of interaction between two living individuals. From a peaceful state of give-and-take, influence and counterinfluence, the relationship extends to a clash of somewhat irreconcilable elements. Conflict, therefore, appears to be a natural quality of the parental images, dialectically moving toward a state of union or synthesis. When parental quarrels are seen from the standpoint of interaction between two individuals, they are readily understandable; however, when they are seen from the standpoint of an idealized eternal truth, the nature of conflict becomes stagnant and threatening and tends to repeat itself indefinitely without finding synthesis and cure.

Many immature individuals solve the problem of conflict between the parental images by seeing no conflict at all in their images. Since the conflict contains traumatic memories of clash, these individuals even suppress the experience of life-generating interaction and freeze the parental images, making them immobile in the mind. The following imagery steps help break the control on threatening contact between parental images.

1. See your parents standing directly in front of you, one on the left and the other on the right.

2. See that the two are fighting with each other with ideas and emotions which take the form of sparks and bolts of electrical light.

3. See the weaker parent more active in throwing the sparks at the other parent.

4. See the parents throwing the sparks of ideas and emotions on each other.

5. As the two parents "electrically" fight, both appear to communicate something positive.

6. Sometimes they behave like two live electrical wires closely tangled together and constantly spitting sparks at each other, and you hear and see the sparks and you experience fear.

7. While the parents fight, they also generate communication between each other. Feel the communication.

8. Concentrate on the weaker parent fighting, and feel the positive side of communication.

9. As you see and feel the image, the sparks coming from this parent form ideas in your mind.

10. While you see this parent fight, form ideas and images of this parent's life perspective.

11. Notice this fight to be a transmission of ideational energy between the two parents. Relax and let the energy flow.

12. See that there is a free ideational traffic between the two parents. Let the energy and the ideas flow, like a dialogue.

13. Relax and concentrate on the flow of ideas and energy, and on the development of the dialogue.

14. List favorable aspects of this interaction between parents, and describe the various chains of dialectical interaction and synthesis between the parental images.

Mother: Communication Image

The previous two image processes reasonably open up contact with the ground structures of the maternal imagery. At this point access to a dialogue with the mother becomes possible and imagery exercises can be started to deal with early difficulties with her. This image exercise opens up relationship with mother at a relatively early level. The initial hurdle in communication with mother, such as her depression, isolation, or anger, becomes the basis of talk with her, and this talking is conducted in an atmosphere of care, flexibility, and persistence.

The adult can pick up the same early unresolved aspects of interaction with the mother and learn how to handle them with initiative, flexibility, and inner assertiveness. This new inner approach involves facing and re-experiencing the negative situation image involving the mother in a manner that the trapped growth potential is released. The approach does not involve overt assertive behavior, but a state of inner consciousness connected with a set of internal images that are developmentally meaningful and re-initiate and redirect growth potential in early development. The following set of images initiates interaction with the unresolved parts of the early relationship with the mother.

1. See your mother in the image. Describe the way she appears in the image.

2. Try to talk with her in the image. How does she respond to you?

3. In the image, ask love from her.

4. Tell her that you feel lonely without her.

5. Do something to mother in the image which presses the point.

6. Does pressing her tend to develop into a negative encounter with her?

7. Allow the meaning of the negative encounter to develop.

8. Let images of negative encounter develop fully.

9. Experience the emotions of fear and assertion during encounter.

10. Now see mother again in the image. See that you are talking with her involving this hurdle with her.

11. See that in the image she is unable to relate to you.

12. Experience the problem in communication with her. She is unable to initiate conversation or maintain it properly.

13. See that she is really not vicious or evilly oriented toward you, but she cannot help it. As a child you are stuck in this problem.

14. If you had been older, i.e., an adult, you would have been able to handle the situation better. You would have been clever and flexible with her.

15. But then you were a child, and you were dependent on her initiative and ability. You could not overcome the hurdle on your own.

16. Now, picture that you are a child, you are relating to her in a flexible manner, and, as you talk, you help the conversation through.

17. Initiate talk with her and converse in such a manner that she does not develop the hurdle. Be caring and flexible in conversation.

18. Initiate conversation with mother, seeing yourself as a child.

19. Experience the difficulty you feel when you initiate some new point. Experience that the ability to converse is stunted within you.

20. Experience that initiating conversation with mother has many crises and can be described in the form of stages.

21. Describe the stages of interaction up to the final successful communication.

22. Experience that, along the way, feelings of apprehension, anxiety, paralysis, distance, contempt, anger, and violence prevail.

23. Each time, try conversation with mother with fresh initiative and flexibility. See how you go through all these stages until you reach the final feeling of communication with her.

After learning the essential structure of initiative, one needs to explore areas where initiative is needed. Make a list of problems concerning mother and the initiatives needed to resolve them.

List of Problems	Initiative and Stages of Crisis
a.	a.
b.	b.
c.	c.
d.	d.
e.	e.
f.	f.

Double-Faced Emotions Concerning Father

Difficulties with the father are usually experienced by the individual after difficulties with the mother have already been established to some extent. After this initial difficulty, problems with father emerge in a complicated manner, and the main emphasis of interaction appears to be the wish that father be stronger in freeing the child from the limitations of the mother, along with a secret fear that the father, in fact, is very strong, and a feeling of indecision and distrust concerning his intention and orientation.

Father: Communication Image

The child reacts to the demands from the father with feelings of incapacity or a desire to please him, and to this picture of interactions is added the original feeling of incapacity experienced with the mother. The images concerning the father thereafter develop around the question of his love, his strength, and his demanding nature, and the child's faith or suspicion regarding father's orientation toward him. To expose the individual to the images which develop his relationship with the father, the following imagery steps are suggested.

1. See your father asking you to do something or asking you a question.

2. Do you feel annoyed, or do you want to please him?

3. See yourself talking with him. Are you able to talk with him freely?

4. Do you feel he is conversing with you comfortably and freely?

5. Do you feel he always expects a right answer from you? What happens if you do not have a right answer?

6. Do you feel he always wants you to succeed? What happens if you do not succeed?

7. As you see him, does he want to converse with you even if you failed?

8. See that deep down he really wants to help you.

9. Image that he is interested in conversing with you and helping you.

10. See yourself conversing with father with more freedom.

11. Choose a topic that you are really afraid of discussing with him.

12. See yourself asking him many questions. What are the questions?

13. Experience various stages of the discussion.

14. See that he can relax and talk about things.

15. See that you can relax and talk about things with him.

16. Choose another crisis topic, and ask him many questions.

17. Experience various stages of discussion. List the stages.

18. Make a list of crisis topics involving the father.

19. Practice images of communication in these areas.

20. See the two of you relaxing and doing nothing after communication.

Positive Father

Since the perceptions emanating from early contact with negative characteristics of the mother exert a limiting influence on the mind, the images of father emerge as a general release function working against the life-defeating pull of a maternal process which had failed in the child's early development. Father symbolizes a release from incorporation by the negative maternal perceptions and entry into the realm of freedom, light, and objects. The child's mind, which is suppressed by the negative ground perceptions, looks at the father's images with a feeling of special hope. To him the images of the father show a rare ability to evoke good feelings, such as euphoria. The historical portrait of the father is experienced as a biological portrait of a releaseful person. This positive, experiential emphasis, which has a biological function, can be a guide to the use of father's imagery. For instance, since it enhances life potential, a severely suppressed individual can benefit from a systematic exposure to positive images of father, selected from pleasurable interactive situations in the mind.

Father in the Evening

The evening appears to be particularly associated with the father's essence, since he returns from work at this time. The images involving this reveal an important portrait of the father: how the child sees him in his psyche, and whether he greets him with feelings of welcome. This imagery is useful when one has no awareness of his relationship with the father or has a fantasy relationship with him based on isolation. Does the father return from work interested, indifferent, aggravated, tired, or looking for an evening of playful interaction with the family? Projection of these images helps the person surface and realize this unknown side and arrive at some understanding of father's orientation to the family. The person comes to understand the need for a gratifying, playful interaction with a forceful reality other than the mother and the difficulties which emerge in the course of such an attempt. The imagery deals with some definite emergent aspects of the father, and is concentrated upon for development of his positive features.

1. See your father coming home in the evening.

2. See how his image appears in your mind as you see him coming toward the house.

3. See that he is still at a distance. How do you feel: pleased, indifferent, or anxious?

4. See whether you do or do not want him to return to the house. How do other members of the family feel about father entering the house?

5. See father entering the house. Does his entrance have overtones of negative or positive feelings? What is the general atmosphere in the house?

6. Describe your feelings concerning your mother in the image. How does she respond to father's entry in the house?

7. Experience your own feelings when you see your father entering the house.

8. Now, see a positive reaction on your part when you see father entering the house. What initiates the positive image?

9. Aid positive entry of the father by consciously remembering other happy images of him. Try to develop various image solutions. It does not matter whether the memory images are based on fantasy or reality.

10. After having structured positive features in the form of mental pictures, gradually build an image of the father entering the house in the evening with happiness, initiating a playful interaction in the family.

11. If father's entry still does not appear to be a happy one, find out why.

12. If the siblings, the mother, or the father appear very negative or fearful, bring the cause of these feelings to the surface.

Images which lead to re-education and dispel the negative atmosphere from the house through awareness and change of attitudes can be developed from the Eidetic Parents Test.

Eidetic Parents Test: Positive Images of Father

The images in the test show both negative and positive imagery relationship with father. These two aspects can be used to develop education concerning father or to induce positive feelings of a happy relationship with him.

1. Select positive images of father from the Eidetic Parents Test and sources directly related to these images (see Eidetic Parents Test section).

2. Project these images routinely for generation of pleasure and euphoria concerning the father.

3. Use the positive images of father to generate imagery experience of release and happiness rather than to prove that conscious opinions concerning him are untrue.

4. Sidetrack any spontaneous tendency to evoke negative memory images of the father from specific events, especially if these are used as a "reminder" of his bad personality.

5. Induce relaxation, and attempt to relate to the positive imagery of father in sufficient depth each time.

6. To strengthen these positive extensions, interactively develop a positive portrait of the father out of various history pieces.

7. Where positive images of the father show a defect due to history, generate new image variations which bring out the positive extensions of experience with father again.

8. Clearly reason out the causes of father's failure through examination of the negative circumstances which did not allow his full, positive character to operate.

9. Make a list of positive objects associated with father in the past, such as his coat, hat, shoes, shirts, umbrella, or walking stick (see Orientation Exercises section). Concentrate on these objects for experience of positive feelings. See a self-image touching, wearing, and using these positive objects both in the past and in the present. Learn to relax while forming these images.

Father: Work Image

A father who is away at work long hours or is psychically needed more due to the maternal handicap generates a negative image based on his absence. Under the pressure of his need for father, the child fantasizes that the father is not happy with him or does not like him. Being under the pressure of this fantasy, the child needs to experience a fantasy against work, namely, that the father does not prefer the work over the child, and that father is ready to leave work for good and come home to stay forever with the child and play with him. This fantasy image aids in turning the picture of an absent, work-oriented father into that of an everlasting playmate who likes to spend time with his child. The imagery sequence proceeds along these lines.

1. See that you want father to come home to play with you.

2. See that the father has left his job for good and he has come to stay at home with you.

3. He has kicked the job for good to be with you forever.

4. See that father likes to be with you and play with you at home.

5. Enjoy the feeling of being with him. See yourself doing many things with father in the home.

6. Do not let ideas of his work interfere with the pleasure of the image. He is not going to go back to his work any more.

7. Relax and see the two of you playing together. See that the mother does not interfere in your play at all.

8. See the playfulness and foreverness of the image as you do things in the home with father.

9. Go around outside the home with him, exploring the world, such as trees and lakes.

10. Return home and do things with him inside the home.

11. Enjoy father's company. He is no longer going to work. He has kicked the work for your sake.

The work-consumed father is an absent father in the psychical sense. This gives the maternal process an unnatural preference in the development of the child, not inferred by biology. This new time-equation involving the duration of time spent by mother and father is not supported by the genetic code because over millions of years, father had always spent, comparatively, more time with children than he does now. Any movement away from the original time-equation creates a psychophysiological trauma in the child.

In the technological society, the mother, being unfavorably placed in a negative time-equation with the father, is bound to isolate him, whether she wishes to do so or not. This psychical isolation is quickly followed by explosive anger in the family and blame of the father for imaginary or real shortcomings. Following such an encounter, the father withdraws into further work or isolation or overt expression of anxiety and anger. His attitudes become outwardly sadistic and inwardly masochistic. As he becomes more embroiled in the negative time-equation, he emerges more isolated and more authoritarian.

The condition of an overworked father, an equivalent of an absent father, generates a fantasy process which attempts retrieval of the father from the work situation. This retrieval is expressed in a complex manner: from a positive formation of the fantasy (in the case of fathers with a consistent work habit) that the father has left the work and has come back home to stay with children, to expression of negative anxiety associated with fear that if father really leaves the job, the family will be in a worse situation (in the case of fathers who actually desert work). Imagery analyses have consistently revealed that bad or unreliable work habits of the father create a need for work at the conscious level. In such cases the fantasy process remains fixated at the work-need level and is unable to touch the deeper core of imagery where the individual visualizes retrieval of the work-consumed father. In such complex cases, one needs to elaborate the total philosophy of work in the mind from the need for work to freedom from work and enjoyment of nature by roaming with father in a pastoral setting of lakes and green verdure.

Father: Humor Image

The work-consumed father obviously needs a little relief from work before he can enter into a meaningful relationship with the family. Imagery studies have revealed that a little bit of humor added to father's imagery eases him into revealing his true dynamics. When the image of the father is seen in a releaseful humorous interaction, the imagery content starts falling into a more resolvable pattern. These studies have also disclosed that such images practiced on the mother do not become releaseful, thus showing that humor is connected with the father in a special way.

The work-consumed father is a humorless father, stuck deep in negative frustration and unable to relate to the family in a positive manner. His cold portrait, however, can be warmed by humor and friendly teasing. It is farthest from the truth to say that all humor is merely ridiculous or sadistic in nature; in fact, when humor is suppressed, the tendency toward friendliness and love is crushed. During image experiments in which father is teased to evoke tendencies toward a friendly relationship within the family, a pure, releasing experience develops. During the initial projection of images, father may appear to be cold, threatening, or angry, but if one stays with the images the humor gradually opens up the father and the fear connected with the father accordingly diminishes, replaced at times by a deep euphoria in the form of visualization of a beautiful pastoral scene with him resembling mythical paradise.

The imagery sequence involving humor with father proceeds along these lines.

1. See that your father is standing near you. The two of you feel somewhat isolated from each other.

2. See that father does something to tease you.

3. See that you do something to tease the father.

4. Now see that both of you are doing something to each other in a lighthearted, funny manner.

5. See that you tease each other physically, with words and funny sounds.

6. See that while you are fooling around with each other, you appear to be moving along together in a certain direction.

7. See that while teasing each other and moving together in this direction, you come across ducks which appear to be walking ahead of you.

8. As you move forward fooling and teasing each other, see that the ducks gradually grow into huge white swans.

9. See that the huge white swans appear extremely pleasing to the eye and lead you and your father to a beautiful, natural place which resembles paradise.

In spite of a negative fallout from a technological environment, we can conclude from all we know that we do not have to be afraid of the image of the father. In it, there is an undoubtable state of pleasure which aids proper growth of the child when handled carefully. Father's image represents the high point of expectation, the point where one makes contact with a new vision of happiness apart from mother, with the mind stuff in ascension, perfumed and permeated with guidance. No doubt all fathers who have problems cause pain to their children. But for those children who do not see the positive side of the father, there is no relief from the suffering. Teasing with father is thus a mind journey, a mental image of release.

Father: Man-Monkey

The teasing image of father achieves a new dimension which joins the lower with the higher, the animalistic with the rational. In this image, instead of anxieties, fears, and laws, one sees a nature image of the father in which his animal aspect is experienced in a state of playful release. At the same time it is experienced that father is in possession of his higher attributes and intellectual functions. At this level one sees the father imagistically as a large monkey of human height or a little larger, with a tail and a red behind.

The man-monkey image of father, which heals the condition of conflict in the mind concerning father, providing it with humor and necessary physical release of the unifying type, is introduced along these lines.

1. See your father as a huge man-monkey with a tail and a red behind.

2. See that your father looks funny with his red behind, and he appears playful.

3. See that you are having fun and experiencing joy with your father, and he is responding.

4. See the man-monkey holding his tail and dancing.

5. See that your father is full of pranks in this form.

6. See the man-monkey playing tricks on you.

7. Concentrate on the red behind of the father and play tricks on him.

Nudging, tantalizing, and teasing father's image will break one's isolation. While in the images one can tease the father and enjoy it, a helpful communication with him has its own special advantages.

Helping Father in His Problem

Children who are raw and weak may react to the father's isolation with isolation. This is determined by the child's condition in history, that he always made an adjustment, but the father always needed to know more about the truth from the child's own tongue. This psychical need is released through the projection process in which the child does, in fact, recognize a problem in the father and wants to make the father become aware of it and help him in dealing with it.

The child extending help to the father at the mental level has a developmental significance. Love of the father, awe of his power, and fear of his authoritarian portrait do not let one see that father as a helpful figure may himself be in need of help. Extending help to the father with the purpose of fulfilling his need to learn new truth and behavior which he may not be ready to recognize due to feelings of authority and shame initiates an interesting interaction with the father.

The projection of a helpful interaction involves the initial fear or embarrassment of opening up the problem and the crisis of bringing father's attention to it, and of sustaining the emotional hassle until a more cooperative portrait of the father develops. It is an imagery process marked with many stages of interaction having many crises laden with stress. Each time, pursuit of the imagery dialogue with father brings the awareness of the problem and the means of solving it to the forefront. This is the creative side of the child in which he formulates solutions for the father, generating in the end a new vision of life meaningful to others. He conceptualizes clearly what father has to do, and he builds his own personal life around it. In this way he becomes a guiding light for others.

1. See your father in the image.

2. Tell him in the image that he has a problem.

3. Tell him that you want to discuss the problem with him.

4. Tell him to put aside his denial, his self-defense, his shame, and his pride, and discuss the problem.

5. Tell him that you really want to help him, and he should trust you.

6. At this point in the image, try to feel out his problem, which he may not be prepared to see for himself. What is the problem?

7. Tell him his problem and that you want to help him and that you are going to help him.

8. Tell him that it is an extraordinary problem which he cannot handle, but he may think he can handle.

9. Hold him firmly in discussion. Do not let him move away from the scene.

10. Tell him to recognize the truth within him, admit it, and discuss it in the open with you.

11. Tell him that children always solve the problems of parents. Parents are at times caught in the confusion.

12. Tell him that children can sense out and search for the solution, because they have a fresh mind and they are gifted that way by nature to help parents.

13. Tell him that innocence makes children aware of father's problems.

14. Tell father that his problems are not petty or ordinary but extraordinary, and he should accept help from you, such as an open discussion of his problem.

15. See that in your own mind by searching the solution for the father you are envisioning a new image of life within yourself. Feel and describe this new vision.

16. See that you have to bring this new image of life into existence by conceptualizing it clearly for the father.

17. See that by teaching father and practicing this new vision of life yourself, you will serve the father.

18. Do not merely discuss with the obstructed father, but practice the solution yourself also.

19. Concentrate on the nucleus of this new vision within you, which is good for him and good for everyone.

20. Hold the conversation with him to create more awareness within you of this nucleus of a new vision.

21. Develop this system of meanings so that you become aware of your own inner light and truth.

22. The system of meanings you see out of these conversations with father represent your inner truth and your vision for others.

The preceding image exercises containing many interactive imagery sequences involve an intricate thought process. The ability of the imagizer to think about thoughts, ruminate about rumination, wonder about wondering, feel about feeling, involves the capacity of the mind to reflect upon itself, a unique form of awareness perhaps manifested only in humans. In this process, the thinker (subject) and what is thought or felt (object) are experienced in a unitary state which in some manner also involves interaction and birth of a new ideation process. Image activity is a form of interaction within the mental content, i.e., a mind reflecting upon a mind-state, generating awareness of truth or error. For instance, if an individual is thinking of parents, the mind is, in fact, thinking of a mind-state in the form of an image; and the statement, "Who are they?" or "I try to be different from them," may be, in the final evaluative sense, an attempt to feel more or find out what is true or false. It is known that a person cannot be different from anyone except through an intimate experience of the one who is involved in the difference. The knowledge of what one is going to be or different from is born out of this exposure. Thus, complete exposure to what one is going to be or different from precedes the birth of the new self or the change itself. This explains why one cannot change without becoming involved in the experience of other people or concrete forms of imagery which represent those people. True change comes through deep experience finally of a concrete mental image. In the case of mental experience of important persons, the experience is invariably loaded with challenge, expectation, and enlightenment, all carried out through the mental image process.

Resolution of Identifications

The imagery processes in general reveal that the individual projecting an image undergoes a certain type of superficial or deep emotional association with the person appearing in the image. This involves three levels: "A-level," superficial association in which the individual does not even see the image lucidly so that he can emote and understand; "B-level," a deeper association in which he covertly unites with the person in the image so that he does not create a problem, i.e., a troubling situation between himself and the person, resulting in a state of undifferentiated consciousness which is classically defined as identification; "C-level," interactive association in which he experiences the image in an interactive fashion. The "C-level" involves two interactive nuclei having two different points of view, with different needs and orientations generating a state of conflict. All imagery situations, to be proper and meaningful for effective change, should involve an awareness of life from A to C. After the person has finally reached the "C-level" in a clear way, he reaches a mental process that deals with a life issue in a new, living manner which is neither passive nor covert. The eidetics, which provide the typical "C-level" imagery, help the individual re-experience his life at a concrete level involving conflict by concrete imagery presentation of it, with its sensory qualities and meanings. As this type of interactive imagery breaks superficialities and covert identifications, the process of encounter finally results in the reassertion of life potential.

Through resolution of these superficial, deep, and interactive barriers, the individual constantly creates his self-image in a new form closest to his original endowment. Identification, which is a shell to this process, like a shell is to the biological egg, must be cast aside finally, to let life itself appear in its true form.

III

The mother and father interacting with the child, and the parents interacting with each other, thus make up the primary pictures of life interactions. We all are pursued by the question: What are parents finally to us? Are they people we can easily disown or cast aside? Are they pure history which affects our physical bodies, but stops short of infiltrating our minds and changing our philosophical attitude to life? Can we reach the core of happiness without their interactive potential? There is an old story about a disciple who came to learn about God and the deeper ways of life. The teacher gave him instructions; but soon the disciple returned, saying he could not carry them out, for every time he tried to meditate, he found himself thinking about his pet buffalo. "Well, then," said the teacher, "meditate on the buffalo that you are so fond of." At this, the disciple shut himself in a room and began concentrating on the buffalo. After some days, the teacher knocked on his door. "Sir," answered the disciple, "I am sorry I can't come out to greet you, but this door is too small and my horns will be in the way." The teacher smiled and said, "Splendid! You have become identified with the object of your concentration. Now fix that concentration upon God and you will easily succeed." Parents are like the buffalo experience.

It is well known that what most attracts our attention is that which completely consumes it by fondness or pain. Parents, personifying this mixture, are the primary distractors of our mind, and loosening our attention from them is not a simple matter. Naturally, the first step on the ladder to proper emotional knowledge would be a body of instructions which helps one experience his parents at the mental plane, in movement, in interaction, and in the performance of life functions as they originally performed them.

We even experience different feelings on the two sides of our body when we see our parents standing in front of us. These feelings are very different from the beliefs we consciously entertain about them. It appears that parents in the brain are neurologically located and cannot be moved from their spontaneous positions without conscious exertion or use of techniques. In these positions each parental image generates specific feelings in the body mechanisms. These implications finally bring us to the question of how we can unify body functions with the mental apparatus and bring about true mental freedom. If parents control our minds to such an extent that they can influence us in a neurological way, what can we do about it? The conclusion is that for as long as we are not conscious of the nature of the influence they exert, we are subject to that influence in our lives in a non-conscious manner. Because they control us at such a subtle level, we should learn structures of influences and select desirable elements of control. As the individual sees the parental experience winding through the terrain of mind, he sees attitudes and feelings that have affected his whole style of life and which he has reacted to or accepted as part of his own fiber. The experience of original innocence is prompted by the assurance that the threat is no longer really imminent, allowing expression with parents, who diverted or thwarted it in some way.

The adult can explore as deeply or superficially as he likes in order to find out what forms him. The individual in search of true fulfillment has to know and overcome the emotions of distance, subjugation, and sorrow concerning these growth images and has to learn to face them in their true biological light. It appears that true knowledge of good and evil is not possible by mere philosophical thought or by ritual and rite, but essentially through the experience of good and evil originating with the parents. By becoming aware of the subtle moral traces operative in the parental images, one becomes aware of good as an experiential event and not as a mere metaphysical notion. Here, instead of being presented as a logical treatise, good and evil *happens* in the mind of the inquirer. If the individual is to know good and evil through his personal life and not through repetitive traumata such as war, sadism, and crime, he can know this through the only source available for such an experience, the parental images.

The awareness of good and evil through images of the parents is not lightly won. The individual who gives up his armchair notions of good and evil and instead experiences the good and evil imposed by the parents' images undergoes a shattering experience of consciousness. The mind liberated by the growth images is the illumined mind which has achieved the stainless existence. The faith which is begotten out of these images is faith not in dogmas but in human capacity. Such a liberation does not extol rituals, but encourages overcoming of the narrow boundaries of mind through personal illumination. The experience does not lead to piling up stocks of dry academic knowledge but to achievement of contact with one's fellow man. The experience of freedom is central to this final achievement of wisdom, as this path relates with pure Nature. All energies must be yoked in this path, and everything must become an illumination of the life process itself.

As no parents are without limitations and only true virtue is stainless, parents without gross limitations represent an even greater responsibility for the special individual who wants to know the nature of complete good. For this individual the path is very subtle and demanding and, unless he puts all his effort and concentration in it, he artificially limits the potentiality of his growth. This individual must experientially understand that his parents do not represent a state of complete good, and he must differentiate between consciousness of parents and the completeness of Nature.

This method bypasses the negative aspects of the ego, but it does not avoid encounter with the problematic aspects of the parents; rather, it enhances their relevance. The method rejects conscious euphemisms, and questions heedless believing and blind living. The "I" being both inside the ego and also in the larger psyche, the ego and the unwanted parts of the psyche become like "I" and "Thou." When the ego lowers the barriers through the parental experience, the rejected parts of the psyche become accessible. Caring for and loving the experience of vulnerability is part of this experience. When the ego opens up to the new experience, it becomes the symbol of the individual's wisdom and availability.

The true relationship between "I" and "Thou" thus lies within this interactive mental process. Once the individual is able to treat the unwanted parts of his own mind with openness and care, the "I" and "Thou" in the external world also become united. By transposing internal anxiety outward, the individual resists the other person. When a true opening has been established within, it results in an opening toward the outside world. Seen in this light, psychology and sociology appear to originate from the same root and to move toward the same goal. The two begin within the individual himself in an interactive dialogue between the two parts of his mind.

2 ∂ High Fidelity Self-Images

What is the true identity of the leaf of life? The ghost part which is now missing is given in mental projection. Unless the missing part is seen again related to the original situation, what injured the leaf of life will not emerge. The leaf will not be able to regenerate itself.

If we look at various memory portraits of ourselves from the past, they appear to be representations of a being in motion, yet the portraits are evidently sections, or space representations. One can move about in physical space easily, but one cannot really get away from the present moment into the absent moment, except through a vehicle which involves a special process of the mind. While experiencing this special process of the mind, i.e., an eidetic, there can be moments when one slides away into the past and then emerges into a new dimension of the world. This special vehicle gives us the freedom to go in any direction of space and time, and as one presses various levers of this "image machine," one glides into the various dimensions of the absent existence. The new emergent machine is emotive, not observational; eventful, not stagnant. It beats like the living heart of life itself in which the universe has become once more accessible.

It is fascinating to see various potentials of the psyche distributed in various time levels. The variety of images which are projected belong to various potential existences. As on a ladder, one can ascend or descend into various aspects of mental existence. Eidetics is a process whereby a person slides into the past, experiencing deeply his self-image in a distinctly different situation. The experience is different from memory recall because it involves a deliberate and structured maneuver by which the experiencer descends to a new point in the past in a realistic manner.

If you examine a movie cartridge, you will find that the smooth movement of a race horse on a movie screen is made out of a series of still frames running at approximately sixteen frames per second. The motion is created out of the perfectly still frames. If you look into the past, you will find similar still frames of events, incidents, people, and objects. A superficial glance reveals all these frames to be motionless, but when you look at them closer, the still frames begin to move and a smooth, perfect motion develops as a result. This reminds one of how a movie projectionist can create motion as he desires so that the movement of the race horse can be seen in slow or fast motion, as he likes. Likewise, in an eidetic, if one concentrates on an incident from the past, one can similarly slow it down to experience the movement in slow motion, and from there, a new, fast movement of another type can be made to emerge. The brain rhythms can run the movie of a past incident at various speeds. Through concentration you can choose your own location and your own speed. You can slow down or speed up a chosen event. You can slow it down to the point where you can observe minute details, or you can speed it up, even faster than it really happened, to the point where you create a vague flicker, a ghost-like eluding awareness in which the details are lost and the ground is set for an illusion.

Concentration slows the speed of the mental movie, revealing more details, while hurried recall or thought speeds up the mental movie, creating illusion. Concentration is like a slow cinematographic process in which you can see the tricky detail at work. In this slow process of the mind, the image shows the structure of the event, the body reaction tells what was caused at the emotional level, and finally comes the meaning of it, i.e., how it related you to life. This cinematographic, or hologramic, image fires many types of waves in the brain. If the event was painful, it creates waves relevant to pain. If the event was pleasurable, it creates pleasurable waves. The rate of brain wave flashing increases or decreases and changes its pattern according to the constant frame of reference photographically presented in the eidetic. If one is consistently seeing a positive picture, one is perhaps firing alpha; occasionally one experiences a jarring burst of beta, associated with a negative eidetic appearing on the mental screen. As these eidetics generate altered states of brain functioning, one can reach or create at will a state of ecstacy or deep depression. One can put one's mind to sleep or flush it with creative insights. It is a dimension of awareness of feeling states induced consciously by summoning up the related image in consciousness.

One can flash any state in a darkened room of the skull, if one can maintain the projection. As the darkened room is lit by the related state through concentration on the image, one can make the event virtually living. As one switches over to a new eidetic, the brain waves pass into a new view of the experience. The previous experience has terminated, and a new one has come to assert itself according to the rules of projection. In this state the person has come to know himself as a self-projector, and has had the first glimpse of his power to handle his own mental states.

The projector of these mental images has come face to face with a new vision of reality. The "out there" of a rigid external reality has been replaced by the "in here" of a whole new inner reality. The person comes to know that he can be as he chooses through these inner dimensions. When the eidetics are still, time stands still, and when time moves, it moves through the eidetics; a motion becomes visible, a reality is born.

Students of brain waves have indicated that it would not be surprising if the discovery were made that people with superior skills are merely those blessed with brain waves firing significantly slower than that of the general population, i.e., people gifted with concentration. The critical difference between the ordinary and extraordinary individual may be precisely this difference in concentration. The brain firing slowly can observe the separate units of detail much more clearly and this gives the individual an upper hand on the event. The superstar baseball player firing the slow moving alpha sees the ball travelling at almost half the speed than his ordinary teammate firing the faster brain wave, beta. Many experienced players have reported such slow motion events during critical hours of the play, suggesting that the same thing happens during peak periods of competition. Eidetic images, which make the experience run slowly, generate more detail, to provide one finally with a better grip of the event. An experience running at less than half its usual speed is obviously more analyzable and, for the same reason, more manageable.

In the slow moving events of concentration the conscious and the non-conscious meet, the known and the unknown unite, unfolding new life perspectives, as a result of which new frames of reality are born. Consciousness is aided, through sequential frames of awareness, into a new shape of history. In this encounter there is nothing truly unconscious; everything is conscious in the sense that it can be known and examined.

Present Looks into the Past

What the mind can miraculously perform really depends on the removal of a certain barrier against it, namely, the barrier of fears and interpretations of the past. This necessitates a certain freedom from present perspectives and willingness to look into the images of the past. The structured present as we know it, blinds and curtains the truth in the past. The individual who has started this journey of knowing the mind in a new way must loosen his stiff views and see the past from a different angle, since it is a gateway to the future. One turns back and goes into the alley of the past a little and this gives one access to the alley of the future. The psychical journey involves this curiosity, and is attended by fear and strength, anguish and hope, entrapment and release.

The entry into and exit from a mental state reflect into each other, like two mirrors standing face to face. Unless the individual is deeply involved in the mental state from the past, he cannot grow out of it, for it is the immediate and direct experience of entrapment in the negative experience which generates release from it. At this point life turns in many directions.

Suppose that a person presently thinks that his relationship with his father had always been a happy one. Suppose also that this person was, in fact, brought up by a disturbed, alcoholic father who would create terror in the family. Presently, this person is trying to suppress the original states of fear and anxiety by rigidly holding onto his present, untrue thought structures that the relationship was good and appropriate. The earlier true states, however, seep through his present, erroneous opinions about the father and create a psychological disturbance. Now, suppose that another person has complaints of ulcers. His attack becomes acute, especially when he is at his job. This person was brought up by a father who did not allow anyone to express himself in the family. The person used to feel angry, but could not do anything about it. Now, the relationship with the boss at work somewhat resembles the relationship with the father, and generates anxiety, frustration, and anger. This gradually becomes a recurrence of physiological states of anger, which become the basis for formation of an ulcer. Imagine still another person, a woman who was brought up by a disturbed mother who would holler at her and chase her up and down the stairs. As a result, she felt anxious and would cry. As the little girl grew up, she became afraid of becoming like her mother, a grown woman, and even delayed her menstruation. Later on, she married a man who hollered at her like her mother. After years of problems with the husband, she developed acute anxiety and started crying over even small frustrations.

The lag between one's relationship with the parents and manifestation of a symptom can be more subtle than the above examples indicate. One may be forced by the parents to develop an orientation which disturbs the natural and balanced functioning of the organism: for instance, an anxious parent may generate unnecessary hurry which later develops into symptoms of restlessness; an overprotective parent may demand overdependence and throttle activity to the point that physiological fatigue is generated in the child and he develops into an individual who is prone to depressions; an isolating parent may generate isolation in the child and consequent fear of relating to other people; or, a parent may generate over-excitement by provoking activity all the time and not allowing the child natural rest. Over a period of time, such various induced unnatural tendencies generate stress for the psycho-physiological system and create either anxiety or a psychosomatic symptom or finally a physiological disturbance.

It appears that the individual's massive problems in identity are based on lack of clarity about the past. As vagueness increases, he becomes self-centered or narcissistic, and with the increased confusion, he no longer has right views, intention, speech, or action, nor is he able to discharge his reactions to the negative situations of the past in a proper way. He compulsively wants to overcome his current pain by various brief procedures without examining its source in past interactions. Between pain and self-centered thought are the functions of aversion. He is no longer able to think, remember, or experience without flight; in brief, he is unable to concentrate. Instead, he guesses the nature of the relationship and, by ignoring or misconstruing what happened in the past, he keeps the cause of his present difficulty suppressed. But the unresolved anxiety and lack of clarity continue to generate offshoots of the original difficulty in the form of more psychological and physiological disturbances.

The eidetic theory indicates that your consciousness in some spontaneous way deals with the objects around you. What material in consciousness forces it to be selective in such a special way that it causes a problem to arise? Consciousness in its ordinary functions has its own objects from memory, with which it is already filled in. Like attracts like and, following that principle, what is already in your mind determines what you will see or choose to see. Examine this brief experiment carefully.

> *EXPERIMENT 1:* Comfortably relax near a pleasant spot such as a natural lake, a rose bush, or a patch of lush green grass. Experience the pleasure associated with the pleasant spot. Next, image an event from the past which was specifically painful to you. Now relax again and experience the pleasure associated with the pleasant spot. After this, image the painful event again. Then again look at the pleasant spot. Alternately experience the painful event and the pleasant spot many times. Notice that each time you image the painful event, the pleasant spot loses its positive effect on you. Finally, deeply concentrate on the painful event. Notice that your mind becomes completely occupied with the image of the negative event and temporarily loses its capacity to return to enjoyment of the pleasant spot. It appears paralyzed under pain.

What is present in the mind in the form of a memory influences the mind in a way that predisposes the individual to see the world with a certain emotional bias. The objects and situations from memory which inundate consciousness color the mind in a special way. How completely absorbed and flooded by the old objects we are is explained by the next experiment, which shows how the mind can spin in the complex web of memories without attempting to create a new experience.

> *EXPERIMENT 2:* Select a few scenes from memory for this experiment, for instance, the school you attended, your friends and classmates, the playground, the games you played, the subjects you liked or disliked. Make a list of these memory objects and scenes. Now, relax completely and pay attention to these memory pictures one by one, and experience your body feelings and thought processes during this concentration. As you move your attention from one picture to another, notice how your body feels and your thought processes change. Notice how you become pleased, angry, frustrated, or perplexed as you concentrate on each of

the various pictures. Notice that you can experience the emotions of pleasure, anger, or perplexity merely by looking at a specific picture. Also notice that you tend to stay with these feelings without changing them in any significant manner.

The above experiment shows that we are affected by what happened in the recent or distant past: an hour ago, a few hours ago, yesterday, many weeks or months ago, even many, many years ago. The memory pictures in our minds not only continue to affect our body and our thought processes, but the same event always creates the same body feeling specific to it. During each brief exposure you become influenced by what is in your mind. In the variety of mental content lies the first glimpse of the flexibility of the mind.

Personality Multiples

There is a fantastic process in the mind which seems almost too fantastic to believe. It demonstrates that a grown person's mind, like a child's, is essentially multiplicity-based, and free in this particular sense. As the individual grows older, he does not lose this freedom to create solutions through new awareness of concrete images of the self. These self-images, called *Personality Multiples,* represent the facts of our life from the moment of birth onward. We are not one but many. "Identity" in the sense of a rational defensive structure is an illusory complex, for in each experience that we participate, we have not yet formed its possibilities in the mind. Our ability to experience each personality multiple through the eidetic, which contains the full spectrum of the experience, is a central issue in eidetic work. Eidetic experience recognizes that the person is not one but many, structured out of many images in the past, and that in their realization lies hope for him. In order to help him reach and fulfill his life, it requires an understanding of who exactly he was in the past, involving his multiplicity, how and why he suffered, and how he could have grown out of his cul-de-sac.

When the individual is eidetically transported into the past, he lives his life experiences in the most lucid fashion, bringing details, conflicts, and polarities to acute awareness. The individual becomes aware of his various selves, experiencing each aspect intensely in the fresh encounter. These personality multiples, or preserved image aspects of the person in many situations where he may have been baffled or traumatized, bring out the potential of change. The individual can collect a measure of understanding out of these multiples by experiencing them in a systematic manner. When he exposes himself to intense experience of them in a structured way, he is able to regenerate the original condition of encounter in all its facets. To know where and how to proceed, the specific terminology that follows, describing the various states of participation, may be found helpful.

P is the person, who suffers from a problem.
P^i is the person in his usual feelings of identity ("i"), with fixed defensive views.
P^o is the person in flesh and blood, the one who can physically experience the complaints or symptoms, or freedom from them.
P^1 is the person in the self-image projected in the mind.

Further divisions and subdivisions of the self-image are possible, but at the present time we will deal only with the above units of experience, and describe the dynamic interaction between these essential, basic aspects to distinguish how the person can work with the experience in a lucid fashion.

If we assume that P undergoes an eidetic experience, in which P^1, an image, is the actor in the experience, and P^o feels the outcome of the experience, then we see that there is a direct relationship between P, P^o, and P^1, and that in this relationship P is ultimately affected and changed in some manner. In fact, what happens to P^i is the experiential change we want to achieve every time we induce an eidetic experience. As the person moves from P^i into P^1, the mediator P^o becomes involved in P^1, and, as a result, P changes and is healed of his symptom.

How P^o changes during eidetic experience, undergoing intense emotional and physiological transformations, should be of interest to us. This dimension gives us a glance into the mechanism of change. During an eidetic experience involving a personality multiple, the individual is not transported into the past in a manner that abolishes his awareness of the present. He as P^o experiences a state of double consciousness in which he is deeply involved in the image, while also simultaneously aware of his immediate surroundings. An experimental psychological environment is generated in which the new experience repeats itself and brings about new awareness, temporarily cutting off the conscious thought processes. Due to this special attribute not found in any other psychological process or phenomenon, the eidetic becomes a healing tool of great potential for the individual, a tool through which he can gradually develop new emotional perspectives at many levels. Clinical history is filled with successful cases in which the individual, during a critical stage of healing, went through such deep exposure to an experience that he lived it in complete depth. During this experience the mind spontaneously develops a certain distance from the present limited consciousness marked by sensitivity to a new emotive experience. The clinical evidence reveals that, as opposed to what usually happens in hypnosis, an intense experience in the eidetic can be effectively relived without complete dissociation. During the eidetic experience the individual deeply lives the critical point in the past where the root cause of the crisis lies and learns how to retrieve his emotional life in the situation where it was originally thwarted. By reliving and progressing the original experience again, the individual builds a new emotional perspective in full view of his present consciousness.

Life is a movie cartridge of frame after frame of subliminal visual involvements. In the stream of such experience, there are little whirlpools of new frames which follow a different vision of reality, vaguely sensed but not fully known. These are optical perceptual images which stand intermediate between fixed views and a new vision. They exist in adults and children, and, from their undiscovered spots, they deal with representative new solutions. In addition to strong visual characteristics, these images display other important features for a depth approach to problems. For instance, while concentrating on such an image, the already known passive image appearing in it may progress and gradually change into an active image. Sometimes, this image emerges slowly and without notice, while at other times one can actually see it even leaping out of the previous personality frame. One sees many new parts of himself in these images, and each expresses significant emotional states and psychological themes. Over a lifetime many of these frames are formed and cast into molds for later use and reference. They survive for indefinite periods of time, until the problem they represent is expressed, lived, and resolved. With each personality frame, new aspects having an important bearing on one's health or difficulties unfold, as in the case below.

> While looking back I saw many images of myself in different negative situations at the Center. I was painfully affected each time by each image of myself. But the most astounding experience was the many image frames of the boy who was constantly picked on by other boys at the place. In the beginning of the imagery sequence I was afraid of even dealing with this unhappy boy. But I took courage and concentrated on the image of the other boys picking on him. Within a short time of seeing this and various images that emerged out of it, I was surprised to see in one image that there was life within this boy. I realized that there was life there in him and life was a very great thing. What happened in the image preceding this awareness was merely a series of images involving persecution. But I became aware that you could not persecute somebody who was not alive. If was as if he was a dead boy, who became alive in my mind through this image and became special and sacred. I had not been aware of life like that before. What a paradox. In life, you may go searching for life and never find it; but as you keep on looking, it leaps out right in front of you.

Emanation Images

Most personality multiples release the eidetic experience contained in them in a progressively unfolding manner. Once the individual comes into contact with an important personality multiple, the experience spontaneously takes him over and leads him to a deep experience in the form of progression of images. However, sometimes an individual may feel such intense emotion due to fear or shame that the experience may come to a complete stop. Interestingly, in such cases another dimension of the image phenomenon, the emanation technique, becomes helpful.

As the eidetic structures show us, each eidetic image has an ability to generate another image through a process that resembles the jump of an electric charge. Each eidetic jump involves a carrying forward of the person's feeling of identity, and as more jumps take place, this identity involves a series of self-images. These strings of self-images can be developed through the emanation technique, based on the electrical capacity in the eidetic toward a new evolvement containing the element of surprise. Eidetic emanation helps break the status quo of an image which is too fixed on a current thought pattern, and is unable to grow independent of the ego defense. The emanation state replaces the frozen state with a fast moving emotional experience.

To break unusual resistances and uncover important mental material, the emanation technique can be highly effective. To visualize how the image progression works, examine this brief description: P is currently seeing a self-image, called P^1; out of P^1 jumps another image called P^2; out of P^2 jumps P^3; out of P^3 jumps P^4, and so on. To know how it actually happens in the mind, study this example involving application of the principle:

> I was experiencing a negative image in which I was frozen with fear before the boys in school. They looked big, tall, and mean. I tried many techniques to give myself a little pep in the image, but none worked out well. Finally, I used the emanation technique. I saw another me jumping out of the scared me. This new me (P^2) looked somewhat less scared but still unable to fend off the attack. Then I attempted another jump and saw another me leaping out of the previous me and this one was a lot more active. It (P^3) quickly and very actively withdrew to a safe distance from the boys. I then saw the fourth me (P^4) jumping out of the third image, and this last image turned back and swooped on the boys and beat up every one of them. I was totally surprised how the whole scene changed into an active scene in which I experienced relief and expression. I beat every one of those nasty, mean kids. I saw them running in all directions under attack from P^4. The imagery scene became bright and full of life energy.

The emanation technique offers a real possibility of progressing and resolving an old image which involved some trauma in the past that could not be resolved in a regular way. Try this experiment regarding emanation.

> **EXPERIMENT 3:** Select a situation from the past in which you faced a problem you could not resolve. See that your self-image is facing the problem in the image. Know the emotions and the problems in an

intense manner and experience how you are blocked as P^1. Now see another self-image jumping out of this self-image, and see how the new image P^2 acts. Experience that the new self-image acts in a way that is different from the previous self-image, and that it resolves the problem. If this does not happen and the new self-image is still unable to break the knot, see yet another self-image P^3 jumping out of the previous self-image. Then see the fourth self-image P^4 jumping out of the third, and the fifth jumping out of the fourth, and so forth. Continue this until you find that the progression of experience in the form of these leaping-out self-images finally resolves the problem. Find another difficult situation in the past and experiment with it in a similar manner.

Parallel Projection

Psychical experience reveals that a person seeing an object unites with the object, becoming one with it. A person experiences an image as if it were he. Psychical experience of water is like "being water." Poets have copiously described this "imaginative" core of deep mental exposure. Like a liquid, experience takes the shape of every container it enters. When a person watches someone suffering, the suffering flows to the person watching it and enters him. Similarly, when a person watches someone who is happy, the happiness flows into the person watching it and enters him. This psychical process, called *Parallel Projection,* enables the individual to experience his identity not from his own side, but from the side of another object or person. Follow closely the experiment given below.

EXPERIMENT 4: Concentrate in your mind on the following natural objects: a flower, a green leaf, a small cloud, an ocean wave, a patch of blue sky. Rest with each object until your consciousness is completely absorbed by it. Notice the change induced in your consciousness by the object. Each object transforms your consciousness according to itself. With the flower your mind becomes "flowery," with the leaf it becomes "leafy," with the cloud it becomes "cloudy," with the wave it becomes "wavy," with the patch of blue sky, it becomes "blue" in color. Now deeply concentrate on the most pleasant image out of these selected images and allow yourself to relax completely. Next, concentrate on this image deeply and experience the relaxation emerging slowly and changing your states of consciousness until you feel you are totally absorbed in a state of complete happiness or bliss. Your mind becomes like the object; it assumes the state of the object.

We can easily see that a child would become depressed with a depressed mother and happy with a happy mother, withdrawn with a withdrawn mother, stiff with a stiff mother and angry with an angry mother. After first changing according to the states of the mother, the child would later change according to the states of the father. At the same time he can be seen changing according to the states of the siblings. All these many states involve parallel projection, and each parallel projection represents a personality multiple. The ability to experience a parallel projection may be considered a heightened state of empathy, almost poetic in nature. The practical lesson in parallel projection concerns the person's ability to experience an image and his personal identity relations with another object or person with profound feeling. The process of empathy prevails in the mind to such an extent and depth that the individual can experience someone else's mental image, if described to him, with such intensity that he can go through that person's feelings of suffering or happiness and experience transformation involving awareness of a new mental horizon never known before. The other person's experience becomes a basis of knowledge about life.

The Magical Behavior of Images

The inner world of images is of such vast potential and so systematic that it is practically magical. One can use certain types of eidetic images for surfacing information which conscious thinking may be unable to produce on demand. The parallel projection imagery demonstrates how certain images in the mind are influenced by other images and made to act in a manner which reasoning fails to explain. Through these images many processes in which the magical behavior of imagery is used can be set in motion. Let us examine this example, in which the Age Projection Test, an eidetic test based directly on this potential in the imagery process, was therapeutically used.

> An individual suffering from anxiety and somnambulism was first asked to see his parents standing in front of him in the form of an image. In the same image setting, he was asked to see himself in the state of anxiety he was suffering from, and to see this self-image standing in front of images of parents. He was then asked to cry in front of his parents, kick up a tantrum, and throw the shirt he was wearing in front of them to create a reaction in them. He saw that the father did not move in the picture, but the mother bent over and picked up his shirt. Thereafter, her image spontaneously walked away from the scene and went to a side room, where she was seen placing the shirt in a box. The individual, who was following her movement in the image, opened the box in the image and looked into it. He spotted his shirt inside the box, but also saw something else alongside it—a pistol. The moment he looked at the pistol, his mind became fogged for a brief period of time. Then, as he continued to look at the image of the pistol, he started shivering and perspiring, and did not know why. Soon, memories spontaneously gushed out, and he remembered that many years ago when he was

travelling to see his grandparents, who were in another city, the train was attacked by robbers. He remembered that, as the robbers entered his compartment, he was half asleep and quickly got up and fled to the fields for safety. The gun in the image was a reminder of the feelings he had. had at that time: fear, humiliation, and the wish that he had a gun. At this moment, he became spontaneously aware that the anxiety which he was suffering from was representative of fixation on the feelings of fear and humiliation experienced in this incident. The mere act of looking at the pistol in the box as he shivered and perspired recovered the forgotten memory and spontaneously healed him of a dissociated feeling state. Through the projection, he was relieved of somnambulism and the feeling of anxiety which had persisted in him since a year after the incident. The intuitive knowledge or omniscience in the mother's image magically provided a link in the mind which had failed to surface through conscious recollection (Ahsen, 1968).

The parents' images contain not only the repertoire of historical relationships, but also omniscient power and ritualistic behavior of magical significance. It appears that these attributes are not accidental, nor a mere oozing of belief on the part of the child during the helpless days of his development, but a segment of a biological relationship. These image structures in the mind have their own power and their own direction; and, if they are handled intelligently, many fantastic maneuvers can be built on them. The magical quality of the parental images appears to run counter to their historical defects, and the two operations oppose each other. In fact, an historically frustrating parent or the patient himself suppresses these magical attributes and replaces them with limiting patterns. These limiting patterns imposed on consciousness and development should be removed and the original qualities released again. The parental images thus contain this bipolar configuration between history and original endowment, in the form of a magical life style resembling the Garden of Eden.

Bipolarity

The eidetic image is a mental event of vast flexibility and possibility, containing many alternatives. The imagery event which happened one way could have happened a different way, and the eidetic contains both the actuality and the possibility. It divides each psychological event into two opposed interpretations, two events, two images. These bipolar images behave in a seesaw of opposition, each with its own configuration and its own specific physiological characteristics that involve the body in a certain manner. Let us see how the principle works regarding the parental images.

EXPERIMENT 5: Select two memories of your parents, i.e., two images, one negative and the other positive. Carefully and clearly see each image in your mind and write down the feelings which it evokes in you. Notice that when you concentrate on the negative and then on the positive image of your parents, your feeling states change accordingly. At one time you feel negative, and at the other time you feel positive. You alternate between the experience of anxiety and relief.

Consciousness cannot be fixed on both poles at the same time; it must choose one and reject the other. Fixation on a negative event leads to negative adjustment, and by reversing the visio-fixation, the negative fixation can be reversed. An event which happened one way could also have happened the opposite way, but ordinary consciousness confirms only one pole. With time, the confirmed pole becomes magnified due to the repeated attention paid to it, while the other pole becomes vague. Visual cues of the suppressed pole do often dimly appear on the fringes of consciousness. If attention is shifted to the suppressed positive pole and is brought to focus on it, the focusing gradually moves it into the center of attention. As it moves into the center, the character of the situation is reversed to a new advantage. Gradually, the ego becomes fixed on the new, positive visual image and the feeling states change accordingly.

Interestingly, the states of consciousness, when pulled to the extreme of painful behavior, as a rule tend to swing in the opposite direction in a spontaneous fashion. The manner in which the states of consciousness can be oscillated from the point of equilibrium represents the basic art of handling consciousness according to its natural and original principles. Try the following experiment, which describes this primary behavior at the level of consciousness change.

> *EXPERIMENT 6:* To demonstrate oscillation of consciousness through a physical analogy, take a string and attach a sufficiently heavy object to it, to construct a pendulum. First, hold the string and let the pendulum come to a state of rest at the middle point, reaching a standstill. Then push the object mildly to one side and watch. As the pendulum moves to one end, it comes back and returns to the opposite side; then it goes to the opposite side and returns again, passing through the middle point each time. This behavior continues until the pendulum stops.

The bipolar behavior of the pendulum resembles the behavior of images not only in the linear forward growth of interpreted perspectives (in the form of image sequences), but also in the mirror opposition between two distinctly opposed interpretations. At this point consciousness behaves like a boat, and the two opposing interpretations (as two opposed series of image sequences) are like two oars. If a person sees one imagery sequence, this oar turns the experiential boat in one direction; but if he sees the opposed imagery sequence, this opposite oar turns the experiential boat in the totally opposite direction. Although the alternatives in the mind go in opposite directions, they emerge from the same essentially unbifurcated point of unity.

Consciousness as an Oscillating Psychofeedback Field

These bipolar and other arrangements in the images can be put to many uses. In our ordinary consciousness, we fix our minds too much on only one aspect of an event. In the awareness of the event, however, we can always hit upon a new aspect or a new alternative. We neglect to notice the deepest mystery of life, that each significant event is not only structured the way we know it happened, but also the way it did not happen or could have happened or should have happened. Reality, if not known in all its varied aspects, can cause problems and symptoms. This unknown alternative reality sends messages to us, saying, "Realize IT; and if you do not, you will remain trapped in the reference points of a fixed illusion." Reality is not fixed, it is the way we see it that determines its definition. By rigidly holding onto a swing of mood in the past, you will overdefine your nature and limit the vision of your true self.

The patterns of bipolarity and other aspects manifest themselves as psychofeedback arrangements at the level of pure consciousness behavior. This field is a complex and intricate system of feedback arrangements at a purely psychological level. These arrangements, unlike biofeedback experiments, use no mechanical equipment; only mental images are employed to create events in consciousness. The previous six experiments described consciousness in its various modes, including swings of consciousness between various states of awareness. Now we will take a total look at the behavior of consciousness through more experiments and show how consciousness as a whole responds to various rules as a self-contained psychofeedback field.

> **EXPERIMENT 7:** Relax completely and become aware of the sensations in your body, such as slight tension along the legs, irritation in the skin, a rumble in the abdomen, tightness in the back and breathing, etc. Experience these body sensations until you become sufficiently aware of how they affect you and how they appear and disappear. Now select two objects in your field of vision: one that you like and one that you dislike. Let us call the object that attracts you Object A and the one that repels you Object B. Now, look at Object A with a relaxed but fixed gaze for about 30 seconds. Become aware of your body response to it, and, as you do so, notice any change in your body feelings, such as in your breathing, etc. Do the same with Object B. Now alternately look at Object A and Object B for a brief period each time and become aware of the character of feelings the two objects create in you. Notice that as you look at Object A or Object B, the body feelings change accordingly each time.

If an object in the environment has negative import for you, viewing it causes negative changes in your body feelings. Similarly, viewing a positive object from the environment influences you, changing your body feelings in the positive direction of pleasure and release. This can be stated in the form of a psychofeedback principle: In order to keep your body feelings in a positive state of release, you must keep a positive object in mind.

However, a person may not know what is truly pleasant or unpleasant for him, because he may impose too much conscious thought on the material of consciousness, causing the experience to appear different from what it really is. In order to train your consciousness to know, at the natural level, what is really pleasant and unpleasant, try the following psychofeedback experiment.

> *EXPERIMENT 8:* Select, instead of two objects, many objects—A, B, C, D, E, and F—from the environment. Now relax and pay attention to these objects one by one. As you concentrate on each object, allow your body and your thought processes to respond spontaneously. Observe how you respond to each object in a certain specific manner. Now change your pattern of attention, and scan all the objects in a different, irregular sequence. Notice that you again respond to each object in a special manner. Object D, for instance, reflects in your body and your thought processes in a manner which is very different from that of Object F. Also, see that you can create all types of emotional sequences at will, through managing the objects accordingly.

This experiment discloses the potency of objects in your environment to induce a change in your body and your feeling and thought processes. Since you are being constantly affected by your environment in this manner, you could determine which objects you want to have around you. However, this principle has a natural limitation: because attention is already selective in nature, it allows only those objects in your environment which are significant to you to emerge in your awareness.

Due to the specific links between the memory picture and the body feelings, we should next try to find out how we can create a specific positive body feeling by merely attending its related image. Interestingly, this gives us access to control feelings along certain memory paths. Having the knowledge that such-and-such memory image is connected with such-and-such nerve path or body feeling, to create a certain body feeling in certain areas of the body, one just summons the related specific image to mind. If one knows the process well, one can make his right arm hot while the left arm remains cold. To learn this basic rule, which has many fascinating possibilities, do this psychofeedback experiment.

> *EXPERIMENT 9:* This experiment uses memory pictures. Make a list

of memory images from the past, some pleasant, others unpleasant, still others which are neutral. Next, relax and see each picture in your mind and examine the related emotion which it induces in your consciousness. Next, select the body feeling or emotion you want to create. Project its corresponding picture, and concentrate on it. You will see that you are able to create the body feeling or emotion on demand by merely attending its mental picture. Go through the whole list of memory pictures and create the body feelings or emotions as you desire. Practice this psychofeedback control on images and their emotions and learn how you can recall and regenerate an emotional state merely by retrieving its memory picture and visualizing it through concentration.

This experiment should make clear that there are objects in memory which are painful and others which are pleasant, and that their related emotions persist in consciousness. Conclusion: an angry person has objects and scenes in his past which made him angry, and, similarly, a depressed or anxious person has objects and scenes in the past which made him depressed or anxious. Once we can actively reproduce the emotions, we can resolve the negative effects from the past.

You might have noticed in the above experiment that some pictures always appear to be more potent than others and generate emotion and thought in a relatively more constant manner. These pictures can be used, as a reliable source, to feed consciousness with a ready emotion to create a desired feeling state or counteract one. For instance, one person recovered from his worst depression by merely looking at the hands of his father in his mind, and another gradually recovered from his muscle aches by wearing the huge coat of his father in the picture. To understand the extreme psychofeedback potency of these mental objects, do this experiment.

EXPERIMENT 10: From memory, make a list of objects associated with father and mother, such as the things they wore or used: hats, coats, shirts, trousers, dresses, shoes, socks, watches, glasses, ties, scarves, walking sticks, handkerchiefs, umbrellas, aprons, and any other such objects you can think of. Concentrate on each object and picture yourself wearing, holding, or touching the object in your mind. Finally, select the object which has the most positive influence on you when you see yourself wearing, holding, or touching it in the picture. Now, list the objects in the order of their influence on you, differentiating those which have the most positive influence from those which have the most negative influence. Notice that you can change your emotional state by wearing, holding, or touching these objects. Practice this often to know the influence of each object on you.

Since objects of memory, whether positive or negative, have a profound influence on our consciousness, they can become a powerful source of feeling states and can influence identity in a demonstrable fashion. Because you are what you feel, your identity state can change from what it is right now if you merely look at an image object from the past.

Mind works in a complex yet completely understandable manner. As a person learns, through the above series of experiments, the various processes involved in feeling and thought, he can differentiate the various aspects of mind. As he contemplates the various aspects of mind, he learns about how his mind behaves and develops personal knowledge of the psychological causation. The freely flowing and changing mind is not an unstable panorama of feelings and thought processes but a sequence of imagery events. As the mind swirls and changes, the mental objects continue to observe the rule of these sequences.

The reality of the self is equally distributed over the lines of imagery sequences and their bipolar configurations. True identity is formed out of these possibilities, whereas mistaken identity is an image nucleus merely accidentally formed. Realization of the self is realization of the perspectives offered by the image nuclei.

Eidetic Images of Parents

The negative orientations in the mind can be spotted in the interaction with parents, and can be treated by specific concentration and discharge methods. Gradually, development of appropriate positive feelings can emerge in place of the original negative feelings as specific location, elaboration, and elimination of negative orientations leads to the cure of the related states. Ordinary memory images of parents in the mind do not give us access to the nature of problems. The conscious thought layers or imagery describe the parents from a defensive angle, while the real layer of imagery dealing with the conflicts and problems associated with the parents is preserved and stored away in the form of eidetic images. The individual obstructs the emergence of these real images by maintaining an attitude of isolation toward these pictures and superimposing on the isolation a romanticized version of life in which parents become an aspect of unreality. Once one breaks through this barrier of unreality and isolation and reaches the real images of parents, one starts experiencing the original source of pleasure and anxiety. Now in possession of the original dynamics, the individual's original vitality can be directed in a manner that enables him to reassert his innate strength and health.

The Eidetic Parents Test images, which help the individual project the original parental imagery in various contexts of development, serve as a key to surfacing the early interactive experience and the attitudes and conflicts which are associated with them. The method of surfacing and treating these images is objective and educational, aimed at development of a new life style.

Symptom's Parallels to Parental Problems

It appears that the symptom is always related to a problem with parents in a direct or indirect manner and originates from an unknown part of the relationship with parents. This unknown is guarded by the inertia of habit. This inertia of habit is further engirdled by myopic behavior. The myopic behavior is fenced in by a form of "pseudo-imagery," which provides a sense of "pseudo-reality." This "pseudo-reality" is defended by "pseudo-reasoning." Finally, the original, "unknown" relationship is replaced by a known relationship which suffers from so many superficialities that it frustrates the natural functions of the mind. This is the symptom. It leads to formulation of further layers of frustration and the individual progressively disintegrates.

Return to the unknown part of the relationship with parental figures involves rejection of the "conscious," the "known," and its various memory forms. This can be done by generating past reality afresh through eidetic rules of imagery projection which gradually cut through the "habits" of memory and pseudo-thought processes, allowing the "original" experiences to emerge again. It is precisely in the dissolution of the outer shell of superficial life and in the understanding of one's precise relationship with the original capacities endowed by nature that the favorable outcome of emotional change lies. If identity is continuous with images of the past, then what we think of ourselves consciously is only a frame of reference serving what is already known and not what needs to be known about the true functions of Nature.

The symptom, which resides and floats in consciousness structures, obeys the rules of nature and of projection mechanisms in the same manner as the rest of consciousness. An individual usually settles himself in a life perspective which involves the pain, conflict, and his adjustment in a state of relative equilibrium. This state, however, is not altogether static because the symptom becomes alternately acute or ameliorated, according to the events and changes around the person. The symptom behaves like the pendulum we described earlier, passing through the midpoints of extremes all the time.

If, then, we make the symptom acute in some way, we will successfully create a state of amelioration spontaneously, as demonstrated by the pushed pendulum returning faster from the high point. Since the symptom shows a natural instability, we can always break fixity of the symptom by making it respond to artificial accentuation, followed by ideas of relief, a technique by which we can push the symptom to its negative extreme and thus cause the positive side to come to the surface. By knowing the symptom's opposite positive relation in the past, we can deal with its structures in a curative fashion. The technique first involves deep concentration on any negative feelings, worries, or concerns you have around the symptom which cause the symptom to become acute. As soon as the symptom becomes acute, then let yourself relax and come back to a normal state again. As this happens and the mental states tend to become more positive, allow your mind to think of positive images from the past. As a positive picture emerges in your mind, you come to know the positive end of what bothers you. To elucidate the nature of the symptom from this angle, let us examine an eidetic test (Age Projection Test) which uses this technique, as described in some detail in *Basic Concepts in Eidetic Psychotherapy* (1968). Although this test was originally developed to treat symptoms, its usefulness in explaining other emotions of the acute type has been established. In fact, the test can be used for any worry, concern, or symptom so that its relationship with unknown past events can be studied with ease and speed.

The Age Projection Test

This test is useful for eliciting material on the symptom and also other negative emotions which the individual has evolved but their cause is no longer available to consciousness. The individual is not able to reach the related themes consciously or connect them with his present condition. The Age Projection Test, also called Symptom Oscillation Test (SOT), points out ideas and themes trapped in the symptom or negative emotions.

The Age Projection Test is a sensitive test which must be administered carefully to obtain maximum results. The steps for administration of the test are the following.

Before the Age Projection Test is administered, a procedure called composing the symptom is used. It aims at assembling the symptom afresh in the clinic in its negative physical and psychological features. The person is asked to talk about the symptom while the therapist takes down notes. During this talk he carefully separates the psychological from the physiological descriptions and records them separately under the two headings in the words of the person. Then the person is asked about ideas of worry and concern about the symptom. These are also listed alongside the other two headings. When a complete picture of the symptom has been assembled, it shows psychological and physiological features and features of worry and concern about these negative conditions. To aid the less introspective person and also to prepare a more accurate picture of his complaints, the therapist should also point to the body of the person in a detailed way and make the person talk about any concern, worry, or negative feelings which he may entertain concerning each body part and organ. He starts from the head, discussing with the person his hair, skull, scalp, brain, temples, neck, eyes, ears, nose, mouth, teeth, tongue, throat, stomach, intestines, genitals, lungs, heart, arms, hands, legs, knees, feet, joints, muscles, skin, etc.

After the therapist has composed the symptom in the above manner, he is ready to administer the Age Projection Test. The therapist asks the person his nickname, first name, and family name, the names commonly used to describe him. These names are later used interchangeably throughout the test so that we do not identify the person with one of the roles signified by the usual name he carries.

Next, the person is educated regarding what he should expect and how he should act during the actual administration of the test. He is told to stay relaxed, eyes open or closed, attending the therapist's words, which will be spoken to him during this relaxed state of attention. After the person has been briefed in this way, the therapist further tells him that after he repeats certain instructions to him over and over again, he will gradually see an image of himself somewhere in the past. The person is warned that in no case should he try to develop this image consciously, but only attend to the words spoken by the therapist in a relaxed state of mind and allow the image to develop gradually out of this state.

The next step involves warming up of the symptom. The therapist, after composing the symptom and giving preliminary instructions, starts the next phase. He repeats the assembled features of the symptom to the person over and over again. While doing so, the person is addressed by his various names alternately. A recitation of the various aspects of the symptom gradually throws the person into an experience of the symptom at a pitch which he has rarely experienced before. The symptom, along with all its details and features, is artificially activated and brought to an unbearable acuteness, at which point the person shows signs of anxiety and a desire to get out of the state imposed by the therapist's procedure.

After the symptom has been brought to this artificial pitch, suddenly and dramatically the opposite tendency toward health is brought into play, the tendency which combats the symptom through the principle of opposition. When the therapist notices acute anxiety in the person, he allows the person to relax for a few seconds and then suddenly starts talking about the past when the person was healthy and happy, and he did not have those symptoms. At this stage the therapist talks about the opposite features of the symptom as if the person were not suffering from the symptom any more and were experiencing the opposite states of happiness and release. As the therapist talks about states of health, the person is emotionally preparing to project a new self-image. This self-image usually belongs to an age one year prior to the emergence of the symptom, outside of the chain of events committing the person to a way of life which finally led him to a state of ill health. The state of health projected in the new image stands in close proximity to this period of crisis.

Once the new image has been projected, the person is asked to see his new self-image over and over again so that it becomes vivid in his mind. Sometimes the image remains vague for a brief while but becomes clear after a few more attempts.

When the person is able to clearly see clothes on the image, we are ready to enter into the next phase of the test, which is connected with making inquiries concerning the year after the age of the new self-image. The inquiry around this critical age in most cases discloses the meaning and origin of the symptom. The person is asked to slowly remember events around this critical period. As he talks, each significant memory is discussed in detail, and the symptom is examined in the light of this information.

The last phase of the test uses parental images to throw light on the meaning of the symptom from another source. This phase is useful especially in case the previous phase of the image failed to elucidate the cause of the symptom.

The next image scene is enacted in the parental house with objects such as the parental images, along with any other person who may appear to be significant, such as a sibling or a grandparent. The self-image of the person stands before the parental images and the significant person, and throws a tantrum and cries to provoke pity and love in them. Then he takes off one article of clothing (especially clothing which looks bright in the image) and flings it on the floor saying, "Take it away, I don't want to wear it." Crying is continued until one of the parents or the significant person picks it up from the floor. After picking it up from the floor, this parent or person is seen going away to deposit it somewhere. The person follows the individual carefully to see where he or she goes and puts it. The person is asked to see where the clothing has been placed, and confirm it by seeing it in the image. The person looks at the clothing where it has been placed, and sees if any other object stands out clearly in the vicinity of that article of clothing. Direct memories are then collected on the new object near the article of clothing, and the symptom is studied in the light of the memories connected with this new object. The symptom then becomes understandable in the light of the new information, revealed through concentration on the new memories.

The Age Projection Test can be used for the following purposes:

1. Discovering the cause of acute symptoms in the events of the past;
2. Discovering the cause of negative emotions in the events of the past;
3. Discovering the cause of minor irritations in the events of the past.

During any difficult analytic phase, the individual can be encouraged to cry in front of the parental images to seek understanding and overcoming of the hurdles of consciousness. In an earlier section entitled "The Magical Behavior of Images," the power in parental images to reveal such information was discussed through a case history. When an individual loses confidence in his own resources, the magical power in the parental images becomes available, and the states of omniscience connected with their images become a new source of strength and information.

Self-Doubt

Self-doubt is a lack of awareness of one's own personality, a state of uncertainty about it characterized by dependency, complacency, and self-effacement. It involves a poor self-image and a lack of confidence in one's internal abilities. When an individual is not in contact with his own experience, he suffers from self-doubt. One should ask these questions about one's self: "Do I suffer from self-doubt?" "Do I doubt my own experience in such a general way that I come to doubt a lot more about my total person?" "Should I find out what happens when I do not really doubt my perceptions?" "Does my self-worth increase if I learn to discover my own perceptions in the images and learn to handle them?" It has been found that by learning to manage one's own experience, one can discover new confidence in one's own way of seeing things. No one should really self-efface himself before views which originated in subtle coercion or hypnotic control of internal mind processes.

How do the emotions proceed from the internal source? In most cases, they flow spontaneously from the images in an uninhibited manner. In some cases, however, they may start in a cramped manner, so that only proper concentration on the images evolves the experience to a sufficient degree. With more concentration and passage of time, the ability for experiencing emotions from the images slowly grows. With this, self-doubt diminishes and self-worth grows. Sometimes, emotions may suddenly break out, as in moments of sadness, crying, rage, etc., but, as more emotions become visible, the ability to view internal life with equanimity grows accordingly. Work with the images increases your capacity to honor your own experience.

Eidetic analysis is the individual's own unfolding. It initiates self-education through internal task-activity, being connected with the pragmatic aim of understanding and overcoming daily anxiety and its origin in personal history. The pragmatic analytic movement leads to progressive integration and harmonization of the individual, releasing and unifying his gifts. Eidetic analysis, a profound study of the self, draws out the individual without an external educator.

Forgetting, Repression, and Unconscious

The heart of the eidetic theory states: There is an activated experiential point in the mind in the form of an eidetic image which reveals personal interactive facts in a spontaneous fashion. Eidetic interaction magnifies the mind material and scans its various layers like a radar beam, detecting, deciphering, revealing, and enforcing expulsion of the negative experience. It leads mental awareness to a culmination point, where another interactive beam, another awareness, enters and initiates another movement of awareness and expansion. When these revealing beams or activated points in the mind are brought to a full interactive view, important aspects of the mind are comprehended in the process.

Forgetting is a natural process in the mind. If we remembered every experience at the same moment of time, our mind would become a scene of utter confusion. However, when someone forgets important and nourishing experiences of life, he denies reentry into consciousness of the content which represents life itself. This well known process is known in literature as repression. Eidetic findings show that these forgotten memories or the unconscious parts of the mind are not truly forgotten but are always available through the eidetic images. Systematic progression of images makes the non-conscious part become conscious within a few minutes. The "unconscious" is mistakenly stated as a region in the mind, but it is, in fact, a condition of noncontact with a relevant emotion, memory, or idea.

If you have forgotten an experience or a memory, it is not lost forever. It expresses itself in the form of blocked images. Once a person rediscovers the image of his true relationship with the parents, the repressions are lifted accordingly. The procedure for surfacing the blocked memories little by little through the parental images is a fairly easy approach to making the "unconscious" part of your personality conscious.

The recovery of emotion or memories—in other words, the lifting of repression—can be accomplished through the procedures mentioned throughout this book, wherein image details, emotions, and meanings are developed through a system of projections. As each detail is developed through repetition, one comes to know the various facets of experiential life not known before.

A subtle form of repression arises from the individual imitating wrongful behavior of parents without critical awareness. Since imitation and reaction start very early, one may practice an emotion or an attitude without knowledge of its origin and consequence. To know the deepest sources of repression in the mind, one needs to know how one has imitated or reacted to the right or wrong influence of parents. Such a study of attachment to the parental figures gives us insight and knowledge. In this process, eidetic analysis searches out the new material not merely in the negative recollection of parents, but also in their positive imagery manifestations, compelling the individual to act in complete recourse to the original self. One must become aware of the elements of personality issuing from the natural parental base. Through searching a source of life in the parents, the individual, in the ultimate sense, becomes a source unto himself.

Attachment to Parents

Attachment is passive reliance on a behavior which at one time was biologically useful but then was pursued beyond the time of its natural usefulness. The individual became attached to the behavior with self-protective tendencies and developed a false sense of security in its practice. Now this behavior creates depression, since the individual has not yet learned to operate in an active and independent fashion, as the parent was always overprotective, creating a relationship of immaturity and ineffectiveness. To know various facets of negative attachment, examine the parents' images to discover whether they force gratifications, demand passivity, and screen the mind from reasonable exposure to life and its situations. Do the parents' images show fear and concern if active interest in the pursuit of new life situations is shown to them?

Imitation of Parents

Imitation is a behavior that copies the action of another individual with or without conscious intention to duplicate it. Do the symptoms reveal imitation of parents? It is possible to take over the problem behavior of parents. Examine which parent's negative behavior patterns appear to have been adopted in life. Was this learning a quiet form of acceptance or had it been initially forced? Unless imitations are uncovered and removed, the individual continues to act under their influence.

Reaction to Parents

Reaction is a behavior which is the direct opposite of another behavior, for instance, in response to a probing parent, the child develops the need to be secretive. Reaction takes many forms: the individual may react with passivity to a controlling parent; with indecision to a critical parent; or with fear to a violent parent. While studying the symptoms, it has to be decided if the symptoms are reactions to some behavior in one or both parents. Take the example of punishment. If one is inappropriately punished, the punishable response, as an impulse, remains strong in the form of a wish and expresses itself through a pattern of seeking overt expression and final punishment. The memory of punishment provokes reenactment feelings so that the individual will create actual life situations in which he would be punished. Unless the original impulse is mentally reenacted, the individual continues to act under the influence of reactions.

Loss

Loss is a feeling state that emerges when a child has been denied one of his biological needs, such as close association with his mother in early development and with his father in later stages of development, predictable feeding schedules on the part of the mother, and appropriate approval or disapproval when the child does the right or wrong thing. The following list of loss behaviors may be found useful in understanding the nature and consequence of loss. Notice any indications of loss from the parental images along these lines.

1. Do you find that you were inappropriately handled while growing up?

2. Discover if your feeding schedules were appropriate.

3. Find out whether one of the parents was more or less absent while you were growing up.

4. Try to recall whether father went out too early in the morning or came home too late at night, and whether mother went out on a job when you were small.

5. Look back and see if a parent ignored you while he or she was at home and paid attention to business or household chores rather than to you.

6. Did a parent give special attention to a particular sibling and ignore you?

7. Were you often caressed physically by mother as well as father, so that you experienced security?

8. Did your parents actively look into your expressed needs and attend to them?

9. Did your parents actively look into your unexpressed needs and attend to them?

Loss means some form of biological rejection and associated attachment to ineffective, inappropriate behavior, which results in lack of happiness and a general failure of life. Finally, loss means being divorced from the basis of life, a lack of enjoyment of life in its original biological condition.

Loss develops into chronic molds of behavior which entrap the individual in a web of self-defeating notions. These stiff molds need to be cracked and the life energies released during a fresh encounter with the foundation of life. The therapy deals with the current experience of past potential, in order to help the individual reach a place in the mind where genuine expression can be experienced. The present, loss ridden, defensive life style barricades this possibility. Only after the individual has experienced his energies from this fundamental side does he come to know his true life.

If one is cut off from natural life and its many pictures, he is cut off from the source of reality. This is how floating begins in the mind. A rigid glance from the state of loss makes life a one–dimensional, linear view; but, if the person knew how to make contact with the many sides of his nature, he would come into contact with diversified reality once again. If he cannot contact that reality, he will continue to journey through the abstract illusions of a constricted mind.

Identification

Identification is a state of closely sharing views and feelings with a parent to the point that one feels almost identical with that parent. One may identify with mother or father to the point that one takes over his or her views and practices them as self-obvious truth. Identification with a parent who has improper views or a behavior disturbance exposes you to having the same problems as that parent.

Identification with one parent leads to rejection of the other parent. If you open yourself to the experience of the rejected parent, it will teach you how to be different toward others. Experience how, over a long period of time, the parent you identify with has impaired your abilities to relate with others. All this is not truly you, and you must make a fresh beginning in the light of this new information. You must discover a new ideal which makes your life better and more useful.

Neurotic Projection

Neurotic projection is attributing one's own inaccurate subjective thoughts to other people. For instance, someone may wrongly attribute a thought or feeling to you which you did not believe or experience yourself. Similarly, you may attribute to another person something which the other person never felt. Speaking in terms of parents, if a parent was generally absent, you may come to doubt that parent's love for you and come to believe that the parent did not like you or, in fact, actively disliked you.

A neurotic projection is basically an inaccurate image of a parent which is not true to history. In this negative clinical sense, the term "neurotic projection" differs from the general process of imagery projection, which is not a morbid process but a method of mental investigation. The neurotic projection shows itself in many ways, in both one's mental imagery and in one's relationship with others. Finally, it corrupts and misconstrues the very fabric of life itself. How do neurotic projections develop from parental figures? A deeper awareness of parental images reveals their source in a direct or indirect way in the presence or absence of interaction with them.

DEEPER INTERACTION WITH PARENTAL IMAGES

Awareness of Symptoms

One way to know more about the images of parents is to experience your symptoms before you experience the parental images. The awareness of symptoms directly creates deeper sensitivity to the images of parents.

Every individual who seeks analysis suffers from some painful symptoms. The individual needs to know not only the obvious and gross forms of the symptoms, but also their subtle aspects. He needs to become aware of his suffering, in all its hidden mental and physical forms. If he proceeds with the analysis by first becoming aware of this suffering, as he knows it in himself, he provides a concrete basis for the eidetic work. When the individual makes a thorough list of his suffering, he can then compare it with what is revealed through the parental images to understand how it all happened. The following method of writing details of the symptoms and then experiencing them in a stepwise manner will be found helpful.

1. I am suffering from the following emotional complaints (write down details of mental symptoms).

2. I have the following physiological complaints (write down details of physiological symptoms).

3. I am worried and concerned that if these symptoms are not cured, they will become worse in the following manner (write down details of concern about mental and physiological symptoms).

Example

1. *I am suffering from* depression. I go through moods of depression and unhappiness. Sometimes, my depressions become very severe.

2. *I have physiological complaints of* pressure around my temples and the skull. I experience loss of physical energy, mental lethargy, and confusion. I also experience tightness in the scalp and the back of my neck, stretching feelings in my cheeks, plugged feelings in my ears, fatigue in my eyes, clogged nose, stiff jaws, irritation and burning feelings in my mouth, a choked throat, bloated feelings in my stomach, and fatigue in the shoulder blades and wrists.

3. *I am worried about* my health, and I have a feeling that something will happen to my body. I am concerned about my physical state, which is not getting better. These moods of depression make me feel terrible and helpless.

Preparing the list of symptoms is the actual beginning of analysis of the parental images. After preparing this list, you should proceed to deepen your awareness of them, for unless you become deeply aware of the symptoms, you will not even begin to experience the nature of conflict between yourself and your parents. Therefore, before you begin projecting the parental images, allow yourself to feel your symptoms as vividly and as deeply as possible. Do not become disturbed if the symptoms become painful. Such an experience of the symptoms serves as a motivating force and increases your sensitivity to what exists in the parental images but may be partly blocked. Although admittedly painful, there is no other way to discover what lies inside you: only experience and awareness of the symptoms tells you about your mental basis in the parental figures. First intensify the symptoms in the following manner.

EXPERIMENT 11:
1. Comfortably lie in bed. Relax completely all the muscles from head to toe. From the neck muscles, go to the shoulder, back, leg, and arm muscles, relaxing each muscle, until you are completely relaxed all over.
2. Next, as you lie relaxed, experience the vague feelings in your head, eyes, nose, mouth, neck, chest, stomach, abdomen, arms, legs, and other parts of your body. Become aware of your breathing rhythms, etc. Note any feelings of tension along the arms, legs, or any other part of the body. Bring these feelings to the focus of your attention.
3. Next, experience the list of negative feelings from the symptom description. Select one negative feeling from the list. Relax and concentrate on the negative feeling. Experience the negative feeling in all its aspects and gradually bring it to an intense experience by slow, gradual concentration.
4. Experience the changes in your body posture as you experience the negative feeling. Allow the rest of the body to respond to the negative feeling. See how the muscles in various parts of the body get pulled in, how the spine becomes tense, and how your breathing changes.
5. Allow the muscular tensions to emerge and develop in a spontaneous manner. Experience the tensions as they deepen and allow them to become acute to the point where you almost cannot bear the tension. Notice if you feel like moaning and crying as you concentrate on the negative experience.
6. Go over the whole list of negative feelings, experiencing them one by one in the manner described above. Allow each aspect of the symptom to develop its body expression completely.

Symptoms in Parents

After having experienced the symptoms in this deep manner, you are now ready to relate the symptoms to the parental figures. By projecting the parental images in the various standardized situations of the Eidetic Parents Test, you will be able to relate the various facts of your symptoms with how you have related to one or both parents and determine whether you developed your symptoms in imitation of or in reaction to them.

Some of the exercises suggested here aim at breaking the monotony of perception and bringing in new vistas of visualization which prepare the individual for a deep knowledge of the parental figures. These exercises may precede administration of the Eidetic Parents Test, and may be carried out in cases where individuals show controlled and frozen ideation and view the test with resistance rather than openness.

EXPERIMENT 12:

1. Lie comfortably in bed. Lightly touch various parts of your body and become aware of the different feelings you experience from these parts. Touch your mother's body and then your father's body in the image in the same way. Compare the feelings you receive from your own body with the feelings you receive from mother's and father's bodies.
2. Become aware of your breathing rhythms. Feel the breath coming into your nostrils, first at the tip of your nose; then experience it flowing upward and then downward into your lungs. After this, feel the breath coming out. Experience your diaphragm while the breath slowly ends and you can no longer breathe. Image your mother breathing in and out similarly. Following this, image your father slowly breathing in and out. Compare your own breathing with mother's and father's breathing.
3. Experience a crying feeling in your throat. Let the crying slowly develop into mild sounds of whimpering and then shrieking. Experience it happening mentally. As you cry out with anguish, let yourself roll with agony. Experience your mother crying in a similar way in the image. Following this, image your father crying. Compare the three images.
4. Experience anger welling up inside you. Let out your anger on a pillow. If you feel like tearing it, tear it apart. Beat the pillow with your fists and bite it. Let the negative verbal expressions flow while experiencing the anger. See an image of mother in which she appears angry in a similar manner. After this, see your father in anger. Compare the three images.
5. See yourself in an imaginary space jumping, leaping, and shouting. See your mother in an image acting the same way. After this see your father's image acting similarly. Compare the three images.
6. Now see your parents standing directly in front of you. Reach out for help to father and mother separately. Express your emotions fully to them as you reach out with your hands and your arms. See how each parent responds. Does the parent stand stolidly, express love to you, or push you away? Reach out with your feelings and see if the parent gives you love. After this see your mother and father individually asking help from you. See them expressing their emotions toward you. First concentrate on the image of the mother and then on the image of the father. Compare the three sets of images.

7. Become aware of the various moods of your parents, such as displeasure, anger, happiness, criticism, appreciation, rejection, control, freedom, etc. Become aware of all the different moods of your parents that are present in the images or can be experienced in the images. Does the parent have only one mood (which shows how limited he or she is and how this has limited your own emotional life)? Are the parents flexible; if not, can they become flexible in your mind? Explore this possibility in the form of images. Follow these suggestions for imagery experience.
8. Test the movement in a parent's image by attempting to cause a new action in it; experience the emotion connected with the result. Under what circumstances is a favorable or unfavorable emotion generated in the image? Compare the original movement in the image brought out in the first projection with the later movements in the image consciously created by you.
9. Notice that the feelings in the image are usually different from what you consciously thought they should have been. As you relate to the images more, you will become aware of many such new areas of information within your consciousness. Learn to bend your conscious views in favor of what is revealed in the images.

An eidetic is a high fidelity image, a vision apart from molded or searching awareness, the original life containing all possibilities and solutions as well as ordinary reality. Placing oneself at the eidetic point of activated consciousness, the eye-center, one travels the route of spiraling pictures, feelings, ideas, concepts, and memories while a new mental structuring takes place in which the past and the present meet and unite the experiencer and the doer.

Eidetic analysis is a novel experience of the mental states in the most complex areas of the mind. You can examine the most minute and intimate details of mental life and discover connections between behavior, thought, and action. You will be introduced to the liveliness of your mind and to its capacity as a clear-sighted and calm projection screen of life. As an involved participant, you will find that you cannot guide the course of an eidetic nor its internal activity, since it has its own course and its own story to tell, according to your innermost fears, desires, and needs. A detail which you thought was insignificant may prove the turning point of progression; an attitude which you believed in for so long may be reversed by the eidetic experience. The orderliness and system in the unfolded material will define clear steps in consciousness like signposts on a fogbound road.

Mental analysis through eidetics is a process of self-evolvement and self-examination through which the individual hopes to learn who he is and why he behaves in a certain way. The images break through his usual mode of perception to help him achieve a self-analytic experience and gain insight into the how's and why's of his personality.

The solution of the issues emphasizes examination through eidetic "seeing" as opposed to thinking. When an individual eidetically sees a situation in his mind, he does not commit errors of thought, memory, or guessing; he lets the high fidelity images formulate the thought. The function of eidetic sight is such that it does not allow the erroneous part of the thinking mind to take over and completely corrupt the rest of the mind. Since this high fidelity "sight" guarantees separation of what is being seen from what the individual "wants" to assume, around this can be built a life of proper thought, memory, and conclusion.

3 ⁂ The Frozen "I"-Image: How to Defreeze It

The self-image developed over the long, drawn out growth process is, at best, a stiff "I"–image. One holds very tightly onto a conscious view of himself and views all psychical events with characteristic fixity. Any shift in events is viewed with anxiety, feelings of distrust, and doubt. As rigidity further develops, feelings of paranoia, restlessness, or phobic withdrawal prevail. After all the resources in previous adjustment have been used, the frozen "I"–image moves to the next stage of either physiological disturbance or misrepresentation of the past, and disruption of the thought process by corruption of meanings to prove and defend the conscious views of the rigid "I"–image. When this final stage has been reached, fears, anxieties, and conflicts become permanently attached to the "I"–self-image, and the individual looks at himself and other members of his family from a characteristic stance.

The frozen "I"–image, which generally represents the known state of identity, originates in extensive interpersonal experience in the past, and contains subtle inconsistencies within itself. One needs imagery constructs to cure these inconsistencies and provide tolerance and continuity to internal life. To achieve this, the individual needs to refer to a central imagery focusing process through which he can discover and remove the inconsistencies and develop feelings of effective selfhood again.

For proper and effective change, one needs authentic facts regarding the past, well founded interpretations of them, and a positive method for reaching these. To deal with the elusive psychological life, one needs a lucid technique which can induce and demonstrate change diagrammatically, in anatomical form. The process utilizing such a technique involves awakening and demonstration of potentialities and awareness of new realms of inner functioning. This psychic transformation through awareness is marked by surprises, intense emotional experiences, and passing through critical stages. Out of experience of many interactions, one finally arrives at the "perfect state," i.e., functioning without fear. This unfreezing of the self is not a static but dynamic process in which willingness to face, decipher, endure, and grapple with presented experience is the guiding light. It is a transition from ignoring to facing the problem and from running away to grappling with it, a process in which long-held conscious "truths" are challenged in favor of true discovery and awakening. The person passes out of his "old condition"; and, while reaching toward a new one, he struggles to know what will bring about the new condition. The recognition of motivations, values, and responsibilities is part of this process of growth and involves confrontation with many choices and decisions along the way. The process of decision is guided by a blend of ideas, perceptions, intuitions, and understandings.

The impulse toward reconstruction is not an ordinary but extraordinary endeavor in the individual, marked by a unique experience of the ground of mental life in which something deeper, more stable, and richer is sought.

Identity with the conscious self represents a state of duality, a contention between two selves: one implicit and struggling to be born; and the other explicit, restricted, limiting, and impositional. True self-identity is born out of relaxation between the two via emergence of a unified center which resolves their conflict.

A MAP OF INVESTIGATIONS

Since the trends within early self-images were not fully explored during original interactions, the very process of self-image formulation needs to be investigated empirically and reconceptualized. Through extensive inner differentiation of these original impressions, a person who never became aware of the original interaction, its alternatives, or its possibilities for growth can discover and change the overall patterning and coherence of the self-image.

To achieve this, the person needs an imagery study process aimed at delineation of the earlier image elements and the emotions and judgments present in them. The ability for feelingful experience of historical images becomes a point of release. A detailed examination of the nature of symptoms, self-images, and images of people associated with one's development in the past becomes a source of gradual awareness. As the individual views mental manifestations of the persons he grew up with in a new way, he experiences the emergence of a new personality in himself. The following procedure should facilitate a reorientation of mental mechanisms toward healthful evolvement.

1. Details of the symptom should be written in terms of conscious mental complaints, the associated physiological symptoms, and your worries and concerns regarding how in time they will become worse

if they are not cured (see chapter entitled "Orientation Exercises").
2. Symptoms in mother should be written down in detail involving her negative habits and behaviors, her physiological symptoms, and her worries and concerns regarding her symptoms (see chapter entitled "Orientation Exercises").
3. Symptoms in father should be written down in detail involving his negative habits and behaviors, his physiological symptoms, and his worries and concerns regarding his symptoms (see chapter entitled "Orientation Exercises").
4. The previous three levels of information are integrated so that symptom parallels between mother, father, and yourself become clear, i.e., that the symptoms have in some way arisen in imitation of or in reaction to the parents' limitations, or out of refusal to see them in their true personality.
5. Concentration on the symptoms should be practiced for a long time so that their effect is enhanced. This should be followed by an image projection in which one sees oneself free of these symptoms somewhere in the past (see sections on the Age Projection Test in the chapter entitled "High Fidelity Self-Images").
6. The Eidetic Parents Test should be administered in detail with a view toward evolving further imagery material which throws light on the symptoms, i.e., how they evolved in the interaction with parents.
7. Treatment of the most obvious problematic experience is conducted first, by reenacting the experience in complete original detail, and treating it in all its components.
8. Relevant expansion of imagery experiences in the distant past is conducted to heal connected areas of psychological development.
9. Treatment of the maternal ground of problematic perceptions is conducted to heal problems due to identification with mother.
10. Treatment of the paternal relationships is conducted through various imagery techniques which help construct a releasing image of father.

The basic barrier to all experience is the experiential stiffness which the individual develops as he grows older. Later, this stiffness becomes the tendency to be defensive and deliberate, self-limiting and containing. Through interaction with the parents' images, one learns to have a vision apart from rigid and defensive awareness. The eidetics filter in new attitudes, minimize isolation, and replace negativism with real life activity.

The above eidetic techniques respect the individual's viability, his inborn ability to explore his internal life, and liberate his will by uniting the experiencer with the doer in the imagery processes.

THERAPIST'S SELF-ANALYTIC MODEL

In clinical literature, the old schools erroneously placed the main burden of analytic awareness on the therapist's own ability for perception. It was assumed that the therapist must be always completely aware of the client's perceptions, including those aspects which even the client was not aware of. The therapist was expected to be the all-knower, one who always made most sensitive and most precise interventions. He was expected to show supreme sensitivity, accurate timing, wording, and keen feelings, in which each emotional nuance in the interchange was communicated with complete logic of purpose. This, of course, was a fairy-tale image of the therapist. Controlled studies have to date revealed a marked cleavage between the intuitions and judgments made by the therapist and the factual material in the mind of the patient. Most studies involving segments from a one-hour therapy interchange have revealed that the two processes (the mental state of the patient and the therapist's knowledge of it) most often did not agree. As a result of these studies, the clinical emphasis has recently shifted from the mere claim of omniscience by the therapist to a need for a clear communication between himself and the patient. The new theory searches out the details of the intrapsychic process through a form of imagery dialogue that resembles a self-analytic process.

Every psychotherapy is, in fact, a self-analytic process of some type. In a successful treatment situation, the individual is guided through mental states until he becomes aware of an important relationship between two parts of his mind. Even when a therapist sees the cause of the problem and presents it to the individual, if the individual did not feel and see the causation in the experience for himself, he cannot benefit from it. Eidetic analysis pursues this link to the utmost. In spite of Eidetic analysis being a complete self-analytic therapy procedure, during difficult periods, the therapist provides special help in initiating and strengthening the self-analytic process. He carefully demonstrates the content of the eidetic over and over again, shows various aspects of the experience to the client, and asks him to recall the demonstrated experience.

Training in Projection of Images

To surface the conflicting psychological forces in useful stages, consciousness during its crisis must be exposed to a systematic experience of the images. During mental experience of these images, the mind comes to understand clearly the origin and meaning of the various forces represented in the experience. Training in deciphering these stages of experience can be given through systematic interaction with Ep1, the first image in the Eidetic Parents Test, or any other image which may be selected for this purpose. Various stages in the interaction should be practiced according to the following basic outline.

a. *Concentration on Picture.* See the selected image in the mind. Repeatedly concentrate on it.
b. *Concentration on Feeling.* Experience the feeling associated with the picture over and over again.
c. *Concentration on Meaning.* As the image is seen clearly, let the meaning come to the mind in a spontaneous manner. Do not force meaning on the picture in a deliberate manner.
d. *Interaction with Picture.* As the image is seen, interact with the image in various meaningful ways by concentrating on its various details, taking notice of objects and persons who appear in the image. For instance, ask questions and talk to the persons appearing in the images, developing interaction toward them.

Therapist's Treatment of Images

a. *Bridging Gaps in Facts and Understanding.* Clearly see the facts in the presented picture and create a deeper awareness concerning objects, people, and events.
b. *Allowing Picture to Progress.* Let the image slowly and spontaneously progress into a new image through repetition and concentration over a period of time.
c. *Allowing Mental Expansion.* Let new experiences, insight, and change slowly emerge at many levels.
d. *Therapist's Empathizing.* During an obstructed image, the therapist aids therapy by empathizing into the obstructed image, providing a solution through his own mental participation in the image (see chapter entitled "Positive Group" and read functions of the moderator).

Suggested Homework for the Patient

It is known that when a therapist gives homework to a patient, the patient progresses much faster. Preferably, each time the image should be written down on a card in a clear way, and the patient should be asked to look at the card and experience the image ten to fifty times each day. At the next session, the therapist should examine the homework exercise along these lines.

a. Did the patient perform the image exercise? If not, why not? Ask the reason.
b. Examine the reason for not performing the exercise at home; does the patient show signs of obstruction to treatment?
c. Examine carefully his report on imagery work at home. Note wheth-

er any new material has emerged during the exercises at home that may be useful in the present session.

d. Develop a new set of imagery instructions involving the new material. Write down the new imagery instructions for practice at home.

THERAPY PROCESS MODEL

To elucidate the above principles of the self-analytic therapeutic process, vignettes from the case history of Mrs. Jay (Wolpe, 1969; Ahsen and Lazarus, 1972) are given below. Mrs. Jay had previously received behavioral treatment at the Eastern Pennsylvania Psychiatric Institute in Philadelphia for more than a year. Mrs. Jay's case history demonstrates the desirability and effectiveness of the experiential approach based on eidetics. The eidetic approach succeeded in swiftly eliminating symptoms which had been previously diagnosed as "psychotic states," proving them to be memories of important events.

The Symptom

Mrs. Jay, age 41, was suffering from symptoms of pain located in the upper left abdomen, chest, and left breast; excessive irrational anxiety involving fear of death, and numerous other manifestations of anxiety, such as palpitations, panting, dizziness, nausea, pins and needles, fainting spells, and strong uncertainties and feelings of personal unworthiness to the extent that she was finding it impossible to go places, especially crowded ones, or perform ordinary daily chores.

Relationship with Parental Symptoms

Mrs. Jay's own conscious thinking and the behavioral questionnaires had failed to bring out any link between the symptoms and her developmental past. In the absence of relevant past material, previous behavior therapy treatment had been administered in the regular way, involving principles of extinction, counter-conditioning, and positive and negative reinforcement, including aversive conditioning and self-imposed punishment with a small electrical gadget which Mrs. Jay was expected to carry with her all the time and shock herself with whenever she entertained a negative idea involving a maladaptive approach to a life problem. Eidetic investigations brought out a totally different picture of her problems.

Detailed examination of Mrs. Jay's symptoms, concentration on and oscillation of symptom details, projection of positive imagery through the Age Projection Test, and administration of the Eidetic Parents Test revealed that her symptoms were connected with father's heart attack during which he was briefly revived by the physicians followed by his death a few minutes later. Mrs. Jay's empathic projection in the heart attack was causing her present symptoms.

Other eidetic imagery material revealed that her positive memories connected with father before the heart attack were buried under the traumatic image of his death. Therapy demanded treatment of this problematic experience of heart attack in all its details so that she would experience it happening dramatically and discharge all the emotions trapped in it. Because of her fear of full reenactment of the experience, specific eidetic techniques were used to make the experience totally accessible. She was led to these experiences with the feeling of the events happening all over again, without abolishing her awareness that this was, in fact, a psychological experience.

Reenactment of the problematic experience involving the heart attack was followed by enactment of positive and other history images connected with the father. This resulted in her awareness of the negative perceptions coming from the maternal ground, that she had been afraid of her mother all along and had been unable to formulate a proper self-image under her condemnatory influence. This led to the examination of Mrs. Jay's own identification with the mother, which had made Mrs. Jay similarly problematic to her own son, influencing his self-image adversely.

A return to the final positive image of the father was made in which her relationship with her own husband was brought into focus and advice for change was given to her for further growth of her self-image in the positive direction. Various gaps between her consciousness and the imagery material were removed along these various levels, resulting in the healing of symptoms.

REENACTING THE PROBLEMATIC EXPERIENCE

Conscious Memory Useless

Evidence has revealed that the conscious memory of the individual proves to be useless in the complete and feelingful reenactment of the problematic experience. An individual who is afraid of a situation in the past prefers to alter it to keep his control over it and keep the event from becoming threatening. This vital difference between a recollection through voluntary recall and through an eidetic is important for healing. In order to arrive at the original detail, one must avoid conscious recall and proceed along the eidetic images which progressively reenact the original event in all its problematic details.

After the critical memory of father's heart attack had been uncovered and its relevance to her symptoms established through examination of imagery details, Mrs. Jay was exposed to the problematic experience in the past through the eidetic images.

How Mrs. Jay tended to describe her symptom, how the symptoms tended to reflect in various parts of her body in the form of somatic feelings and how, particularly, they tended to localize in a certain area of the chest were recorded in the words of Mrs. Jay. A graphic picture of the symptoms emerged as a result. After this, the procedure of repeating the symptoms back to Mrs. Jay in her own words was carried out. As she listened to the repetitions, her concentration on the symptom developed and her symptoms gradually became so acute that she begged that the repetition be stopped. At this point she was asked to relax and experience a self-image of herself somewhere in the past, a self-image in which she did not suffer from the present symptoms. She saw an image of herself around age 25.

Initial Confusion

In the early stages of experience, the person usually relates to the symptoms as well as the revealed picture material with complete lack of comprehension.

> Mrs. Jay, while concentrating on her self-image around age 25, did not remember anything significant around that year or a year earlier or later. She, in fact, appeared somewhat confused about how this period of her life was connected with her symptoms.

Initial confusion and other forms of reaction, such as resistance to an evoked picture and its attendant psychological material, are commonly evidenced in the initial stages of the projection. The person facing the experience shows a lack of precise recall and inability to relate to it in a full manner. To avoid the experience, he becomes passive, confused, or critical. Or, because the experience happens to be quite different from the emotional life to which he is consciously accustomed, he may feel that the exploration does not represent meaning or reality to him. One needs to aim at this target centrally.

Feeling of Contact with Target

It is common to see a person go at a verbal tangent, even indulging in rationalizations as an attempt is made to remove the initial resistance. The strategy at this point is to evolve the picture experience and not allow the verbal side to develop too much.

When Mrs. Jay was asked to concentrate more on her self-image, she formed a vague connection. She reported that her father had died the year after the age at which she imaged herself, and that his death had been traumatic for her. Her mind, however, was still confused as to the real significance of this recall.

While attempting to revive the event, one should not hurry toward a detailed contact with the picture, but instead activate the vague recall over and over again, even if it is difficult to concentrate on. Repetition soon links consciousness with the underlying image. Vagueness is a phase in evolution of the experience, rather than a defect or proof of absence of an image. One experiences feelings of contact with the target.

Target Recollection

In the initial stages of eidetic projection, the person becomes aware that something important is present in the area. He experiences a state of definite awareness, but does not see detail.

> As Mrs. Jay concentrated more on the image of her father's death, she reported progressive involvement with the material and evolved a definite awareness. The experience generated was more real than anything she could possibly have recalled consciously from memory. During recall she saw flashes of doctors temporarily reviving the father through cardiac massage. She saw herself begging them not to massage his heart, but to let the father die peacefully. She saw that the doctors did not listen and she saw herself watching them performing cardiac massage. Seeing the father returning to life and then dying again was traumatic. As she saw these images, she experienced choked hysteria inside.

Complete target recollection, demonstrated above, is an important phase of progression of experience. In some cases, body reaction to the picture content appears first, while in others it is the visual panorama which first becomes clear. While projecting the images, the more physically oriented person reacts strongly through his body, while the visually oriented individual partly inhibits his body reactions, allowing the picture content to appear first and then responding to it physically. One should allow either course of awareness to take place without interference.

The target recollection has access to the original images which are always more real than conscious memory, and even more complete than the original event. These images help reproduce scenes and events with realistic, original detail as well as the symbolism which was not expressed at that time. Consequently, the image panorama forces itself upon the attention and the individual attends it as he would attend a real event. The fuller reality of the experiential images gives access to the details so fundamentally important for structuring of the problematic event.

Target Amplification

Complete evocation of the experience is a full and final awareness of the event, panorama, people, objects, time, and dynamics. When a clear recollection is finally tracked down, the identity of the event is established beyond doubt. At this point, the event can be finally reenacted for therapeutic discharge and correction of its problematic aspects.

> Mrs. Jay's gradual recollection of the target event contained many details, which emerged as she thought of the event under eidetic management. The flashes of actual images contained image elements covering the main event of father dying, the doctors attempting to revive him, the father temporarily reviving and then dying, her own experience of hysteria during cardiac massage, and her desire that the physicians not attempt to revive him but let him die peacefully, since he had had previous heart attacks and this was the final one. While experiencing these flashes in the form of clear images, Mrs. Jay showed a tendency to experience acute symptoms whenever she thought of the cardiac massage, and amelioration of the symptoms while thinking about the father's relapse and death. Her symptoms clearly displayed this oscillation between the cardiac massage and death, as if these two events were opposite in her mind. She appeared to be extremely favorable to the idea of his death, and her hysteria appeared to be the expression of her inability to control the physicians. This involved a certain idea of force on her part which she could not use or express since things were in the physicians' hands and not hers. In the image flashes she saw a pillow on the hospital bed, which she recalled clearly without it having any meaning or significance. She said she only knew one thing, that she wanted her father to die in peace. Reviving him was a false hope and it had no use. Following the emergence of all these details, it was decided to expose Mrs. Jay to an amplified experience of father's heart attack. It was decided to present various images in a slow and systematic manner, allowing the event to evolve and settle as naturally as possible according to its own dynamics.

As the person repeats the pictures over and over again, more interpretation filters into consciousness. Repetition not only increases further recollection of the experience as to panorama, people, and objects, it also surfaces the meaning connected with the experience. These two processes, namely, image concentration and interpretation, emerge in an interdependent manner, so that one tends to generate the other.

During target amplification each recollected image is repeated separately over and over again until it becomes lucid in the mind. Various levels of images are kept separate and repeated separately to allow each level to progress in its natural direction. Finally the links are allowed to develop and relationships established. This finally leads to a clear therapeutic handling of the most central part of the event, called the *target center*.

During target amplification each image is experienced like a present experience with its original situation and emotion, the visualizer becomes a part of the situation, becoming both an actor and an audience, each fantasy is treated as a fact and each fact as a fantasy, emphasizing that we are essentially dealing with a mental process. The inmost problematic part of the experience, the target center, is treated in a manner that the conflictual parts become resolved either through progression of the event or through bipolar resolution.

The following description of the amplification process may be found useful in managing a problematic event.

Like a Present Experience

In the evocation of an image, the vividness of the experience should make a strong, direct impression. As a result of this, the person experiences past scenes and events as if they were happening now and becomes aware of what he saw, felt, and understood when the event originally happened.

The evocation as a present experience creates again the experiential state which was present when the image was first formed. In it, all the participating elements are revealed again. Current experience of the image is necessary, and without this, neither recapturing of the original situation nor therapeutic work is possible.

> Concentration on the image as a present experience exposed Mrs. Jay to a direct experience of father's heart attack. Each time she saw the image clearly, she recollected the hour, the day, and the atmosphere around the event in the most lucid fashion. Each repetition took her all the way back into the past, as if the event were happening all over again now.

Original Situation

Each evoked image contains the dynamics of the original situation, captured without falsification. When all the elements of the original situation regain their original panorama, the experience then generates reliving of the situation at the optimum level of encounter.

> During the projections of each image, Mrs. Jay uncovered the original situation, in which she experienced all the details with a sense of total recall. The visual panorama of people around the father, cardiac massage, revival of father, father's relapse and death, and her hysteria over the doctors' attempt to revive him, all flowed back to her one by one as they had originally taken place.

Original Emotion

> While projecting the image of her father's heart attack, Mrs. Jay was helped to reproduce the feelings of suffocation, nausea, and even distrust of the doctors around her as she had felt them at that time. As each body response and emotion emerged in its original form, she was fully conscious and aware of its impact. She passed through many emotional impacts, including trembling, panting, and crying hysterically.

While experiencing the image, the person spontaneously experiences the emotion along with the interpretation he was experiencing at the original moment. Events appear to him again as they did earlier: strange, threatening, frustrating, difficult or easy to master. He feels involved as he felt involved at the time of the original event.

Visualizer, A Part of the Situation

The individual seeing an experiential image becomes an inalienable part of the situation represented in it.

> At the critical point in the image progression, Mrs. Jay became an intimate part of the situation and was totally involved in it. Her visualization was no longer a process of looking at the image, but of real involvement. The situation was relived by her with new responses, and her reactions were more than a process of mere recall. As she recollected a new detail, she reacted to it as if to a new situation happening right now, with a current challenge in it.

The experience is achieved through nonverbal participation involving only a remote verbal awareness. During this image experience, the person is not transported into the past in a manner that abolishes his awareness of the present;

rather, he experiences a state of double consciousness in which he knows himself to be deeply involved in the experience, but also to be aware of the present and his immediate surroundings. A momentary exception at times occurs in cases where the intensity of the original experience blurs awareness of the present to the point that the individual shows a trancelike state of consciousness, following which he may gradually go to sleep due to development of an underlying deep relaxation state. However, at the peak of evocation, the state of double consciousness remains the important feature which integrates present consciousness with an arrested piece of old consciousness. It is at this point that the drama of change within the evocation takes place in an explicit eidetic manner.

Both Actor and Audience

Whatever the person has experienced in the past, he remains that person in the past dealing with the same situation in the present. He is a composite of personality multiples living, feeling, and breathing through many separate identities. What he or anyone else did then, he is doing now; and what was left unfinished is being finished and completed through the medium of images.

> In the next stage of projection, Mrs. Jay was made to experience the image fully as both actor and audience. She was made to experience the image in a manner that there was a complete empathic reliving of all the roles: father, doctors, and herself. In this imagery experience she was many persons dealing with many images of various potentials. On the image-stage in her mind the whole drama of the critical situation was reenacted in all its facets in an authentic way.

The experiential image is a psychical stage on which various needs, desires, apprehensions, confusions, etc., become so many actors. One must set the image-stage in such a manner that each action is portrayed lucidly. The main actor, the experiencer, should be attuned through keen empathy so that he can differentiate each aspect of the action like the sensitive audience watching the events. Unless the experiencer reproduces all actions on his own, there is no progress.

Fact = Fantasy

The original interpretation present in an evoked image may present a complex problem in reasoning. To all appearances, reality-oriented, two-dimensional, logical reasoning does not apply to the experiential evocation. Here a three-dimensional reasoning operates, the third dimension being magicality, i.e., the wish or fantasy.

By the end of these recalls, it was found that two lucid images had been clearly arrived at connected with cardiac massage. Mrs. Jay showed a clear tendency to react to (1) the image of the cardiac massage by developing acute symptoms and to (2) the image of stopping of the cardiac massage and father's death by becoming relaxed. The doctors wanted to revive the father, but Mrs. Jay wanted to let him die, amounting to a form of "murder fantasy." Then was seen an unusual phenomenon. To finish off the father, Mrs. Jay spontaneously saw images in which she suffocated him with the pillow (mentioned earlier) and put him to death on the hospital bed. As she did so, she bitterly cried and then became completely peaceful, as if the storm had passed. After she enforced the death image with the help of the pillow, her somatic symptoms of panting and suffocation disappeared.

After her father died in fantasy, Mrs. Jay accepted her father's death in a real way for the first time. Only through replay of her own wish, leading to his death as she wanted it, did the father's death become factual in her mind. The original reality of his dying following brief cardiac massage was a "crude" one ridden with unresolved conflict. When the underlying wish in this crude reality was released, the event became complete, and, being complete, it also became more real.

The traumatic memory of Mrs. Jay's father precipitated the symptoms. By concentrating on this magical part which had never happened, Mrs. Jay removed from her mind fixation on the remembered course of the event and moved her mind onto a new visualization of the event. In terms of the past, both parts of the memory were real; but in ordinary terms the event as it happened and was consequently remembered was "reality," and Mrs. Jay's imagined action was a "magical" picture of it. By concentration, the actually present elements in her imagined-memory were realized and the real memory became less effective. By removing concentration from its fixation on the real memory, the experience was drained of its crude memory rigidity and the true reality was instituted in its place.

The important questions—What is "real" and what is "magical" and what is "fact" and what is "fantasy" in the mind?—cannot be answered by separating fact from fiction on the basis of what is rational or irrational, but on the basis of functions. At the mental plane, what produces results is fact and what does not is fiction. Fantasies are a real part of the psyche and satisfy psychological needs. They generate tangible events, and are a powerful source of action dedicated to goals which cannot be achieved otherwise. A psychology which does not consider magicality as real as reasoning cannot be expected to deal with the mind. The mind contains magically conceived images which control our destiny, as real objects do. The proof that a stone exists is that when you hit it, it hurts your toe; and the proof that a magical image exists is that it can either create a symptom or heal one. Thus, concrete objects are equal to fantasied objects. An individual can use this knowledge very well, toward the noble purpose of healing.

Target Education

In the heart of the target recollection lies the center, which contains the most pivotal event around which turns the question of health. This center is developed next as a lucid structure of imagery events. The most central part of it is assembled with extreme care and demonstrated to the person in the most clear fashion. This demonstration, conducted carefully with emphasis on image, body feelings, and meanings and aimed at elucidation of the centermost structure, creates the healing.

> Mrs. Jay's recollections involved many events around the father's heart attack. However, the centermost part of these recollections was the discovery that when she concentrated on father's death or her own suffocation of him, the symptoms would definitely subside. In the next phase of the treatment, Mrs. Jay was exposed to the various facets of this observation through the following demonstrations.
>
> *Demonstration 1:* Her reported images were split up into two distinct image configurations: (1) cardiac massage and (2) father's death after cardiac massage. Concentration on image-1, i.e., cardiac massage, produced chest pain, profuse sweating, shortness of breath, and feelings of giddiness and nausea, whereas concentration on image-2, i.e., father's death, created feelings of relaxation and comfort. This was repeatedly demonstrated to Mrs. Jay through alternate concentration on the two images.
>
> *Demonstration 2:* After oscillation of the symptom states through the two images, Mrs. Jay was instructed in how she could consciously repeat the two images and produce the two states herself. In following these instructions, Mrs. Jay was able to handle her symptoms on her own. Awareness of this generated a new feeling of confidence in her, that she understood the nature of her symptoms and that her symptoms were not altogether mysterious and unmanageable.
>
> *Demonstration 3:* Next was demonstrated the vivid experience of smothering father with a pillow as being composed of elements from her love for father. Careful analysis made evident to Mrs. Jay that the experience of smothering father to death was built out of her desire that father be allowed to die peacefully.

TARGET MEDIATION INTO HISTORY

Careful questioning and evoking of the various images connected with the central experience brings about movement of the target area away from the target experience in the direction of earlier target-related events. As this is done systematically, many new incidents are surfaced, become part of the new movement, and bring about further awareness of the experiential history. The technique involves careful listing of each important image and the material it indicates. Questions are systematically asked until the related history material starts surfacing.

> As Mrs. Jay concentrated on the images further, she recalled father's two previous heart attacks. With further concentration, her mind became occupied with the memory of his first heart attack, which suddenly developed while her mother was boiling water. This image was induced and its emotional impact was so strong that Mrs. Jay was thrown again into a mild experience of symptoms around her heart. This image, however, left her stronger in the end, as its memory passed like a cloud, bringing to the surface another important memory in which a thief attacked and robbed her father in their store, which was directly below their apartment. The memory pertaining to the robbery brought out other hidden fears concerning strangers and her own feelings of aggression. She experienced an image of herself attacking the thief in the store, which helped her actively master the traumatic memory. All these memories were relevant to the suffering image of the father and were laden with strong feeling. The extensive and systematic repetition of these images proved very therapeutic to her.

The images produced by target mediation provide direct access to the life processes outside of the target area. Such access evolves in the direction of events which directly produced weakness in the individual. To achieve proper development of this phase, all related images in the past are listed and explored in detail, and the events are treated along appropriate lines.

GENERAL HISTORY ANALYSIS

The next phase in the imagery progression shows the experience travelling from directly connected emotions toward a releaseful exit in new indirect material that is characterized by fresh perspectives evidencing one's ability to deal with the situation with more openness. This definite phase in recollection and development of emotions shows the individual in the process of exit from immediate fixed recollection, moving toward an interactive relationship with people in the distant past.

As Mrs. Jay concentrated on the revealed images, her memories moved away from a feeling of concern for the father's life into an experience of him as a whole person. She could now enjoy conflict with this more complete father without fear that she was going to hurt him in some way. After this readjustment with father came memories of her stealing candy from the store, and her own as well as her father's concern about her weight. Either in humor or seriousness, her father would insist that if a customer came into the store, she should try to hide herself behind the counter because she was too fat. As a result of this memory, Mrs. Jay saw herself clobbering the father on the head. The image was releasing as well as somewhat curiously similar to the thief attacking the father. Anger and humor were mixed in the experience of these images. As she repeated them, Mrs. Jay became more and more preoccupied with other events outside of the original theme of father's heart attack.

As a result of further concentration on the images, Mrs. Jay's memories moved in the direction of her fears at school, where her classmates ridiculed her for being fat. As Mrs. Jay remembered some of these classmates, she saw their images and she understood why she had grown to be so passive toward people. She let loose her anger on these classmates in the images and experienced relief. After this came images pertaining to her first menstruation involving feelings of apprehension. The onset of menstruation had come without any prior education, and the sight of menses had generated fear in her about growing up. Following repetition of these images along with education, she witnessed the progress of the image, and developed new confidence in the menstrual process as a normal expression of life. The eidetics in this area gradually led to her fears concerning conception. A range of additional images (Ahsen, *Basic Concepts in Eidetic Psychotherapy*, 1968, pp. 258–261) enabled her to work through this conflict and led to various realizations. She recalled images of a miscarriage and many mishaps around the event. Loss of the baby was followed by a period of jealousy concerning pregnant women, during which time she started noticing pregnant women in the stores and on the sidewalks and reacted with severe feelings of inferiority. Wherever she looked, she saw so many pregnant women that she withdrew. At this point a series of expressive images released her from withdrawal, the associated phobia of going places, and the feeling of personal unworthiness.

When a past experience is successfully broken down into its parts, the self is experienced in the form of inner potentials. Through past personality multiples, i.e., a variety of self-images involving various situations in the past and containing one's views and reactions to them, the individual can experience an old event vividly. When the experience of a past multiple achieves a certain intensity, the timeless, placeless potential finds time and place and becomes connected with history, thereby becoming real. The individual becomes timeful and placeful and deals with his possibilities again in a concrete manner. No longer is he held down by abstract notions; his selfhood is revitalized and becomes instructed by experience.

One may find the personal return to the past painful, especially if, at first glance, it offers a bad self-image. A voice inside him says, "You should not look back, because you have a bad self-image there," and causes him to turn away. But this bad self-image in the past is a door to the truth, however undecorated and unflattering.

If we superficially look into the past, we think that events are what they appear to be. But mental states, like time, are not linear, one-dimensional events; they are constructs. Mental events are what one makes of them and what they are capable of becoming through relating to them. The present is a battleground between many constructs, and this is where the hope lies. The present also is what we make of it, but it starts from the past, for it is the past which provides the raw material for the new construct we wish for ourselves.

The ability to bridge the gap between himself and the past psychical experience depends directly on the individual's ability to interact with the problem images. When the individual visualizes his problems in the form of images and exposes himself to the content of these images, the re-experience of personal history begins. When he is able to deal with these images without distance, without fear, and without any need to defend himself from the pain associated with the situations, the self-protective barriers in the ego are lifted and the original strength and harmony of the self is experientially revealed. Because large amounts of energy stay bound with these past images, unless they are freed, the individual has very little strength to work with.

CONSCIOUSNESS-IMAGERY GAP

Through systematic examination of the images, fresh avenues of awareness can be opened in consciousness. By revealing what is not known, consciousness is educated to handle what is known. The eidetic is a three-dimensional unity composed of a vivid image (I), a vivid emotional or somatic response (S), and a vivid meaning (M). Each eidetic shows these three ISM aspects clearly. Superficial attention on a memory may evidence a lacking in these aspects, resulting in the individual's incapacity to handle the event effectively. This basic gap in the awareness of a problem is called the *Consciousness-Imagery Gap (C-I-G)* and represents three types of gaps, those pertaining to the image, the somatic state, and the meaning. When trained in locating these gaps, consciousness is able to recover a large amount of experiential material composed of event recollection, original body feelings, and meanings. When the individual is encouraged to actively pay attention to the eidetic, elaborating these three aspects, he uncovers and bridges gaps between what he already knows and what is revealed. This leads to development of a new outlook and spontaneous therapeutic change.

IMAGE GAP: Concentration on the vague visual aspects of an image can reveal new information. Through this, consciousness can be encouraged to yield its contents and evolve a new awareness without undue fear and dependence on previous thinking or learning. A methodically induced optical clarity can complete an otherwise incomplete or vague picture of an event or enrich the already available visual features of a fantasy or a memory.

 a. Make repeated attempts to complete incomplete features in the picture, such as absent eyes, voice, or limbs of a person.
 b. Introduce and repeat concentration on behavior which should have been a part of the picture, such as positive and loving behavior of a parent.
 c. Introduce and repeat concentration on a person who should have been a part of the picture of the family scene but is absent, such as mother, father, a sibling, or a grandparent in a problematic image.

SOMATIC GAP: While experiencing a visual image, one's physical and emotional attitude toward it can disclose a lot: e.g., does one withdraw from the visual image or approach it in a warm, empathic manner; does one allow oneself to experience the pain or the pleasure present in the image; does one plunge into the image experience or skirt around it; while concentrating on the image, is there any lacking in the physical feeling, avoidance, or tendency toward an over-response which does not really belong to the image? One should bridge such somatic gaps by carefully interacting with the eidetic, allowing the body response to develop while repeatedly concentrating on the image and experiencing its specific relationship with the situation represented in it. If one cannot bridge the gap in this way, why not? Gaps in the somatic feelings should be carefully searched for and bridged by bringing in new information which fills in the gap and generates the feeling. For instance, one may ask, "Why does such-and-such somatic response develop in relation to an image when it really does not belong to the presented situation in the image?" or, "Why is such-and-such somatic response not present when it does belong to the presented situation?" Searching into the incidents which bring about the required relationship comprises the therapy process.

Why does one surface an inappropriate somatic response? Concentration during repetition of a visual image may reveal a problem in body feeling while the image is being seen. If this happens, the following procedure should be helpful.

a. Allow the body response to develop slowly, as the image is repeated.
b. Detect any overt avoidance of body feeling. Set up an imagery sequence to find out the cause and develop procedures to remove it.
c. Detect a false body response ascribed to the image. Investigate the imagery to restore the original situation in which the appropriate body response is present.

MEANING GAP: There are many meanings possible from an image. One may react with a complete lack of understanding of a meaning. Or, while waiting for the meaning to emerge or become clear, one may react with panic, haste, or anxiety, and consciously impose a meaning on the image. One can arrive at the precise meaning of an image in a spontaneous fashion only over a long while, by merely looking at an image with passive attention. During this time, a part of the mind spontaneously ideates and formulates the meaning. One must not be impatient with the image; actively looking for a clear meaning in it is obviously a form of anxiety. Being with the vague meaning is being with the image experience as it is, a state which is full of rest and without anxiety. Such passive attention paid to an image is a form of therapeutic rest from which the positive thought process develops spontaneously. Following are helpful rules.

a. Do not be impatient.
b. Develop confidence in new meanings coming from the images.
c. Remove misunderstanding caused by a superficial thought barrier.

An eidetic image is a self-evident unit of experience that represents a self-obvious meaning. The task of knowing new meanings concerning life does not become hazardous, contrary to what has been found concerning dreams and forced imagery formation processes. The individual is able to see the first layer of meaning of an eidetic image without much aid or support. Mental precision at this level proceeds to the deeper level and dispels the thoughts that confuse the experiences of life through manipulation.

One who obtains knowledge of the nature and content of the superficial layers of the mind finally obtains knowledge of the deeper mind. The first recognition—that we are not in true contact with our own selves as we had thought—is replaced gradually by the awareness that experiential knowledge of this fact is a genuine mental liberation. Interestingly, concentration on deep images may be interrupted by a mind activated to stay distant from itself. For instance, a conscious fixed orientation toward corrupted memories, fantasies, rationalizations, intellectualizations, all may emerge along the way. This occurs as the natural process of mind emerges and helps the individual in life, generating true discriminations in the mind.

We grow up through our own experience. We do not receive impressions from teachers like blackboards. We exist in a state of perfect union with our own experience which is, unfortunately, marred with imperfection. This scar we carry with us forever; for as long as we have eyes to see, bodies to feel, and minds to know, we cannot escape these impressions. Here begins the first enlightenment and the union of a mind divided.

MATERNAL GROUND

The wandering mind cannot be stilled, because it tries to go beyond the corrupted experience into true life. The parents in the mind are not only emotional but social issues. A doting father who is always away because he is a salesman, a working mother who is loving but absent because she needs more money, represent problems in the transmission of loving contact.

After target mediation into history and general history analysis in remote areas of the past, the person comes to deal with that aspect of mind where the mental processes appear to be issuing from, i.e., the "maternal ground." During this phase the individual shows an explicit relationship with the maternal upbringing, so much so that the mother's personality shows through his own characteristics.

Emergence of the maternal ground initiates a phase of the analytic process which determines the historical character of the mother apart from her positive role as a nourishing mother. The maternal ground shows two strands: (1) the negative character limitations of the mother and (2) the positive maternal interest which creatively helps the child relate to the world.

Analysis of the maternal ground is conducted with the explicit purpose of separating the above two strands—character and creation—and showing the individual where he needs to learn anew the basis of life and where he needs to unlearn the negative influences. This phase is aimed at correcting and freeing the positive biological perceptions and restoring them to their original natural forms. At this stage of analysis, the creation aspect of the mother must be clearly differentiated from her character aspect, and the person must clearly decide what distracts from creation or contributes toward it.

> Mrs. Jay's treatment proceeded by first throwing the father's eidetic into the forefront to resolve the main issue connected with his death. As Mrs. Jay became stronger through recollection of positive and other memories, the mother's figure came into full relief. Mrs. Jay had not yet related her consciousness to the mother's image, but near the end of the treatment, she became centrally aware of a lacking in the mother. In these recollections and the Eidetic Parents Test images, Mrs. Jay's mother seemed to lack warmth, understanding, and tolerance for the daughter. She emerged as an impatient and critical person who did not hide how disappointed she was in her daughter. She was a martyr with a cold,

loud voice, who dominated her husband and had infused her daughter's mind with feelings of worthlessness and guilt. The mother's main concern turned out to be her daughter's overweight, a theme which at the upper level was ascribed to father. Mrs. Jay finally recollected that this theme had been started by the mother, and father had been made to enforce it. In fact, father had been an especially understanding person in Mrs. Jay's life. Out of this reversal, Mrs. Jay experienced feelings of tension and rage toward her mother. As a next step in therapy, Mrs. Jay experienced a series of images covering situations of extreme frustration with the mother and her reactions to them involving the discharge of anger.

The reason why one forgets maternal defects lies in the fact that children start their educational process with the mother, and that all children, irrespective of sex, show extreme attachment to this primary identification. In fact, from this deepest core of relationship with the mother emerge, as from a ground, all perceptions and interactions, which then spread in various directions. One must reach this ground structure, bare its dynamics, and expose oneself to its various implications and associated solutions, tracing the process through adulthood.

Eidetic Parents Test Interaction with Parental Images

Interaction with a life-defeating behavior of a parent is shown in the person himself reproducing the same interactions in real life. A severe state of fixation on these behaviors covers up a knowledgeful awareness of the defect in the parent or in the person himself. This is precisely where the Eidetic Parents Test becomes helpful.

In Mrs. Jay the Eidetic Parents Test images, administered in a systematic fashion, induced a decisive awareness and created an understanding of her psychological interactions with the mother. She began questioning whether her mother had normal attitudes toward life and whether her mother's feelings of martyrdom were directly responsible for creating feelings of martyrdom and guilt in herself. By understanding the source of her guilt and knowing in an experiential manner how it affected her, Mrs. Jay then drew a parallel between herself and her mother, inquiring if she was acting in the same manner toward her own family.

It was through these systematic images that Mrs. Jay gradually came to feel that she needed to separate herself from the mother. All along she had been bringing her mother to the clinic as an escort, but now she decided to try and come on her own. She understood that by remaining passive and afraid she was allowing herself to be destroyed by the mother.

The parental interactions can be dealt with clearly by establishing nuclei of active imagery in the area of the parental defect. The defect becomes accessible when interaction is induced through the imagery process. In general, to develop the parental defect, interaction should be developed along the following lines.

1. Make a list of the parent's negative images.

2. Make a list of the parent's positive images.

3. Make a list of the parent's vague images.

4. Interact with the parent in the visual images involving a problem.

5. Show frustration, anxiety, anger, pleasure, or confusion to the parent in the images.

6. Act in the image in a manner that you receive pain from the parent in the image.

7. Act in the image in a manner that you receive pleasure from the parent in the image.

8. Act in the image in a manner that you clarify the vague situation in the image.

9. Express in a parallel way to the parental image, showing anger where the parent shows anger and love where the parent shows love in order to see how the sameness effects the interaction.

10. Express bipolarly to the parent, i.e., where the parent shows love, show anger, and where the parent shows anger, show love, in order to know the true nature of emotions involved.

11. See the parent acting in a manner opposite to the revealed defect in the form of a clear image.

12. Use the therapist's or someone else's empathy to inject new images of awareness and reaction to the parent in the area of the defect.

Mental problems are characterized by lack of insight, fixed emotional responses, and thought blocking. The fixed thought symbols of a disturbed mind make discussion without personal evidence an empty and meaningless pursuit. The new mental process must start from an inner eidetic state and the interpretation which is usually vague or problematic at the beginning of the picture soon becomes clear and the individual becomes more expressive with progression of the interactions.

Many individuals consider expression of certain natural drives bad; others consider any natural drive sinful, stretching the point to a limit which is obviously ridiculous. Expression of natural anger, sorrow, or frustration over real issues cannot be held immoral because these emotions describe the natural functioning of the human organism. Natural energies should not be put away or suppressed, but released and integrated and brought into harmony with life through interactive imagery.

Integration is facilitated by activated experience of inner perception. After the person has witnessed an interactive resolution of the historical and symbolic elements, he is prepared to deal with the questions of his own behavior in an intensive way: how exactly did the behavior of his parents affect him and how has he modified his real character to suit the imposition from the parental images? The person then enters into what may be called the discovery and resolution of these issues.

The interaction with images of parents helps the individual connect his consciousness to parental figures firmly and integrate the whole gamut of imagery in a proper way, generating a relevant and timely encounter along the line of self-discovery.

> Mrs. Jay's imagery made it clear that in certain areas she could not interact with her mother because she was negatively identified with her. The realization that she was negatively identified with the mother and was oriented toward her own family in a similar way was the next step in the therapy. These feelings of identification became more obvious when Mrs. Jay reported that her son had recently complained of heart symptoms somewhat similar to her own and that she had felt frightened on that account. She was now preoccupied with the idea of her son's having all kinds of ailments. She said, "Yesterday my son had mowed the lawn. After he was done he came in and said that for a few minutes his circulation went fast. I think he meant his pulse was rapid and his heart pounded. He did not seem frightened. He said he thought it may have happened once before, a few years ago. I get petrified inside when he is sick. I felt that yesterday he may have had an epileptic attack. I thought the doctor should check his blood sugar level for diabetes. My father had diabetes before he died. I also thought maybe he had a sort of allergy attack, as he is allergic to many plants."
>
> It was pointed out to Mrs. Jay that she was overconcerned and had been reading physical symptoms into her son and, especially, since she had been doing it for so long, she had made him "invent" these illnesses. She had given him the thought that people were unkind to him, and had given him the idea that he might die. She was helped to overcome her

negative identification with the mother by reorienting her attitudes to her own family.

DEEP INTERACTION WITH FATHER

All mental change aims at sufficiently loosening the individual so that he can experience his true identity without confusion or fear. A rigid and narrow emphasis on one's relationship with the mother runs counter to the aim of self-discovery. As a result of fixation on mother, the individual insists on his customary negative portrait of life. This is a position which is contrary to the task of separating oneself from the womb, if one wants to follow the course of development set by the biological basis of life.

Consciousness strikes a relationship with the external environment through the image of the father, which exists in consciousness as a problematic image. Consciousness which is overattached to the mother always selectively concentrates on the negative side of the father. Considering the need for separation from the ground perceptions, the positive portrait of the father becomes a necessity. Overattachment to mother compels consciousness to see all external experiences as negative, and prohibitive.

The father's image has many possibilities. He is not only the person one consciously knows him to be (the negative person), but another person, a biological symbol, which spontaneously evolves in many positive directions. Growth involves becoming aware of this possibility in the father. The journey starts with giving up the limiting, narrow portrait of him, and pursuing the positive symbols attached to his identity.

> Mrs. Jay, in the beginning of her treatment, had shown negative conscious attitudes toward the father. The underlying eidetic imagery, however, disclosed a more loving relationship with him. As gradual release of further material instead brought the failure of the maternal process to the forefront, the negative portrait of the father was further reversed. This positive portrait was further strengthened through elaborate exposure to the positive father imagery schedules, areas where Mrs. Jay's personality needed to be further strengthened.

Through bringing the positive portrait of the father into the center of consciousness and strengthening its details through various imagery schedules, the individual goes through a reorientation, drops apprehensions, sees new meanings, and develops new insights, resulting in a reappraisal of the original life perspective. One who learns to change his negative consciousness concerning father learns to handle his mind in a manner that mental states offer no barrier to him and he relates to them in an effective and fruitful manner.

4 ⚡ Orientation Exercises

I

The impulse toward realization of inner potentialities, wholeness, and self-fulfillment sprouts from the innermost core of human nature. The person wants to experience his true nature vividly and without doubt. The search for this fulfilling self-image is a quest for a state of well-being, free from conflict.

Mental analysis through eidetics is a procedure involving principles of self-analysis, a highly practical form of knowing oneself. This procedure is based on revelation of the natural truth within the mind and provides self-educational techniques for attaining basic clarity, whereby sources of confusion and anxiety states are understood and the pleasure of normal consciousness is reinstated. As a result of such a study one can differentiate problems arising in present situations on the pattern of old situations and can understand the life-defeating nature of certain negative habits. One can also understand how the present environment generates anxiety and symptoms, and can appreciate the relevance of internal life and self-motivation.

The various mental imagery exercises presented in this chapter can be used toward this goal of self-awareness and self-change. The study initiated through these exercises assists in the recall of memories, correction of false impressions, discharge of inhibited emotions, and elaboration of positive experiences by developing undeveloped nourishing aspects of life. Some of the applications of this technique are discussed in this chapter in brief sections. The reader should acquaint himself with the sections listed below, select the type of application he needs, and follow the Orientation Exercises accordingly:

    Individual or Personal Analysis
    Mutual Analysis by Two Individuals, known as "Consciousness Friends"
    Family and Marriage Counseling

Group Therapy
Professional's Analytic Guide

The above types of applications can be developed through the Orientation Exercises, which are experienced or introduced carefully along the suggested lines. These exercises expand consciousness in a self-analytic manner, creating change in the areas of problems and symptoms. As the information is evolved through personal concentration, or during interaction with another individual or the whole family exploring facets of their relationships or groups working together to generate empathic growth and awareness, a sure change is always witnessed in the participating individuals. The methods of examining consciousness, and methods of interaction, create the capacity for fruitful communication and personal enjoyment of consciousness.

The individuals using the Orientation Exercises should pursue them with an awareness that they are a sensitive psychological system and that they have to be handled with finesse. No carelessness or sloppiness in carrying out of the exercises should be shown. Consciousness should be progressed with a sense of discipline. The reader should acquaint himself thoroughly with the spirit of the self-analytic technique and with the self-educational emphasis which the self-analytic technique implies. He should try to clarify what promotes or hinders the self-analytic process and the obstacles which present themselves as self-education takes place. The intricacies involved in handling of the experience should be examined carefully and any problems which are spotted should be eradicated.

The usages of the Orientation Exercises will now be described below in small individual sections. The reader should, however, remember that to all these various applications, individual or personal analysis is fundamental. Therefore, special attention should be given first to the next section and then to other specific sections of interest.

INDIVIDUAL OR PERSONAL ANALYSIS

The eidetic experience connected with the individual pictures reveals that experience is a flexible function and various altered states of consciousness can be generated by slowing down or speeding up, and by repetition backward and forward of these pictures. The fact that we can repeat the mental content precisely in slow, fast, backward, forward motion gives us a technical power over the past, and through this, a definite hand in the formulation of our personal image.

By repetition of mental pictures, we can examine facts and introduce change. Without repetition of pictures, we would not know where and how to introduce change. This principle adds another dimension to the mental rhythm. Since we can repeat and experience an event over and over again, we can adjust to it also in the meanwhile. The principle of repetition generates high fidelity in the exploration and management of events. Through the repetition, we can intervene in the picture, at any selected point, by bringing out suppressed reactions or introducing new ideas which should have been present in it. We are free to look at the image, the feeling, or the meaning as we prefer and change it accordingly. We can intervene wherever and whenever we like, since we can study, and dissect, the event and react to it in slow motion. Through repetition we can transform the event and change ourselves, too. When a person images the eidetic picture over and over again, he profits through exposure and reaction at many levels. Repetition is the source of regeneration of high fidelity consciousness in which the facts are more authentic than in the ordinary states of consciousness and are reacted to with more flexibility than in the ordinary rush of life. During slow-motion repetitions we become subliminally conscious of new details. We get spaced out projections during which conscious awareness of elements grows in richness and detail. The spaced out arrangements allow things to happen from a new angle. During the gap between various repetitions and during slowdowns, the mind is ready to look into the infinite depth of new consciousness. During these periods the mind plunges into the infinite possibilities inherent in the mind stuff. A new interface develops between old perspectives. A new configuration of connections emerges spontaneously. The repetition creates what may be called "sequences," in which old interpretations are hammered into new ones. As the motion of the shifting consciousness happens smoothly over a period of time, new perspectives are revealed one after another. The new experience is a function of consciousness shifting itself sequentially in the form of progression of pictures. The progression in pictures is a progression in perspective, a shift in self-perspectives, a new birth of self-image and identity.

Individual analysis can be conducted through slowed down experience of the Orientation Exercises by writing down responses to the psychological questions presented from Step 1 through Step 16 (see pages 154–176). The analysis starts with a careful dissection of the symptom, a deeper awareness of the symptom through concentration exercises, symptom analysis in mother, symptom analysis in father, and comparison of these analyses to study whether there is evidence of imitation or reaction involving a parent. This is followed by a detailed administration of the Eidetic Parents Test. Naturally, important in personal analysis is the individual's native ability to see the eidetic images, which means that he is still in contact with the life-initiating forces of the eidetic. When it is clear very early that an individual is unable to see an eidetic, Step 17 gives preliminary instructions on how to overcome this basic defect. Once this defect has been removed, all 30 items of the Eidetic Parents Test are administered at one time and then each item is projected again according to its breakdown in ten concentration steps. Experience of significant images of the Eidetic Parents Test and of the other suggested imagery schedules, over a period of time, comprises psychotherapy. These images involve the person in interaction with the mother, father, siblings, and other significant persons, and revitalize emotional behavior through regenerating a new relationship with these figures. The aim in these exercises is to overcome the consequences of a previous negative relationship which resulted in misguidance, starvation, or strangulation of natural biological propensities.

The process of analysis involves weeks and months of concentration exercises on various levels of imagery, during which time consciousness is progressively developed from a surface understanding of situations present in the symptom to the deeper levels of information, to experience and resolve the various layers of conflict. The analysis is conducted along the following lines.

BASIC ANALYSIS LEVELS

ORIENTATION EXERCISES

Step 1: The Symptom
Step 2: Awareness of the Symptom
Step 3: Symptoms in Mother
Step 4: Symptoms in Father
Step 5: Integrating Information on Mother's Symptoms
Step 6: Integrating Information on Father's Symptoms
Step 7: Eidetic Parents Test Images
Step 8: Analysis, Concentration, and Dialogue
Step 9: Negative Images
Step 10: Positive Images
Step 11: Negative-Positive Alternation
Step 12: Mother—Positive Body
Step 13: Mother—Positive Objects
Step 14: Father—Positive Body
Step 15: Father—Positive Objects
Step 16: Nature Images
Step 17: Can You See an Eidetic?

During individual analysis, Eidetic Parents Test imagery is developed separately for concentration exercises on positive, negative, and vague images. A short therapy course can be based on the Orientation Exercises, which involves careful selection of some or all the significant images from the Eidetic Parents Test. If more treatment of mental states through other imagery levels appears necessary, the interested reader can use further schedules of imagery along the following lines.

Analysis of a Problematic Event

During the imagery exercises a problematic experience, such as a complex traumatic event, may come to light which needs to be handled in a thorough, extensive fashion. To treat various facets of the event for further psychological development, the chapter "The Frozen 'I'–Image: How to Defreeze It" should be studied. This chapter shows how a problematic experience is located and how recollection of the event is sharpened by staging it like a current experience. The chapter also shows how to transition from the problematic event into a general analysis of history in a relevant, smooth manner.

Analysis of Parental Ground

After the problematic event has been resolved and history analysis has been expanded, the new level of information deals with the larger significance of the parental figures, understanding of their functions, and treatment of their personality deficiencies. The exercises can create consciousness change in the area of their deficient behaviors and limitations. The following imagery schedules from the chapter "Psycheye" will be found useful for conducting imagery work in this area.

1. Inversion Process
2. Early Anger and Pity Associated with the Mother Image
3. Images of Depressed Mother
4. Quarrelling Images of Parents
5. Mother: Communication Image
6. Double-Faced Emotions Concerning Father
7. Father: Communication Image
8. Positive Father
9. Father in the Evening
10. Eidetic Parents Test: Positive Images of Father
11. Father: Work Image
12. Father: Humor Image
13. Father: Man-Monkey
14. Helping Father in His Problem
15. Resolution of Identifications

CONSCIOUSNESS FRIENDS

A person who has studied eidetics learns the importance of internal images which give guidance in a personal way, as a healing experience. However, the question in the form of a feeling always persists in his mind: "Can I similarly help another person?" The technique suggested here answers this question.

Although one uses eidetics as a way of experiencing personal life where it was stifled, still it appears natural that somehow people think of themselves also as therapists. Yet, in no way are they accepted as "therapists" in the technical sense. We have not yet begun, in our technical journals, to discuss this possibility, brought into focus by experience. It appears that a decisively positive orientation must be provided to those who are learning the technique for also helping others, and that a restrictive definition of the therapist-patient relationship discourages the potential in these people. Unless a clear departure in philosophy is made at this point, it is feared that when these people will act in order to help others, they will not be effective, for they will not feel that they have a legitimate framework for operating in this manner.

The basic philosophy is not so much the need to raise an army of therapists at the grass roots level but to discover an answer to the finding that there is a great percentage of individuals who are seeking help while, at the same time, they want to extend help to others in the epidemic of emotional illness. More and more of these concerned people are searching answers for mental health problems. It is known that almost all therapists, in fact, start their careers in this manner. Those who are outside of the profession proper, however, experience a deep sense of isolation and a feeling that they have been bereft of their essential human trait, their desire to help and heal others. These individuals cannot be truly helped unless they can also be shown a way to help others in the mental health field. They are bringing into focus the central question which the mental health field must face, that it is not self-ingratiation and dependence but service to the other and a positive activity in that direction that makes a person relate to his own fundamental nature in a complete manner. This is especially true regarding those persons who are conscious of the frustration of this central need, causing a tremendous amount of disturbance and a destruction of wholeness in them. Thus, it can be recognized that many individuals live their lives with this sentiment, and are patients in the initial stages of therapy but would be healers in the later stages of therapy. A complete cure in them would demand recognizing the fact that the later part of the treatment will fail if the healer is not recognized.

For such a person to receive a greater degree of help, it is a necessary ingredient that he also help someone else, since his helping of another person is conducive to improved health in himself. The two functions of helping and being helped can be combined in a single structure of therapy in which two individuals help each other by alternating the roles of therapist and patient.

The imagery exercises described above can be used by two individuals, called here *Consciousness Friends,* who cooperate in a program of mental exercises to evolve consciousness in a self-educational manner. In a regular self-help program, the consciousness friends meet at least once a week or more, during which time they administer the imagery processes to each other. They operate from two separate books, and experience the roles of therapist and patient with one another. Each records his own responses in his own personal book. During a meeting one third of the time is spent in individual analysis, one third of the time on empathy exercises, and one third of the time on dialogue or discussion. For details on the procedures for empathy and discussion, see the chapter "Positive Group."

FAMILY AND MARRIAGE COUNSELING

The problems in a family originate from an unknown part of the relationship between parents and children. This unknown is guarded by lack of introspection and inertia of habit in the family members. This inertia of habit is further defended by bias or myopic behavior. The myopic behavior is fenced in by a form of pseudo-diagnosis of the troubled member, which provides the blindness to other members of the family for behaving in a negative way. This negativity is usually expressed through pseudo-reasoning. In the end the original natural relationship is replaced by a known negative relationship which suffers from so many superficialities and defects that it frustrates the natural functions of the family members. This leads to anxiety and formulations of layers of symptoms and disturbances, and the individuals in the family thereafter progressively isolate themselves and enter disintegrative life styles.

Discovering the unknown part of the relationships within the family nucleus involves rejection of the "conscious" and the "known" in its negative and isolating forms. This can be done by generating a fresh reality in the form of experience of family images. Rules of imagery projection gradually cut through the "habits" and isolating thought processes, allowing the unifying experiences to penetrate through.

A careful looking at family images in the mind does not, of course, involve any value judgment on the parents themselves. Since the aim in the family is not to judge the members but to know them, the individual who is oriented for or against them will not be truly investigative. It is precisely this outer shell of isolation and defense which needs to be broken through. The members of a family should collectively approach the parental and sibling images with an open consciousness. The difficulty they may find in accepting what is revealed in them is the beginning of change in the family. The mechanical behavior of this isolating consciousness directed toward the family members must be penetrated in order to break the frigid molds of behavior in the individual family members who may be causing the symptoms or problems.

The imagery exercises can be used by a whole family toward the goal of understanding and healing the conflicts in the family. The family, under the guidance of one person from within the family, introduces the exercises, and each individual writes down his own responses in his own book. In the case of an individual who is unable to write, someone else takes over the responsibility of recording the material. The imagery is recorded and projected at least once a week, during which time the imagery is empathized into and discussed according to the procedure laid down in the chapter entitled "Positive Group."

The family as a group notes down the areas of conflict and carries out imagery exercises to resolve problems in those special areas. Attempts are made to reach and free the positive areas of interaction by locating the relevant areas of imagery and projecting them together as a group to develop understanding and empathy in those areas.

In the case of an individual with severe problems, the family should especially concentrate on his or her images to develop empathic projections and enlarge the consciousness of the individual as well as other members of the family with the aim of correcting negative behaviors in the related areas.

The above instructions can also be applied for self-education in the areas of marital conflict. The couple should use separate books for recording of responses and should write their images in their own respective books.

GROUP THERAPY

While analyzing images, one faces the problem of separating truth from fiction and what is being really seen from what is being imposed on the sight, in the form of imagination, fantasy, or thought, through social pressure. For this reason, it becomes necessary to develop a group process that provides social analysis by showing which aspects of mental life are real and which represent corruption. In a group setting, the picture is experienced as a social object and described as one would describe any natural object, such as a tree. Just as by looking at a tree, one can distinguish the trunk from the branches, the birds in the tree from the branches they are sitting on, the shadows from the real leaves—in the same way one can look at the mental pictures, discovering their biological significance and also discovering, at the same time, how their nourishing nature is affected through cultural pressures.

In group therapy, 3–15 members, with or without a moderator, participate through regular meetings in a program for general expansion of consciousness or for a specific psychotherapy goal. This is achieved through empathic regeneration of positive potentials, in which expansion of consciousness follows the general rules for individual expansion of consciousness through imagery procedures. If the aim is psychotherapy, the procedure remains the same, except more effort is centered on the presented symptoms in the individual members. While the goal for expansion of consciousness remains enrichment of experience and knowledge of interactions, the goal of the psychotherapy group is specifically limited to the abolishing of symptoms.

The group procedures for imagery exercises have been presented in detail in the chapter entitled "Positive Group." These groups are formed as leaderless or self-motivated groups out of college students or socially-oriented individuals, and function as psychological clubs. These positive groups aim at the study of consciousness through a self-educational experience of imagery. When a group is raised by a professional therapist, the leaderless spirit should be maintained in the sessions to achieve positive results.

PROFESSIONAL'S ANALYTIC GUIDE

The instructions for a therapist's use of the imagery exercises, in fact, covers the whole scheme of this book. The therapist who wants to use these exercises should experience all of them himself first in the sequence described under "Individual or Personal Analysis." After knowing the material in this personal fashion, he will develop a fair grasp of the nature of imagery projection and the art of managing the flow of the exercises. The therapist should also read the chapter "More on Adjustment" and formulate an overall picture of administration of therapy with regard to a variety of symptoms. A detailed guide for reading on the treatment procedures has been provided in that chapter and he should acquaint himself well with the suggested reading material.

II

Eidetic Therapy involves repeated summoning of images in the mind. The repetition of a single image over days and weeks generates a new experience in consciousness which may, at times, seem like too much too fast and, therefore, confusing to the mind. How exactly does one see the images? To know how the process moves, think of how you will observe a flower from many angles: the design, the color, the texture, the fragrance, even the environment in which it is found. This observation involves looking again and again. This is how repetition of an internal image proceeds.

Sit comfortably in a chair, or just relax.
With eyes open or closed, whichever you prefer, allow a selected image from the Eidetic Parents Test or from memory to form on its own.
Allow time to elapse before describing the image so that it will be clear in your mind.
First, pay attention to the whole image in a relaxed way.
Do not exert or force the image or think about it. Just report what you see.
Project the image for only a few seconds and write down what you see. If the image is not clear, project it for only a fraction of a second, tantalizing it through brief flashes of attention. Paradoxically, many a time briefer projections help the vague image become more clear.

Consider how the image appears visually. Note any emotions present in it. Note any change in your usual state of feeling, and try to see how the feeling emerges from a detail displayed in the image. To see this, try to handle various parts of the image by actively repeating them in your mind.

Let your attention travel over the various parts of the image or the series of images that have emerged so far. Wherever a whole image or an image detail spontaneously catches your attention, stop and concentrate on it, feeling your emotions and what you like or dislike about it.

Experience whatever emotional reactions come naturally, such as love, doubt, greed, disgust, hatred, anxiety, or even anger against a person in the image to express the feelings of frustration in you.

The eidetic images revealed at various levels are repertoires of important life situations, and in these images appear a variety of concrete experiences, memories, and fantasies. Most of what is revealed can be interpreted at face value. And if it is unclear, it represents something which you are not yet emotionally ready to understand; but the very fact that you are dealing with it in an experiential manner is preparing you to understand it eventually. Waiting for the interpretation to emerge on its own as you expand your awareness is the process of working with the eidetic images. Interpretation follows the initial meaning and its progression as one concentrates on the image. To discover the meaning of an eidetic, ask the following questions concerning the image:

1. What do you see in the image?

2. How do you feel when you see the image?

3. Do you feel the presence of a vague or clear meaning in the image? This is its meaning.

4. Do you experience the meaning at first glance? If not, continue to look at the image until some meaning emerges in your mind.

5. What is your conscious understanding of the situation presented in the image? What has been your long-standing view in this area?

6. Now, can you compare your conscious understanding with the meaning in the image? Try to solve the contradiction, if one is present.

7. Do you know that each person responds individually to the image and that the meaning of the image is always personal and private? Try to overcome gaps by concentration and introspection.

What is your manner of relating when you look at the images? Do you try to see in the images what your parents have told you? Do you expect to find something different? Are you timid or furtive with images? Do you dig hard for new information and experience? Do you remain tangled in your preconceived notions or do you let some fresh air in and allow some new angle of looking at things to emerge? If most of what you see coincides with your conscious thinking, you are imposing your conscious views and what others have taught you on your internal possibilities without letting them speak for themselves.

How do we know that we have our own perceptions, not imposed by others? If we did not have our own perceptions, we would be without a center. If we lived according to our perceptions, there would be no conflict between what we feel and what we think. When there is no conflict, there is no division. So, when we return to our own original perceptions and allow our minds to experience them, it takes away the pressure and the conflict, and a healing process in the mind begins.

The individual who intends to conduct eidetic analysis must learn to regard the whole question of symptoms and their relationship with the parents from a new angle. Of course, this does not involve a judgment on the parents, but an experience of how they actually appear in the mind and influence one's emotions.

You should look at the images and describe them in a simple fashion: "Now I see . . ." "Now I experience . . ." "Now I feel . . ." "Now I react . . ." "I am aware . . ." "I wish . . ." "I understand . . ." As you see the image, try to separate its various aspects: the visual elements, the events, actions, reactions, physiological sensations, feelings or tensions, emotions, thoughts, and conclusions. Concentrate on each aspect, analyzing it in the light of the other aspects. Carefully practice deep concentration and awareness in connection with the images. Body awareness through images is not difficult if you are prepared to experience, and not resist, anxiety and pain. If you have special difficulty in this area, it will be fruitful to spend even hours relating to your images bodily.

SUGGESTIONS

Here are some suggestions to help you do the imagery exercises according to the eidetic instructions, and to elicit a rich response from the instructions.

Read the eidetic instructions aloud or silently, as you prefer. Experience each phrase as a total unit, allow the image to form, then continue with the next phrase. Let the imagery emerge gradually in a relaxed way, keeping your eyes open or closed as you prefer.

A good eidetic response is an image with three qualities: it is pictorial, emotive, and capable of repetition and further investigation. If you do not experience an image at all the first time, read the instructions and repeat them until you notice that you are responding in a fixed manner, for instance, with a clear image or with a feeling that there is a vague image somewhere in your mind. Repeat this pictorial feeling in your mind until you get a clear picture. Record the picture response to the instruction. Allow any associated memories to emerge and record them too. If any significant fantasy material enters, it may contain important depth material and may prove useful for structuring self-analytic awareness. If, instead of the picture, you experience anger, passivity, resistance, doubt, etc., this, too, throws light on the internal experience. At this point, you may question whether one or both of your parents behave as you are behaving. If you tend to describe an eidetic briefly by answering the inquiries with "yes," "no," or half-phrases that are incomplete and nondescriptive, try to give a more complete response containing more details: more picture, more feeling, more meaning. If you respond to the image with feelings of moral aversion, because it contains negative information concerning you or your parents, this imagery must be experienced because it contains a story of your life. It tells how your parents related to you, how they view things, and how you have related to them.

If the parent's images do not appear clear or whole—for instance, you see vague limbs, a head with a vague body, a body without hands—it tells you that you have experienced a problem with that parent in that area. Look carefully into each vagueness or mutilation to find out its meaning for you.

Now, select and repeat one of the pictures over and over again in your mind. At first you may experience a lot of material, or very little. As you continue concentrating, the amount of material may diminish or increase. If repetition of the eidetic bores or annoys you, or you relate to the image in a nonintrospective manner, by insisting on what you call or define as "real," by fearing it, arguing about it, not seeing it clearly, blaming yourself or the person imaged, or feeling inferior as you picture it—you have set up a barrier between yourself and the image. To break this barrier, repeat the eidetic with the openness that characterizes all genuine investigation.

- Be accurate, clear, and faithful in seeing and reporting the image.
- Be certain about what you see and feel, and do not allow such phrases as "I think," "maybe," or "but" to enter the description.
- Be patient, and sort out an image difficulty through repetition of the picture.
- Be willing to relate with feeling to whatever is revealed, no matter how painful.
- Be vigilant in your concentration on the eidetic and do not allow distractions to carry you off the mark.
- Be open and let the meaning filter in and pose questions to the mind that contradict or expand the current beliefs and life concepts you hold.

ROUTINE

Notice how you project your images. Do you concentrate on them clearly and regularly or think of them in a half-hearted and casual manner? Do you put the image work away for long periods and then complain of absence of progress? Do you have an efficient routine for work on your images? Do you use a regular routine for writing further information on your images? Go back over your images and occasionally examine how they change and progress over a period of time. Keep an eye on the images and their content as it slowly changes. Try to experience the various flavors and textures in the new experience. Do not skip over experiences; try to re-create the important ones over and over again.

After you have learned to project eidetics, you will experience that the eidetic images start flowing like a stream. You will find them developing from earlier images and evolving the hidden layers of your mind in more spontaneous forms.

See the image steps three times a day or at least once a day—morning, noon, or night. Do the image exercise a minimum of once a day without breaking the routine unless it is impossible to keep.

Experience your images while lying comfortably on a couch or a bed, during free time while doing daily business, during walks, while preparing to go to sleep or while waking up in the morning. Images do not interfere with the normal, day-to-day duties of life. In fact, they keep your mind directed on what is important for you.

Some persons become wakeful when they do the images; others become sleepy. Therefore, you can also do the images to create the necessary mood, i.e., make yourself sleepy or wakeful, in the morning or evening.

Keep the image exercises going at an easy pace. Do not overdo it.

Example

How do the image exercises proceed? Here is an example of someone's response to the first instruction of the Eidetic Parents Test (Ep1) with concentration exercises and comments.

PICTURE:

I see my mother in the house. My father is in the yard. He's cutting the grass. I don't feel like seeing him in the image. What do I feel in this picture? I don't feel anything.

STEPS:
1. I see my parents at home. My mother is reading and my father is cutting the grass.
2. Does the house give me a feeling of a home? No, the house does not give me the feeling of a home. I don't believe it ever has, except on some occasions, a few times.
3. Where do I see my father? I see my father in the yard. He is cutting the grass.

4. How do I feel about this father who is cutting the grass? What kind of a mood do I develop when I concentrate on his picture? He appears annoyed and I feel offended. There is a clear feeling of anger and retaliation in me.
5. The image where my father is cutting grass in the yard is very striking. As I concentrate, this image gradually changes and I see him, instead, watching television in the living room, and I am asking questions and he is expressing annoyance. Why did I see him first in the yard and then in the television room, and what is the difference between the two images? I have no answer to it at this moment.

    My memories and thoughts concerning my father? I am thinking about my father and myself and want to write something about my relationship with him.

    I know that I am a strong-willed person. When I was growing up, my father would tell me to do something in a specific way, but I felt my way was better. So, I went ahead and did it my way, and, in many cases, it turned out to be the wrong way. During these battles with my father, he would usually yell or hit me. Sometimes he would say nothing about what I had done and I would expect him to; other times, when I least expected it, he would be completely enraged. I would be so surprised by his reaction.
6. Where do I see the mother in the house? Unlike my father, my mother is seen in two places. One is in the kitchen; she is standing by the sink looking out of the window. The second picture shows her sitting in the living room.
7. How do I feel when I see my mother in the pictures? I feel very comfortable, but also I've felt at times that she works hard or does all the work in the house and she receives no help. I feel badly that I did not help her more when I lived with my parents. For some reason, I never felt any responsibility for performing the needed tasks.
8. I see my mother in the house. She is usually in the house. Either in the kitchen or the living room. At present, she is making dinner. She is doing all the work of preparing the dinner. I never helped too often with dinner. I never felt that I had to do anything. We were never given specific chores on a "must-do" basis. It was either hit or miss. Many times she complained that she received no help. But I think that if it were mandatory that we had to do certain jobs, this problem wouldn't have existed. The discipline was lax and erratic. Really, talking about the past this way makes me feel very bad.
9. Where are my siblings? I had one older brother who died. I was very little then, maybe two years old. I have one sister. She is four years younger than I. I think that we share some of the same problems, e.g., lack of self-worth, hostile feelings, anger, defiance, wanting not to conform, lack of respect and perhaps . . . One big difference is

that I always knew that I wanted more out of life. So, I tried a little harder to accomplish something.

My sister and I are not close—or perhaps one might say that we cannot communicate. She feels that I have always been the favored one. I don't think this is so. I love her and I wish I could help her or at least be a friend to her.

10. Can I see myself in the picture? No, I cannot. If I am not in the picture, where am I then? I do not know where I am.

I can't stand the feeling of being left out. I don't understand people who are not nice to other people because of jealousy. I think I am a nice person and I can't understand it when other people are not reciprocal. If only I could look at the picture closer, I might find myself. Is it because I feel inferiority and feel that people naturally do not like me? This clouds my ability to differentiate and look at situations and individuals objectively.

I can feel that my relationship with any man stems from my relationship with my father, that I am usually defensive and battling with him and I cannot control it. I put the man to a test.

When I repeat these images, I find that either I'm closed or there is too much emotion in me. In fact, the first image reproduces exactly the same feeling in me as it did originally. It just cuts off everything. However, when I repeat the image and I start asking father questions and the battle develops, I become aware of my anger in relationship with my father. Imagewise, this anger cannot be brought to the surface through the first image in the steps for concentration, it is kind of a "safe picture." It is interesting. This explains my need to forget my problem with my father. I wanted to see my father cutting the grass rather than watching the television, when the battle becomes really severe.

So, I go back to the picture in which he is watching the television, and there is anger between us. When I see my father yelling at me, he says something which makes me feel inferior or undermined. I want to hurt him just as he has hurt me. If he criticizes me, I lose my confidence and feel like nothing.

During the course of my marriage, this seeking of reassurance or attention has been recurring. It has caused much anxiety and pain for both my husband and me. After I have achieved the desired effect that I want my actions to produce, I feel satisfied and perhaps secure that I have achieved my goal—whatever that may be.

I always feel that I have been wronged—never trying to weigh the other person's reasons. Maybe I have been hurt more than I realize. I find it very easy to cast blame and thus absolve myself.

A

Preliminary Note

on

ORIENTATION EXERCISES

The following pages containing imagery exercises should be read slowly. All the blank spaces provided for writing personal images should be filled in carefully. Concentration on these images should be practiced each day at a slow, steady pace, one image or a few images each day, and each image should be practiced at least 10 to 20 times, usually through 10–15 second projections, except when deep concentration is needed. Deep concentration exercises require a longer projection period involving a duration of time from 30 seconds to a few minutes. During all mental exercises, deep projections are encouraged as a rule, unless there is inability to sustain longer concentration. If you hit upon important material, stay with it until you feel you have explored and absorbed all the information contained in it by concentrating on it.

Step 1: The Symptom

The symptom, similar to an iceberg, is usually not wholly accessible to the consciousness of the individual; only its tip is. The person shies away from its complete awareness. A clear outlining of the symptom in its mental and physiological manifestation can create a systematic view of the problems. A full awareness of the symptom can be developed by answering questions on specific details. For the purpose of elucidation, descriptions should be filled in the blank spaces below along the suggested lines.

1. I am suffering from the following emotional complaints:

    a.

    b.

    c.

    d.

2. I also have the following physiological complaints:

    a.

    b.

    c.

    d.

3. I am worried and concerned that if these symptoms are not cured, they will become worse in the following manner:

    a.

    b.

    c.

    d.

Step 2: Awareness of the Symptom

Awareness of the symptom detail is a step toward clarity of mind, and one should remove vagueness in the area by seeing what is really present. Awareness can be created by concentrating separately on each symptom detail given on the opposite page. The negative feelings should be fully developed by slow and repeated mental concentration. This total exposure generates an ability to handle the symptoms in a spontaneous manner.

1. Deeply concentrate on each emotional complaint on the opposite page and write down further feelings as you concentrate.

    a.

    b.

    c.

    d.

2. Deeply concentrate on each physiological complaint and write down further feelings as you concentrate.

    a.

    b.

    c.

    d.

3. Deeply concentrate on each worry and concern. If these symptoms are not cured, how will they become worse? Write details.

    a.

    b.

    c.

    d.

Step 3: Symptoms in Mother

To understand the origin of a personal symptom, the presence of symptoms in the parents should be examined, starting with the mother. When the information on an individual's symptoms matches with the information on mother's symptoms, this indicates the possible source of the person's symptom in the mother. Similarity of symptoms with the mother indicates imitation of or identification with mother, and contrast shows reaction to her symptoms. This will determine the relationship of symptoms with mother. First, fill in information in the blank spaces below.

1. Mother usually suffered from these negative feelings or behaviors:

    a.

    b.

    c.

    d.

2. Mother usually suffered from the following physiological complaints:

    a.

    b.

    c.

    d.

3. Mother usually worried about her symptoms, and when they became worse, she would behave in the following manner:

    a.

    b.

    c.

    d.

Step 4: Symptoms in Father

A symptom may originate from some problematic interaction with father just as it may with mother, the difference being that interaction with father occurs much later in time. Similarity of symptoms with the father indicates imitation of or identification with father, and contrast shows reaction to his symptoms. This will determine the relationship of symptoms with father. First, fill in information in the blank spaces below.

1. Father usually suffered from these negative feelings or behaviors:

   a.

   b.

   c.

   d.

2. Father usually suffered from the following physiological complaints:

   a.

   b.

   c.

   d.

3. Father usually worried about his symptoms, and when they became worse, he would behave in the following manner:

   a.

   b.

   c.

   d.

Step 5: Integrating Information on Mother's Symptoms

After filling in all the sections regarding the personal symptoms, the mother's symptoms, and the father's symptoms, you have amassed an initial spectrum of information. How does the information fit into a meaningful pattern of similarity or reaction? Next, you need to outline the connecting links between personal symptoms and symptoms in parents, starting with mother.

1. *Imitation or Identification:* Compare the information in Step 1 and Step 3. If certain emotional complaints, physiological complaints, and worries are *similar* between you and your mother, write descriptive information here.

    a.

    b.

    c.

    d.

    e.

    f.

2. *Reactions:* Compare the information in Step 1 and Step 3. If certain emotional complaints, physiological complaints, and worries appear to be present in you as a *reaction* to mother's emotional complaints, physiological complaints, and worries, write descriptive information here.

    a.

    b.

    c.

    d.

    e.

    f.

3. *Sympathy, Fear, Avoidance, Anger, or Isolation:* Circle any of these emotions that you feel concerning mother.

Step 6: Integrating Information on Father's Symptoms

After information regarding the symptoms of the person and his mother has been filled in, the same information should be developed concerning the father. Notice whether father has really been related to in the mind or he has been avoided altogether. If father has been feelingfully related to, the picture of interaction will emerge clearly. Fill in information in the blank spaces below.

1. *Imitation or Identification:* Compare the information in Step 1 and Step 4. If certain emotional complaints, physiological complaints, and worries are *similar* between you and your father, write descriptive information here.

    a.

    b.

    c.

    d.

    e.

    f.

2. *Reactions:* Compare the information in Step 1 and Step 4. If certain emotional complaints, physiological complaints, and worries appear to be present in you as a *reaction* to father's emotional complaints, physiological complaints, and worries, write descriptive information here.

    a.

    b.

    c.

    d.

    e.

    f.

3. *Sympathy, Fear, Avoidance, Anger, or Isolation:* Circle any of these emotions that you feel concerning father.

Step 7: Eidetic Parents Test Images

Just as a person may be unaware of the details of his symptoms, he may be vague about their causes in his interactions with the parents. Obviously, this important material needs to be further developed in a careful, stepwise fashion. The Eidetic Parents Test (see chapter 5) achieves this needed information through systematic pictorial experience. Briefly called the EPT, this test enacts 30 image situations involving parents' body images.

Each EPT image situation is induced through an instruction. The instructions are read out slowly for visualization, and time is allowed for the image response to develop. The instruction is repeated until the picture is formed. When the same picture appears in the mind the same way every time, this picture is described, with the feelings and memories that accompany it, along with some comments. The response is written in the blank space provided under the word "picture" as specified below (see the page after next for example).

PICTURE:

STEPS:
Analysis of the main picture response, also called the *Primary Picture,* is carried out in 10 further steps along suggested imagery lines and responses are written in the blank spaces provided for this purpose. Since the complete Eidetic Parents Test contains 30 image situations broken down into 10 steps, the complete spectrum of imagery information on the parents' body images contains 300 different facets.

From these basic steps a comprehensive analysis of the relationship with parents can be developed. The individual can do these images during current work and return to them any time later and elaborate an associative chain of images from them for self-education.

The reader should not underestimate the importance of the material revealed through these 10 steps covering 30 items of the test. Considering the extent of information and its levels, the value of this multi-levelled material remains basic to the needs of systematic analysis. Therefore, whenever the analysis meets a blind alley, one should return to this source material and make a fresh start again. Similarly, when material in a certain area appears to be exhausted and need for a fresh angle of looking at the problems is indicated, one can return to this material and go through it carefully, choosing points of imagery from where fresh analytic work can be started. The basic importance of this extensive material should be kept in mind, and one should even occasionally consult the material as a matter of routine for injecting new orientations in analysis.

Step 8: Analysis, Concentration, and Dialogue

After the 30 test items of the Eidetic Parents Test have been developed into steps for concentration, consciousness can be further developed through personal exercises, empathy exercises, and dialogue. Concentration is practiced on three selected images out of the 10 image-steps to the primary picture, and also on the primary picture, for the following benefits (see the page after next for example).

1. *POSITIVE IMAGE:* Concentration is practiced for pleasurable release.

2. *NEGATIVE IMAGE:* Concentration is practiced for elucidation of the problem.

3. *VAGUE IMAGE:* Concentration is practiced for clarity of detail.

EMPATHY: Each person's primary, positive, negative, and vague images are empathized into in order to create change and expansion of experience. Understanding of images is developed by empathy and friendly dialogue. As a result of these communication exercises, the consciousness of the participating individuals matures and expands. As they accumulate experience and knowledge, resistances and conflicts are overcome. The four spaces (Empathy 1, 2, 3, 4) provided under the heading "Empathy" can be used for writing responses for the following types of imagery work: *(i) Groups:* for expansion of consciousness; *(ii) Family and Marriage Counseling:* for knowing each other's feelings and views and also enhancing mutual understanding; *(iii) Consciousness Friends:* for consciousness expansion; *(iv) Therapist:* for writing empathy responses to a patient's obstructed imagery.

Empathy 1:

Empathy 2:

Empathy 3:

Empathy 4:

Image: House (Example)

READ the instruction below slowly and allow the image to be formed.

    Ep1:   *Picture your parents in the house where you lived most of the time with them, the house which gives you the feeling of a home. —Where do you see them? —What are they doing? —How do you feel when you see the images? —Are there any memories connected with this picture?*

PICTURE: Write here what is seen in the mind.

    I see my mother in the kitchen and I feel insecure or feelingless. My father is in the basement and he is building a concrete column. I am playing, making firecrackers near him. I am not sure what I feel concerning my mother. I feel warm toward my father.

STEPS: Concentrate on the above picture in the following stepwise manner and write the experience in each blank space in detail.

1. Picture your parents in the house. Where do you see them?
   I see my mother in the kitchen and my father in the basement.

2. Does the house give you the feeling of a home? Describe it.
   The house gives me a feeling of a home.

3. See your father. What is he doing in the picture?
   He is working, building a concrete column.

4. Do you experience positive or negative feelings when you see him?
   I experience warm feelings toward father.

5. Relax and recall memories about the place where father appears.
   I used to play sometimes in the basement, work on the bicycle, or make firecrackers.

6. Now, see your mother. What is she doing in the picture?
   She is standing at the sink cutting string beans.

7. Do you experience positive or negative feelings when you see her?
   I have no feelings toward my mother one way or the other.

8. Relax and recall memories about the place where mother appears.
   Memories of eating meals, washing machine, clock on the wall with the flag on it.

9. Where are your siblings? What are they doing?
   Warm feelings for siblings, for all of them.

10. Now, see yourself in the picture. What are you doing?
    I am sitting. I am inactive, more inactive than my siblings.

Analysis, Concentration, and Dialogue (Example)

READ each response (1–10) on the opposite page. Then select and write below three significant images for concentration: a positive, a negative, and a vague image. Repeat them according to the directions below.

> *1. POSITIVE IMAGE:* Concentrate for pleasurable release.
>
> *I see myself playing in the basement making firecrackers.*
>
> *2. NEGATIVE IMAGE:* Concentrate for elucidation of the problem.
>
> *I am sitting. I am inactive, more inactive than my siblings.*
>
> *3. VAGUE IMAGE:* Concentrate for clarity of detail.
>
> *I have no feelings toward my mother one way or the other.*

The above images should be repeated mentally over many days and weeks to stabilize the positive experience, to resolve the negative experience, and to lift vagueness from forgotten and inaccessible areas.

EMPATHY: Ask the person(s) working with you, "Please relax and pay attention to the image I am going to read to you. Empathize and experience the image as if it were your own." Then, from the opposite page, read the image written below *picture* aloud and allow sufficient time for concentration and development of empathy. Then say, "Describe what you see." Write the empathy response below. The spaces below can be used by a group, a family, two individuals, or a therapist for recording empathy and re-empathy experience, and expansion of consciousness.

> *Empathy 1:* (By Group) I see that I am in the basement and I especially feel secure with my father. When a firecracker makes noise, I laugh.
>
> *Empathy 2:* (By Group) I am sitting alone in the basement, and I feel as if I am bound in chains. I am waiting for my father to come home.
>
> *Empathy 3:* (By Group) When I see my father in the basement, I feel relaxed in my diaphragm. I feel I had been suffocated by my mother. I am unable to speak to her. She does not let me.
>
> *Empathy 4:* (By Group) I am in the basement. I am a little secretive when I set off the firecracker. My father hears the blast and he laughs.

Step 9: Negative Images

The negative images are painful to the person and he usually avoids them in his mind. Considering this fact, mental exposure to painful images greatly benefits the individual by expanding his consciousness beyond the circle of narrow fears and apprehensions. After the Eidetic Parents Test has been induced, the positive and negative images in the test are marked out. The negative images are experienced to enhance awareness in the following manner.

Model: The negative images should be experienced in an intensive manner according to the model presented on the opposite page under *Concentration*. This model should be applied faithfully, yet with sufficient flexibility to allow experience to flow in a natural fashion.

Image Experience: The mind should be exposed to the visual situation in the image. The ability to handle details of imagery should be developed. Minute facets of imagery should be brought to attention through repeated visualization.

Catharsis: The negative image is experienced in an intense manner, resulting in catharsis. Pain in the image is suffered to the point where one feels totally exhausted and can no longer experience the pain. As the mind is exposed to the unpleasurable situation, one experiences discharge and toleration of pain, and the ability to handle pain progressively increases.

Body Experience: When the body responds to the pain in the image, one should see how the rest of the body joins in the experience of pain. The local response should be developed to the point where the whole body gets involved in the experience of pain.

Situation Elements: Carry out a systematic dissection of the events appearing in the image. How does the mind respond to each aspect of the painful situation? This will generate a full knowledge of what causes pain, when and how, and increase knowledge about the meaning and structure of pain.

Justice and Wisdom: Knowing where pain comes from and experiencing overt anger in response to it comprises justice in the psyche. When this justice is suppressed in favor of another emotion, such as sympathy or a naive and premature expression of charity, the mind tends to close down. When the true emotions attached to the negative image are lived and the elements of the situation are understood in all their varied facets, this spells out the awareness of universal wisdom.

Concentration

To study how concentration on a negative image is carried out, select a painful negative image from memory or from the Eidetic Parents Test responses. Experience the selected image clearly in the following manner, and describe it in the blank spaces. Later, use this model for all negative images.

1. Select the negative image, and describe it.

2. See the image visually. See what causes the pain.

3. Experience the *pain* by repeatedly concentrating on the painful aspect.

4. Allow your body to *respond* to the painful aspect in the image.

5. Suffer the painful aspect fully, until you feel completely exhausted.

6. Again, clearly see the situation in the image which causes pain.

7. See yourself doing something in the image to solve the situation.

8. See your father doing something in the image to solve the situation.

9. See your mother doing something in the image to solve the situation.

10. Comment on any aspect of the image which seems difficult to handle.

11. Comment on what can overcome the problem.

Step 10: Positive Images

When too much pain floods a person's life, the ability to experience pleasure progressively diminishes, setting off a state of incapacity in the organism to enjoy life. The ability to enjoy positive images, even fresh air, the green grass, and the blue water, which is naturally gifted in the human organism, is tarnished. The absence of pleasure manifests itself as a general hindrance to awareness of life. The positive images thus exert a bipolar action on the suppressed painful areas, and the individual can be induced to let himself go and experience life as it is. The positive images from the Eidetic Parents Test are used for pleasurable experience along the following lines.

Model: The positive images should be experienced in an intensive manner according to the model presented on the opposite page under *Concentration*. This model should be applied faithfully, yet with sufficient flexibility to allow experience to flow in a natural fashion.

Image Experience: The mind should be exposed to the visual situation in the image. The ability to handle details of imagery should be developed. Minute facets of imagery should be brought to attention through repeated visualization.

Pleasure Experience: By giving positive images to the mind when it is threatened by negative images, one opens up the mind. In this way one can provide initial relief or initiative to the resistant mind so that it will eventually relinquish its guard against the general flow of images.

Body Experience: As the positive image is seen, help the whole body respond to the pleasure in the image. See where the positive image reflects locally in the body. As you concentrate, see how the rest of the body also becomes relaxed. Finally, let the whole body become totally relaxed.

Final Positive Potential: When the person shows no fear of any type of image and he can respond to the problems in the images with openness, flexibility, and resourcefulness, more of the positive images should be introduced. The person should be encouraged to develop his psychical potential for a pleasurable style of relating to the world. A person who goes away from therapy having experienced only negative images has no idea of the positiveness of life. Experience of therapeutic imagery should, therefore, involve a final stage in which only Nature Images are projected, and a contact with the positive ground of life is developed in a systematic manner (see Step 16: Nature Images).

Concentration

To study how concentration on a positive image is carried out, select a positive image from memory or from the Eidetic Parents Test responses. Experience the selected image clearly in the following manner, and describe it in the blank spaces. Later, use this model for all positive images.

1. Select the positive image, and describe it.

2. See the image visually. See what creates pleasure.

3. Experience *pleasure* by repeatedly concentrating on the pleasing aspect.

4. Allow your body to *respond* to the pleasing aspect in the image.

5. Experience the pleasurable aspect fully, until you feel completely relaxed.

6. Again clearly see the situation in the image which creates pleasure.

7. See yourself doing something in the image which increases the pleasure.

8. See your father doing something in the image which increases the pleasure.

9. See your mother doing something in the image which increases the pleasure.

10. Comment on any aspect of the image which tends to stop the pleasure.

11. Comment on what can overcome the problem.

Step 11: Negative-Positive Alternation

Concentration on a negative or a positive image changes the consciousness mood accordingly. On this principle, opposite images can be introduced to neutralize a fixed thought or emotion. This technique works with two images—one positive and one negative—which are repeated in an alternate fashion. As a result, the painful image becomes neutralized, with noticeable reduction of anxiety. Command on one's consciousness is simultaneously expanded by seeing how these two patterns behave almost mechanically, and one can enjoy the voluntary manipulation of anxiety and pleasure in the mind.

1. *EXPOSURE TO THE NEGATIVE IMAGE:* First, a selected negative image is seen in a systematic way in the following manner.

    a. Repeated attention is paid to the negative image.
    b. Concentration on the negative image is practiced and anxiety is allowed to develop.
    c. Anxiety is intensified to a maximum tolerable limit by repeated concentration.

2. *EXPOSURE TO THE POSITIVE IMAGE:* Immediately following exposure to the negative image, a selected positive image is concentrated upon. This positive image is introduced to create release and balance, in the following manner.

    a. Repeated attention is paid to the positive image.
    b. Concentration on the positive image is practiced and a pleasurable feeling is allowed to develop.
    c. The pleasure is intensified to the maximum extent through repeated projection of the image.

3. *ALTERNATION OF NEGATIVE AND POSITIVE:* After initial exposure to the negative and positive images, these two images are repeated alternately in the following manner until benefit results.

    a. Introduction to the negative image is followed immediately by introduction of the positive image.
    b. The negative and positive images are repeated in an alternate manner.
    c. Comparatively more repetitions of the positive image are made, if toleration to the negative image is very low.

Training in Psychical Autonomy

By experiencing alternate states of anxiety and pleasure, the ability to master and control mental processes increases. Autonomous functioning is basic to this process. All the eidetic maneuvers revolve around the model of "Psychical Autonomy," i.e., psychical change through self-generation of experience, in which one learns to initiate anxiety or pleasure, develop mental structures, and interact with them, on his own. A thorough knowledge of this autonomy is most helpful in management of consciousness along negative-positive alternations.

The following training exercises in the form of experiments will be found most useful for learning about management of mental states. These exercises contain descriptions of consciousness behavior when mental states are handled in a certain way. (For more details, see the chapter entitled "High Fidelity Self-Images.")

Training Exercises

Experiment 1: Alternation of consciousness between pleasant and painful

Experiment 2: Influence of selected memory scenes on consciousness

Experiment 3: Self-images that leap out from previous images and break status quo in consciousness

Experiment 4: How consciousness becomes simliar to what is present in consciousness

Experiment 5: Bipolar seesaw behavior of two opposite images

Experiment 6: How consciousness oscillates between two opposite states, like a pendulum

Experiment 7: How pleasant or unpleasant objects present around a person change his consciousness

Experiment 8: How one can change consciousness as one wants by attending a previously selected image

Experiment 9: Image control of memory through selection, a psychofeedback control of the past

Experiment 10: Selection of positive objects and scenes connected with parents

Experiment 11: Awareness of symptoms through deep rest and concentration

Experiment 12: Deep concentration on the symptom and associated states

Step 12: Mother—Positive Body

The imagery of mother in the Eidetic Parents Test may reveal her body as generally negative, depending on the historical relationship with her. However, parts of her body may contain some positive feelings, behind which the real potential of the mother may lie concealed. Considering this, the various parts of her body, the objects usually associated with her, and her activities should be experienced for evidence of positive aspects. These aspects should then be developed and concentration exercises should be practiced in the following manner for evolving a positive relationship.

1. *List of Positive Body Images:* Touch and experience various parts of mother's body, such as her head, hair, eyes, ears, nose, throat, mouth, arms, hands, legs, lap, feet, chest, heart, and image her breathing, voice, thinking, etc. See which part is pleasurable, and write below the nature of the positive feeling in detail.

    a.

    b.

    c.

    d.

2. *Early Image:* Reconstruct your early childhood relationship with mother by forming positive images along these lines.
    a. See yourself as very young.
    b. See the house where you lived when you were very young.
    c. See the room where mother used to sleep.
    d. See mother resting in bed.
    e. See yourself as a child resting with her in the bed.
    f. See that your mother is caressing you.
    g. See that she is calling you by endearing names and by your nickname.
    h. See that she is stroking your forehead and is kissing you. She is hugging and embracing you.
    i. See that she is rubbing your back. You feel pleased. Allow the relaxation to develop.
    j. You are feeling kisses and embraces all over your body. You feel wonderful.
    k. Experience the image deeply, to the point where you almost go to sleep with relaxation.

Step 13: Mother—Positive Objects

After mother's body has been experienced deeply, think of all the objects associated with mother's body. Especially image things from the distant past, such as her hat, coat, jacket, blouse, skirt, watch, glasses, shoes, stockings, belt, scarf, handkerchief, and other objects such as kitchen objects. Explore all these objects one by one. Follow her in the house, or if she works, at her work activities. Describe the places and objects which are especially pleasing, and write the images with feelings below.

1. *List of Positive Images with Feelings:*

   a.

   b.

   c.

   d.

   e.

   f.

   g.

   h.

   i.

   j.

2. *Exercise:* Concentrate on the positive images you have described above along the following lines.
   a. See yourself in the positive place, and experience pleasure.
   b. See yourself interacting with the mother in the positive place.
   c. See yourself repeatedly touching and handling the positive object.
   d. See yourself wearing or using this object in the image as a child.
   e. See yourself wearing or using the object at your present age.
   f. Experience the pleasure of the positive images repeatedly, to create deep relaxation.

Step 14: Father—Positive Body

The imagery of father in the Eidetic Parents Test may reveal his body as generally negative, depending on the historical relationship with him. However, parts of his body may contain some positive feelings, behind which the real potential of the father may lie concealed. Considering this, the various parts of his body, the objects usually associated with him, and his activities should be experienced for evidence of positive aspects. These aspects should then be developed and concentration exercises should be practiced in the following manner for evolving a positive relationship.

1. *List of Positive Body Images:* Touch and experience various parts of father's body, such as his head, hair, eyes, ears, nose, throat, mouth, arms, hands, legs, lap, feet, chest, heart, and image his breathing, voice, thinking, etc. See which part is pleasurable, and write below the nature of the positive feeling in detail.

   a.

   b.

   c.

   d.

2. *Lifting Image:* Reconstruct an early positive body relationship with the father by forming positive images along these lines.
   a. See yourself as very young.
   b. See father standing and holding you in his arms.
   c. Experience the height and the space feelings from your high position in his arms.
   d. See yourself being lifted from the ground by father.
   e. See yourself being carried around in the arms of father.
   f. Experience the movement of the space as he carries you around.
   g. Now, see yourself seated in the lap of the father.
   h. See that from the lap of the father you are watching the world in a relaxed manner.
   i. Experience the contact with father's arms as you sit in his lap.
   j. Experience the above images deeply, to the point where you feel completely rested or activated.

Step 15: Father—Positive Objects

After father's body has been experienced deeply, think of all the objects associated with father's body. Especially image things from the distant past, such as his hat, walking stick, coat, jacket, shirt, trousers, watch, glasses, shoes, socks, belt, tie, handkerchief, and other objects, such as his office or work tools. Explore all these objects one by one. Follow him during his walk, and at his office. Describe the places and objects which are especially pleasing, and write the images with feelings below.

1. *List of Positive Images with Feelings:*

   a.

   b.

   c.

   d.

   e.

   f.

   g.

   h.

   i.

   j.

2. *Exercise:* Concentrate on the positive images you have described above along the following lines.

   a. See yourself in the positive place, and experience pleasure.
   b. See yourself interacting with the father in the positive place.
   c. See yourself repeatedly touching and handling the positive object.
   d. See yourself wearing or using this object in the image as a child.
   e. See yourself wearing or using the object at your present age.
   f. Experience the pleasure of the positive images repeatedly, to create deep relaxation.

Step 16: Nature Images

Parental figures have been associated with development of the mind and with the phenomena of Nature, such as sailing clouds, the blue sky, thunder and lightning, fire, rocks, streams, and forest creatures, since antiquity. In the technological environment, isolation from parents also involves insensitivity to natural phenomena and distance from the nourishing aspects of Nature. The stress generated by the artificial mechanical environment can be relieved by seeing oneself and the parents in a setting of Nature, performing some natural task involving contact with Nature. In the projection of images the person sees first himself performing the natural task, then father and then mother performing it. In the last phase of imagery projection, all the siblings join in and the whole family is seen performing the natural task. Discussion is held on resultant images, if a group uses this imagery step.

Each Nature task is concentrated upon in a deep fashion until the person feels and lives the images in all their details, feelings, and meanings, and experiences a refreshing physical feeling and a new awakening. As the burdensome artificial feelings of day-to-day mechanical life melt away during concentration, one no longer feels isolated and lonely, but relaxed, peaceful, and united with Nature.

A list of Nature images covering a variety of basic primary scenes is presented on the opposite page under *Concentration on Nature*. These images involve descriptions of natural phenomena: wind and water activity, colors, landscapes, and animal life, experience of daylight, evening, midnight, and daybreak, and images of relationship with soil, such as tilling of the land. The images should be visualized and concentration should be practiced on them along the following lines.

STEPS FOR CONCENTRATION ON NATURE IMAGES

a. See yourself experiencing the Nature image.

b. See the father experiencing the Nature image.

c. See the mother experiencing the Nature image.

d. See the siblings experiencing the Nature image, each sibling separately.

e. See the whole family, including siblings, experiencing the Nature image together.

f. See the family together discussing the Nature image.

Concentration on Nature

Visualize the Nature images below, deeply experiencing each image according to the steps for concentration given on the opposite page. See yourself experiencing Natural phenomena along the following line of images.

1. Sitting facing the twilight on a summer evening, looking up through the trees at the midnight blue sky; it is peaceful and relaxing.
2. Hearing the rain, the lightning, and the thunder, it is awesome, even fearful. You wonder at first whether someone up there is angry, but it is not so. Then you relax in the awesome feelings of the experience. The rain and the wind in the bushes make sounds, and the smell of freshness gets into your nose. It is an experience of pleasure when you can feel all the three: sound, smell, and sight.
3. Sitting on a high ground and watching the blue sky on a clear day after the clouds have just rained and dispersed, there is not a speck of cloud and the sky is all blue and cool.
4. Relaxing near a pond of rain water, watching a toad as it croaks. You can feel the pleasant vibration of the croaking in your mind. Hear the frog croaking in the water. See the frog hopping back and forth in the water.
5. Watching the ants go in and out of a partially wet anthill, carrying food back and forth.
6. Standing in a running stream, in the middle of the water. You are fishing with a pointed stick.
7. Seeing a small green mound of earth being buffeted by wind. You are standing on it, and you experience the breeze hitting your face.
8. Relaxing near the ocean, watching the ocean rolling in and out on the sand. Look at the fish leaping near the shore, and feel the sand and rocks under your feet. Feel the undercurrent, an initial coldness and gradual warmth.
9. Being in a forest, the earth is moist under your feet and the ground rustles. There are numerous sounds—birds, animals. All sounds are harmonious and blend. The smell is fresh and clean and it seems to rejuvenate you. Relax and enjoy being in the forest.
10. Walking in the woods, you find yourself on the top of a hill from which you can see trees with leaves of many colors. There are trees in front and below you, down in the valley, and all along up the mountain in front of you.
11. Looking at the bark of a tree, see all the tiny animals on the tree bark and a small caterpillar climbing up. Put it on your finger and then put it back

again. Feel the bark; it is rough. The tree is very tall, awesome. You do not feel small, just awed. It seems like a world in itself.

12. Watching a huge mountain in front of you. Where the peak is you cannot see, but the many snow caps of the mountain are stretching in front of you and go on and on until you can no longer see them; yet you know there are more snowy hills in front. As you progress upward, the snowy hills appear that you could not see before.

13. Watching a land stretching ahead as far as you can see. The grass is high and moves a little because of the breeze. The crickets chirp continuously. Occasionally, there is a small bush or a short tree. The undulating land keeps stretching on forever.

14. Watching the rolling hills and shallow valleys covered with grass. Hear the sound of a few lambs calling out competing with the cricket noise.

15. Watching a cow feeding a calf, how the calf suckles and the cow's tail keeps swatting and both seem unperturbed by anything, it looks like the way it should be. The experience is restful and makes you feel secure.

16. Collecting dry leaves in the middle of the forest, burning them in a pit, and watching the flames rise. Watch the tongues of flames crackle, break, and chew the leaves. Feed the fire and watch it devour the forest leaves.

17. Tilling a vast land in the morning with a bull yoked to a crude plow. You are spreading the seeds as you till and move.

18. See the parted and tilled earth, experience the smell of the fresh, overturned soil spreading in front of you. Look at its moist freshness.

19. Experience the early morning light, concentrate on the slowly growing morning light before you know that the sun is going to rise.

20. Experience and watch the midnight hour of pitch darkness in which nothing is visible, it is awesome and silent. All objects and images invisibly reside in this hour of darkness.

21. Experience darkness, your eyes do not see, but you walk with the feeling that your foot knows the path.

22. Wake up a sleeping person and ask the person to watch with you from the midnight hour to sunrise. With this person, know the mental process progressing in each shade of darkness as it moves to light.

Step 17: Can You See an Eidetic?

It is not difficult to experience an eidetic. However, some individuals habitually use conscious thinking, memory, and reasoning, and give the impression that they do not see eidetics. These individuals are usually resistant to imagery due to the difficulty in interaction while growing up. The following simple image situations based on memory should be practiced for gradual release of eidetics in these individuals.

1. Recall a pleasurable vacation with father in the past. See it like a picture in your mind. Develop details and concentrate on them over many weeks. Describe the picture here briefly.

2. Recall a very pleasant event involving the mother. See it like a picture. Develop details and concentrate on them over many weeks. Describe the picture here briefly.

3. Recall the school you attended. See it like a picture. See yourself in the classroom, in the hallways, or playing games. Develop details and concentrate on them over many weeks. Describe the picture here briefly.

4. Recall an event from the remote past which was particularly worrisome or painful to you. See it in the form of images. Develop the details and concentrate on them over many weeks. Describe the images here briefly.

5. If the eidetic imagery is still difficult to evoke in the experience, use the imagery steps described on the next page under *Eidetic Concentration on Objects*. These imagery steps aim at reinstating natural eidetic capacity starting with the basic experience of objects.

Eidetic Concentration on Objects

Some individuals show an extremely rigid fixation on conscious thinking and have a fear of relating to their real emotions. They feel secure in what they consciously know and compulsively use this conscious manner of thinking, which results in hiding of their true feelings. This defect is not only found in many adults but also in children, who have been forced to assertively learn an inappropriate way of viewing life. Due to extreme usage of conscious concepts, such individuals can no longer see eidetic imagery. These individuals may show "imagination," but if one looks closer at their images, one would notice emotional alienation from them. They have to be brought back to a genuine contact with imagery through slow exercises, starting with simple objects presented to them visually.

1. During these eidetic exercises, the individual is asked to describe a simple object from the room, or a formless object with certain intense characteristics, such as a rug, a simple painting, or a lamp. Objects such as ornate statues, typewriters, or other overly formed or mechanical objects are unsatisfactory for this purpose, since they elicit a well-formed meaning response. They catch the concept-building interest and generate thinking and curiosity rather than description.

2. As an introduction to the procedure, the person is told, "When you are outside and see a tree, you just look at the tree and enjoy it. You do not think how the tree is made. I will ask you to look at an object. Just see the object and describe it to me as you see it."

3. One cannot trust what a person is seeing internally, even after one has given him instructions. For this reason, he is asked to describe every detail of the object, without thinking or too much embellishment. The description should be as full as is necessary to give a clear image of the object that is being described. Neither stories nor fantasies nor concepts are allowed—only the pure perceptual description. Consider this example of describing a tissue box: "The box is rectangular, and has flowers on it, some with light green and some with white centers. The flowers are on a light green background and the stems are black and leaves are brown. The flowers look like daisies. Out of a slit in the top, which is also rectangular, there is a greenish-blue tissue coming out, resting on the box. The box is sitting on a brown wood desk with papers to the left side and a yellow pencil on top of the papers."

4. Sometimes, individuals experience difficulty describing an object. When they see a lamp, they do not look at its details. They just say, "It is a lamp," and consider that a complete description. While describing a painting, a person may say, "It is just a man." In such cases, the attention of the person is drawn

to the visual details as follows: "See that the lamp is made of wood and is brown; in the painting, the man has an axe in one hand and a rope in the other. There is hay on his back and he is wearing unusual clothes. He is sitting on a rock and the sky is blue. There is an expression in his face and his eyes." The person should begin to see description from the view of perception, not as a result of thinking about the object.

5. Next, it is pointed out, "When you look at the man in the painting, you get feelings." After it is agreed, the feelings are examined: how the person feels looking at the ground, the sky, the hay, the man in general, his eyes, his clothing. The feelings are clearly localized and evaluated, e.g., "I like it" is localized and evaluated as "It makes me feel warm and relaxed in my mind."

6. The individual now is finally "trained" to visualize, feel, and report faithfully. Following these exercises, the ability for imagery experience and accurate reporting increases. The person becomes accessible to his internal imagery state, which he is now able to concentrate on and repeat accurately.

7. Suggested objects for concentration: a lamp, a paperweight, a rug, a simple painting, a pencil, and other simple objects in the room.

A

Preliminary Note

on

EIDETIC PARENTS TEST

The following pages containing imagery exercises should be read slowly. All the blank spaces provided for writing personal images should be filled in carefully. Concentration on these images should be practiced each day at a slow, steady pace, one image or a few images each day, and each image should be practiced at least 10 to 20 times, usually through 10–15 second projections, except when deep concentration is needed. Deep concentration exercises require a longer projection period involving a duration of time from 30 seconds to a few minutes. During all mental exercises, deep projections are encouraged as a rule, unless there is inability to sustain longer concentration. If you hit upon important material, stay with it until you feel you have explored and absorbed all the information contained in it by concentrating on it.

Note: The instructions for the Eidetic Parents Test were originally written for use by therapists. The instructions, therefore, allude to the therapist's voice speaking directly to the patient. During self-use, the instructions should be read with this in mind.

5 & Eidetic Parents Test

INTRODUCTION

Read this instruction before doing the Eidetic Parents Test

Try to recall an event which happened up to five minutes ago, and concentrate on it mentally. Do you clearly remember the event, almost see it in your mind's eye? This image is vivid and lively because the event happened so recently. We will be dealing with images of this type in this test.

Now, turn the page, read the instructions one at a time, and write answers in the blank spaces provided for this purpose. Write each response clearly and faithfully.

Turn the Page for the Eidetic Parents Test

Image: House

READ the instruction below slowly and allow the image to be formed.

> Epl: *Picture your parents in the house where you lived most of the time with them, the house which gives you the feeling of a home. —Where do you see them? —What are they doing? —How do you feel when you see the images? —Are there any memories connected with this picture?*

PICTURE: Write here what is seen in the mind.

STEPS: Concentrate on the above picture in the following stepwise manner and write the experience in each blank space in detail.

1. Picture your parents in the house. Where do you see them?

2. Does the house give you the feeling of a home? Describe it.

3. See your father. What is he doing in the picture?

4. Do you experience positive or negative feelings when you see him?

5. Relax and recall memories about the place where father appears.

6. Now, see your mother. What is she doing in the picture?

7. Do you experience positive or negative feelings when you see her?

8. Relax and recall memories about the place where mother appears.

9. Where are your siblings? What are they doing?

10. Now, see yourself in the picture. What are you doing?

Analysis, Concentration, and Dialogue

READ each response (1–10) on the opposite page. Then select and write below three significant images for concentration: a positive, a negative, and a vague image. Repeat them according to the directions below.

    1. POSITIVE IMAGE: Concentrate for pleasurable release.

    2. NEGATIVE IMAGE: Concentrate for elucidation of the problem.

    3. VAGUE IMAGE: Concentrate for clarity of detail.

The above images should be repeated mentally over many days and weeks to stabilize the positive experience, to resolve the negative experience, and to lift vagueness from forgotten and inaccessible areas.

EMPATHY: Ask the person(s) working with you, "Please relax and pay attention to the image I am going to read to you. Empathize and experience the image as if it were your own." Then, from the opposite page, read the image written below *picture* aloud and allow sufficient time for concentration and development of empathy. Then say, "Describe what you see." Write the empathy response below. The spaces below can be used by a group, a family, two individuals, or a therapist for recording empathy and re-empathy experience, and expansion of consciousness.

    Empathy 1:

    Empathy 2:

    Empathy 3:

    Empathy 4:

Image: Left-Right Position of Parents

READ the instruction below slowly and allow the image to be formed.

> Ep2: *Now, set aside this picture of the house and see your parents standing directly in front of you. —Tell me, as you look at them, who is standing on your left and who is standing on your right? —Now, try to switch their positions. —Do you experience any difficulty or discomfort when you do this? Try to switch their positions again. —Do you again feel any difficulty? Do you feel that these images are independent of your control?*

PICTURE: Write here what is seen in the mind.

STEPS: Concentrate on the above picture in the following stepwise manner and write the experience in each blank space in detail.

1. Picture your parents standing directly in front of you.

2. As you see them, who is on the left and who is on the right?

3. Now, try to switch their positions. Are you able to switch them?

4. Describe any difficulty you experience when you switch them.

5. Now, see your parents standing in front of you again.

6. Who is standing on the left and who is standing on the right now?

7. Switch your parents' positions again.

8. Do you again experience a problem when you switch them?

9. Notice the two different feelings: spontaneous and forced.

10. Notice that you have no control over parents' spontaneous images.

Analysis, Concentration, and Dialogue

READ each response (1–10) on the opposite page. Then select and write below three significant images for concentration: a positive, a negative, and a vague image. Repeat them according to the directions below.

    1. POSITIVE IMAGE: Concentrate for pleasurable release.

    2. NEGATIVE IMAGE: Concentrate for elucidation of the problem.

    3. VAGUE IMAGE: Concentrate for clarity of detail.

The above images should be repeated mentally over many days and weeks to stabilize the positive experience, to resolve the negative experience, and to lift vagueness from forgotten and inaccessible areas.

EMPATHY: Ask the person(s) working with you, "Please relax and pay attention to the image I am going to read to you. Empathize and experience the image as if it were your own." Then, from the opposite page, read the image written below *picture* aloud and allow sufficient time for concentration and development of empathy. Then say, "Describe what you see." Write the empathy response below. The spaces below can be used by a group, a family, two individuals, or a therapist for recording empathy and re-empathy experience, and expansion of consciousness.

    Empathy 1:

    Empathy 2:

    Empathy 3:

    Empathy 4:

Image: Parents Separated or United

READ the instruction below slowly and allow the image to be formed.

    Ep3:   As you see your parents standing in front of you, do they appear separated or united as a couple? —Describe the character of the space each occupies. Do the spaces differ in temperature and illumination?

PICTURE: Write here what is seen in the mind.

STEPS: Concentrate on the above picture in the following stepwise manner and write the experience in each blank space in detail.

1. Picture your parents standing in front of you.

2. Do they appear separated or united as a couple?

3. Describe your father as he appears alongside your mother.

4. Describe your mother as she appears alongside your father.

5. Describe your father's space with regard to warmth and light.

6. Describe your mother's space with regard to warmth and light.

7. Do the father's and mother's spaces appear friendly or clashing?

8. Which space appears stronger, mother's or father's?

9. Does friendliness between parents' spaces create security in you?

10. Does conflict between parents' spaces create conflict in you?

Analysis, Concentration, and Dialogue

READ each response (1–10) on the opposite page. Then select and write below three significant images for concentration: a positive, a negative, and a vague image. Repeat them according to the directions below.

    1. POSITIVE IMAGE: Concentrate for pleasurable release.

    2. NEGATIVE IMAGE: Concentrate for elucidation of the problem.

    3. VAGUE IMAGE: Concentrate for clarity of detail.

The above images should be repeated mentally over many days and weeks to stabilize the positive experience, to resolve the negative experience, and to lift vagueness from forgotten and inaccessible areas.

EMPATHY: Ask the person(s) working with you, "Please relax and pay attention to the image I am going to read to you. Empathize and experience the image as if it were your own." Then, from the opposite page, read the image written below *picture* aloud and allow sufficient time for concentration and development of empathy. Then say, "Describe what you see." Write the empathy response below. The spaces below can be used by a group, a family, two individuals, or a therapist for recording empathy and re-empathy experience, and expansion of consciousness.

    Empathy 1:

    Empathy 2:

    Empathy 3:

    Empathy 4:

Image: Active-Passive Parents

READ the instruction below slowly and allow the image to be formed.

> Ep4: *As you see them standing in front of you, which parent seems to be more active and aggressive in the picture? —Is he/she extremely active, very active, or just active? —How is the other parent in comparison? Is he/she extremely passive, very passive, or just passive?*

PICTURE: Write here what is seen in the mind.

STEPS: Concentrate on the above picture in the following stepwise manner and write the experience in each blank space in detail.

1. Picture your parents standing in front of you again.

2. Which parent seems to be more active in the picture?

3. How is the other parent in comparison?

4. Is this active-passive relationship pleasant or unpleasant to you?

5. Does the more active parent appear to have proper attitudes?

6. Does the less active parent appear to have proper attitudes?

7. Who is more of a controlling type, mother or father?

8. How do you generally relate in life to an active person?

9. How do you generally relate in life to a passive person?

10. How do you generally relate in life to a controlling person?

Analysis, Concentration, and Dialogue

READ each response (1–10) on the opposite page. Then select and write below three significant images for concentration: a positive, a negative, and a vague image. Repeat them according to the directions below.

   1. POSITIVE IMAGE: Concentrate for pleasurable release.

   2. NEGATIVE IMAGE: Concentrate for elucidation of the problem.

   3. VAGUE IMAGE: Concentrate for clarity of detail.

The above images should be repeated mentally over many days and weeks to stabilize the positive experience, to resolve the negative experience, and to lift vagueness from forgotten and inaccessible areas.

EMPATHY: Ask the person(s) working with you, "Please relax and pay attention to the image I am going to read to you. Empathize and experience the image as if it were your own." Then, from the opposite page, read the image written below *picture* aloud and allow sufficient time for concentration and development of empathy. Then say, "Describe what you see." Write the empathy response below. The spaces below can be used by a group, a family, two individuals, or a therapist for recording empathy and re-empathy experience, and expansion of consciousness.

   Empathy 1:

   Empathy 2:

   Empathy 3:

   Empathy 4:

Image: Running Faster

READ the instruction below slowly and allow the image to be formed.

> Ep5: *Now set aside this image and picture your parents running in an open countryside. —Are they both running? —Who seems to be running faster? —Is he/she running extremely fast, very fast, or just fast? —How is the other parent running: extremely slow, very slow, or just slow?*

PICTURE: Write here what is seen in the mind.

STEPS: Concentrate on the above picture in the following stepwise manner and write the experience in each blank space in detail.

1. Picture your parents running in an open countryside.

2. Describe the countryside in which they are running.

3. See both parents running. Who is running faster?

4. How is the other parent running?

5. Does the parent who is ahead help the other parent?

6. Does the parent who is behind desire help?

7. If the leading parent does not extend help, what is the problem?

8. If the leading parent does extend help, what is the problem?

9. What do you understand about father from this picture?

10. What do you understand about mother from this picture?

Analysis, Concentration, and Dialogue

READ each response (1–10) on the opposite page. Then select and write below three significant images for concentration: a positive, a negative, and a vague image. Repeat them according to the directions below.

    1. POSITIVE IMAGE: Concentrate for pleasurable release.

    2. NEGATIVE IMAGE: Concentrate for elucidation of the problem.

    3. VAGUE IMAGE: Concentrate for clarity of detail.

The above images should be repeated mentally over many days and weeks to stabilize the positive experience, to resolve the negative experience, and to lift vagueness from forgotten and inaccessible areas.

EMPATHY: Ask the person(s) working with you, "Please relax and pay attention to the image I am going to read to you. Empathize and experience the image as if it were your own." Then, from the opposite page, read the image written below *picture* aloud and allow sufficient time for concentration and development of empathy. Then say, "Describe what you see." Write the empathy response below. The spaces below can be used by a group, a family, two individuals, or a therapist for recording empathy and re-empathy experience, and expansion of consciousness.

    Empathy 1:

    Empathy 2:

    Empathy 3:

    Empathy 4:

Image: Pattern of Running

READ the instruction below slowly and allow the image to be formed.

> Ep6: *Continue watching your parents running in the open countryside. —Now pay attention to the way in which they run. —Describe how each parent is running, the style and pattern of his running. —What seems to be the purpose in their running? —Why are they running?*

PICTURE: Write here what is seen in the mind.

STEPS: Concentrate on the above picture in the following stepwise manner and write the experience in each blank space in detail.

1. Picture your parents running in the open countryside.

2. Pay attention to their running.

3. Concentrate on the pattern of your father's running. Describe it.

4. What seems to be the purpose in his running?

5. Concentrate on the pattern of your mother's running. Describe it.

6. What seems to be the purpose in her running?

7. Does the pattern of your father's running remind you of anything?

8. Does the pattern of your mother's running remind you of anything?

9. Do you want any change in father's pattern of running?

10. Do you want any change in mother's pattern of running?

Analysis, Concentration, and Dialogue

READ each response (1–10) on the opposite page. Then select and write below three significant images for concentration: a positive, a negative, and a vague image. Repeat them according to the directions below.

1. POSITIVE IMAGE: Concentrate for pleasurable release.

2. NEGATIVE IMAGE: Concentrate for elucidation of the problem.

3. VAGUE IMAGE: Concentrate for clarity of detail.

The above images should be repeated mentally over many days and weeks to stabilize the positive experience, to resolve the negative experience, and to lift vagueness from forgotten and inaccessible areas.

EMPATHY: Ask the person(s) working with you, "Please relax and pay attention to the image I am going to read to you. Empathize and experience the image as if it were your own." Then, from the opposite page, read the image written below *picture* aloud and allow sufficient time for concentration and development of empathy. Then say, "Describe what you see." Write the empathy response below. The spaces below can be used by a group, a family, two individuals, or a therapist for recording empathy and re-empathy experience, and expansion of consciousness.

Empathy 1:

Empathy 2:

Empathy 3:

Empathy 4:

Image: Freedom of Limbs

READ the instruction below slowly and allow the image to be formed.

Ep7: *As you see your parents running, do their limbs appear stiff or relaxed? —Whose limbs appear more stiff and whose limbs appear more relaxed?*

PICTURE: Write here what is seen in the mind.

STEPS: Concentrate on the above picture in the following stepwise manner and write the experience in each blank space in detail.

1. Picture your parents running in the open countryside.

2. As you see them running, concentrate on their bodies.

3. Now, see the father running. Do his limbs appear stiff or relaxed?

4. Now, see the mother running. Do her limbs appear stiff or relaxed?

5. Concentrate on the parent whose limbs appear more relaxed.

6. Describe your feelings concerning the relaxation in this parent.

7. Look at the parent whose limbs appear more stiff.

8. Describe your feelings concerning the stiffness in this parent.

9. Describe the mental states of the relaxed parent.

10. Describe the mental states of the stiff parent.

Analysis, Concentration, and Dialogue

READ each response (1–10) on the opposite page. Then select and write below three significant images for concentration: a positive, a negative, and a vague image. Repeat them according to the directions below.

    1. POSITIVE IMAGE: Concentrate for pleasurable release.

    2. NEGATIVE IMAGE: Concentrate for elucidation of the problem.

    3. VAGUE IMAGE: Concentrate for clarity of detail.

The above images should be repeated mentally over many days and weeks to stabilize the positive experience, to resolve the negative experience, and to lift vagueness from forgotten and inaccessible areas.

EMPATHY: Ask the person(s) working with you, "Please relax and pay attention to the image I am going to read to you. Empathize and experience the image as if it were your own." Then, from the opposite page, read the image written below *picture* aloud and allow sufficient time for concentration and development of empathy. Then say, "Describe what you see." Write the empathy response below. The spaces below can be used by a group, a family, two individuals, or a therapist for recording empathy and re-empathy experience, and expansion of consciousness.

    Empathy 1:

    Empathy 2:

    Empathy 3:

    Empathy 4:

Image: Brilliance of Parents' Eyes

READ the instruction below slowly and allow the image to be formed.

> Ep8: *Now set aside this picture and see your parents standing directly in front of you again. —Look at their eyes. (Do not recollect their real eyes.) —Whose eyes are more brilliant? —Are they extremely brilliant, very brilliant, or just brilliant? —How do the other parent's eyes appear?*

PICTURE: Write here what is seen in the mind.

STEPS: Concentrate on the above picture in the following stepwise manner and write the experience in each blank space in detail.

1. Picture your parents standing in front of you again.

2. Look at their eyes in the picture.

3. Whose eyes appear more brilliant?

4. How are the eyes of the other parent in comparison?

5. What kind of brilliance or dullness do the father's eyes have?

6. What kind of brilliance or dullness do the mother's eyes have?

7. Look at the parent with brilliant eyes. How do the eyes affect you?

8. Look at the parent who has dull eyes. How do the eyes affect you?

9. Relax and recall memories as you look at father's eyes.

10. Relax and recall memories as you look at mother's eyes.

Analysis, Concentration, and Dialogue

READ each response (1–10) on the opposite page. Then select and write below three significant images for concentration: a positive, a negative, and a vague image. Repeat them according to the directions below.

    1. POSITIVE IMAGE: Concentrate for pleasurable release.

    2. NEGATIVE IMAGE: Concentrate for elucidation of the problem.

    3. VAGUE IMAGE: Concentrate for clarity of detail.

The above images should be repeated mentally over many days and weeks to stabilize the positive experience, to resolve the negative experience, and to lift vagueness from forgotten and inaccessible areas.

EMPATHY: Ask the person(s) working with you, "Please relax and pay attention to the image I am going to read to you. Empathize and experience the image as if it were your own." Then, from the opposite page, read the image written below *picture* aloud and allow sufficient time for concentration and development of empathy. Then say, "Describe what you see." Write the empathy response below. The spaces below can be used by a group, a family, two individuals, or a therapist for recording empathy and re-empathy experience, and expansion of consciousness.

    Empathy 1:

    Empathy 2:

    Empathy 3:

    Empathy 4:

Image: Object Orientation

READ the instruction below slowly and allow the image to be formed.

   Ep9: Now set aside this image and look at me. As I look at objects, my eyes focus on one object and then another. Now, I am staring into space and my eyes focus on nothing. —Now see your parents' eyes in the image again. —Whose eyes focus on objects more easily? —Are the eyes extremely object oriented, very object oriented, or just object oriented? —How are the other parent's eyes?

PICTURE: Write here what is seen in the mind.

STEPS: Concentrate on the above picture in the following stepwise manner and write the experience in each blank space in detail.

   1. Picture your parents' eyes focusing on objects.

   2. Whose eyes focus on objects more easily, mother's or father's?

   3. How do the eyes of the other parent focus in comparison?

   4. Now, concentrate on your father focusing on objects.

   5. Does his focusing on objects feel pleasant or unpleasant to you?

   6. Relax and recall memories as you see father's eyes focusing.

   7. Now, concentrate on your mother focusing on objects.

   8. Does her focusing on objects feel pleasant or unpleasant to you?

   9. Relax and recall memories as you see mother's eyes focusing.

   10. Do you focus on objects more like your father or your mother?

Analysis, Concentration, and Dialogue

READ each response (1–10) on the opposite page. Then select and write below three significant images for concentration: a positive, a negative, and a vague image. Repeat them according to the directions below.

> 1. *POSITIVE IMAGE:* Concentrate for pleasurable release.

> 2. *NEGATIVE IMAGE:* Concentrate for elucidation of the problem.

> 3. *VAGUE IMAGE:* Concentrate for clarity of detail.

The above images should be repeated mentally over many days and weeks to stabilize the positive experience, to resolve the negative experience, and to lift vagueness from forgotten and inaccessible areas.

EMPATHY: Ask the person(s) working with you, "Please relax and pay attention to the image I am going to read to you. Empathize and experience the image as if it were your own." Then, from the opposite page, read the image written below *picture* aloud and allow sufficient time for concentration and development of empathy. Then say, "Describe what you see." Write the empathy response below. The spaces below can be used by a group, a family, two individuals, or a therapist for recording empathy and re-empathy experience, and expansion of consciousness.

Empathy 1:

Empathy 2:

Empathy 3:

Empathy 4:

Image: Story in the Eyes

READ the instruction below slowly and allow the image to be formed.

Ep10:   *Continue concentrating on your parents' eyes in the picture. —Do they give you any feeling or tell you any story?*

PICTURE: Write here what is seen in the mind.

STEPS: Concentrate on the above picture in the following stepwise manner and write the experience in each blank space in detail.

1. Picture your parents' eyes again.

2. Concentrate on your father's eyes in the picture.

3. Do his eyes give you any feeling or tell you any story?

4. Concentrate on the story in father's eyes.

5. Do you experience pleasant or unpleasant feelings?

6. Now, concentrate on your mother's eyes in the picture.

7. Do her eyes give you any feeling or tell you any story?

8. Concentrate on the story in mother's eyes.

9. Do you experience pleasant or unpleasant feelings?

10. Which story do you feel is more true?

Analysis, Concentration, and Dialogue

READ each response (1–10) on the opposite page. Then select and write below three significant images for concentration: a positive, a negative, and a vague image. Repeat them according to the directions below.

    1. POSITIVE IMAGE: Concentrate for pleasurable release.

    2. NEGATIVE IMAGE: Concentrate for elucidation of the problem.

    3. VAGUE IMAGE: Concentrate for clarity of detail.

The above images should be repeated mentally over many days and weeks to stabilize the positive experience, to resolve the negative experience, and to lift vagueness from forgotten and inaccessible areas.

EMPATHY: Ask the person(s) working with you, "Please relax and pay attention to the image I am going to read to you. Empathize and experience the image as if it were your own." Then, from the opposite page, read the image written below *picture* aloud and allow sufficient time for concentration and development of empathy. Then say, "Describe what you see." Write the empathy response below. The spaces below can be used by a group, a family, two individuals, or a therapist for recording empathy and re-empathy experience, and expansion of consciousness.

    Empathy 1:

    Empathy 2:

    Empathy 3:

    Empathy 4:

Image: Loudness of Parents' Voices

READ the instruction below slowly and allow the image to be formed.

> Ep11: *Now set aside this picture and see that you are hearing your parents' voices. —Whose voice sounds louder to you? —Is it extremely loud, very loud, or just loud? —How does the other parent's voice sound to you?*

PICTURE: Write here what is seen in the mind.

STEPS: Concentrate on the above picture in the following stepwise manner and write the experience in each blank space in detail.

1. Picture your parents and hear their voices.

2. Whose voice sounds louder to you? Describe the voice.

3. How is the voice of the other parent in comparison?

4. Concentrate on father's voice. Is the sound pleasant or unpleasant?

5. Relax and recall memories as you continue to hear his voice.

6. Concentrate on mother's voice. Is the sound pleasant or unpleasant?

7. Relax and recall memories as you continue to hear her voice.

8. Whose voice do you pay attention to less, mother's or father's?

9. What is this voice you attend less saying to you?

10. Why do you pay less attention to this voice?

Analysis, Concentration, and Dialogue

READ each response (1–10) on the opposite page. Then select and write below three significant images for concentration: a positive, a negative, and a vague image. Repeat them according to the directions below.

    1. POSITIVE IMAGE: Concentrate for pleasurable release.

    2. NEGATIVE IMAGE: Concentrate for elucidation of the problem.

    3. VAGUE IMAGE: Concentrate for clarity of detail.

The above images should be repeated mentally over many days and weeks to stabilize the positive experience, to resolve the negative experience, and to lift vagueness from forgotten and inaccessible areas.

EMPATHY: Ask the person(s) working with you, "Please relax and pay attention to the image I am going to read to you. Empathize and experience the image as if it were your own." Then, from the opposite page, read the image written below *picture* aloud and allow sufficient time for concentration and development of empathy. Then say, "Describe what you see." Write the empathy response below. The spaces below can be used by a group, a family, two individuals, or a therapist for recording empathy and re-empathy experience, and expansion of consciousness.

    Empathy 1:

    Empathy 2:

    Empathy 3:

    Empathy 4:

Image: Meaningfulness of Voices

READ the instruction below slowly and allow the image to be formed.

> Ep12: *Now hear your parents' voices again. —Do the voices seem meaningful, or are they merely patterns of sound in the air? —Whose voice carries more meaning? —Is it extremely meaningful, very meaningful, or just meaningful? —How does the other parent's voice sound to you?*

PICTURE: Write here what is seen in the mind.

STEPS: Concentrate on the above picture in the following stepwise manner and write the experience in each blank space in detail.

1. Picture your parents and hear their voices.

2. Are the voices meaningful, or merely patterns of sound?

3. Whose voice carries more meaning, mother's or father's?

4. Concentrate on your father's voice.

5. What message does your father's voice carry for your mother?

6. Concentrate on your mother's voice.

7. What message does your mother's voice carry for your father?

8. Concentrate on the voice that you hear more. How do you react?

9. Concentrate on the voice that you hear less. How do you react?

10. Which ear do you use more, your right or your left?

Analysis, Concentration, and Dialogue

READ each response (1–10) on the opposite page. Then select and write below three significant images for concentration: a positive, a negative, and a vague image. Repeat them according to the directions below.

> *1. POSITIVE IMAGE:* Concentrate for pleasurable release.

> *2. NEGATIVE IMAGE:* Concentrate for elucidation of the problem.

> *3. VAGUE IMAGE:* Concentrate for clarity of detail.

The above images should be repeated mentally over many days and weeks to stabilize the positive experience, to resolve the negative experience, and to lift vagueness from forgotten and inaccessible areas.

EMPATHY: Ask the person(s) working with you, "Please relax and pay attention to the image I am going to read to you. Empathize and experience the image as if it were your own." Then, from the opposite page, read the image written below *picture* aloud and allow sufficient time for concentration and development of empathy. Then say, "Describe what you see." Write the empathy response below. The spaces below can be used by a group, a family, two individuals, or a therapist for recording empathy and re-empathy experience, and expansion of consciousness.

> *Empathy 1:*

> *Empathy 2:*

> *Empathy 3:*

> *Empathy 4:*

206   *PSYCHEYE*

Image: Story in the Voices

READ the instruction below slowly and allow the image to be formed.

　Ep13: *Continue listening to your parents' voices. —Do they give you any feeling or tell you any story?*

PICTURE: Write here what is seen in the mind.

STEPS: Concentrate on the above picture in the following stepwise manner and write the experience in each blank space in detail.

1. Picture your parents and hear their voices again.

2. Concentrate on your father's voice in the picture.

3. Does his voice give you any feeling or tell you any story?

4. Concentrate and hear the story in your father's voice.

5. Do you experience pleasant or unpleasant feelings?

6. Now, concentrate on your mother's voice in the picture.

7. Does her voice give you any feeling or tell you any story?

8. Concentrate and hear the story in your mother's voice.

9. Do you experience pleasant or unpleasant feelings?

10. What do you understand from these two stories?

Analysis, Concentration, and Dialogue

READ each response (1–10) on the opposite page. Then select and write below three significant images for concentration: a positive, a negative, and a vague image. Repeat them according to the directions below.

    1. POSITIVE IMAGE: Concentrate for pleasurable release.

    2. NEGATIVE IMAGE: Concentrate for elucidation of the problem.

    3. VAGUE IMAGE: Concentrate for clarity of detail.

The above images should be repeated mentally over many days and weeks to stabilize the positive experience, to resolve the negative experience, and to lift vagueness from forgotten and inaccessible areas.

EMPATHY: Ask the person(s) working with you, "Please relax and pay attention to the image I am going to read to you. Empathize and experience the image as if it were your own." Then, from the opposite page, read the image written below *picture* aloud and allow sufficient time for concentration and development of empathy. Then say, "Describe what you see." Write the empathy response below. The spaces below can be used by a group, a family, two individuals, or a therapist for recording empathy and re-empathy experience, and expansion of consciousness.

    Empathy 1:

    Empathy 2:

    Empathy 3:

    Empathy 4:

Image: Hearing by Parents' Ears

READ the instruction below slowly and allow the image to be formed.

 Ep14: *Now see yourself talking to both your parents. —Who seems to hear you better or has good ears for you? —Does he/she hear you extremely well, very well, or just well? —Describe how the other parent hears you.*

PICTURE: Write here what is seen in the mind.

STEPS: Concentrate on the above picture in the following stepwise manner and write the experience in each blank space in detail.

1. Picture yourself talking to both your parents.

2. Who seems to hear you better?

3. How does the other parent hear you in comparison?

4. Concentrate on how your father hears you in the picture.

5. When he hears you, do you feel secure or insecure?

6. Concentrate on how your mother hears you in the picture.

7. When she hears you, do you feel secure or insecure?

8. Concentrate on the parent whose hearing creates security in you.

9. Concentrate on the parent whose hearing creates insecurity in you.

10. Which parent do you approach more, for listening to you?

Analysis, Concentration, and Dialogue

READ each response (1–10) on the opposite page. Then select and write below three significant images for concentration: a positive, a negative, and a vague image. Repeat them according to the directions below.

   1. POSITIVE IMAGE: Concentrate for pleasurable release.

   2. NEGATIVE IMAGE: Concentrate for elucidation of the problem.

   3. VAGUE IMAGE: Concentrate for clarity of detail.

The above images should be repeated mentally over many days and weeks to stabilize the positive experience, to resolve the negative experience, and to lift vagueness from forgotten and inaccessible areas.

EMPATHY: Ask the person(s) working with you, "Please relax and pay attention to the image I am going to read to you. Empathize and experience the image as if it were your own." Then, from the opposite page, read the image written below *picture* aloud and allow sufficient time for concentration and development of empathy. Then say, "Describe what you see." Write the empathy response below. The spaces below can be used by a group, a family, two individuals, or a therapist for recording empathy and re-empathy experience, and expansion of consciousness.

   Empathy 1:

   Empathy 2:

   Empathy 3:

   Empathy 4:

210   *PSYCHEYE*

Image: Understanding by Ears

READ the instruction below slowly and allow the image to be formed.

> Ep15: *As you talk to your parents in the image, do they seem to understand you? —Who seems to understand you better? —Does he/she understand you extremely well, very well, or just well? —Describe how much the other parent understands you.*

PICTURE: Write here what is seen in the mind.

STEPS: Concentrate on the above picture in the following stepwise manner and write the experience in each blank space in detail.

1. Picture yourself talking to both your parents again.

2. Who seems to understand you better, mother or father?

3. Concentrate on how your father understands you in the picture.

4. Do you feel understood?

5. Concentrate on how your mother understands you in the picture.

6. Do you feel understood?

7. See father. What kind of ideas would you like to exchange with him?

8. See mother. What kind of ideas would you like to exchange with her?

9. Which parent exchanges ideas with you more?

10. Which parent do you feel should exchange ideas with you more?

Analysis, Concentration, and Dialogue

READ each response (1–10) on the opposite page. Then select and write below three significant images for concentration: a positive, a negative, and a vague image. Repeat them according to the directions below.

    1. POSITIVE IMAGE: Concentrate for pleasurable release.

    2. NEGATIVE IMAGE: Concentrate for elucidation of the problem.

    3. VAGUE IMAGE: Concentrate for clarity of detail.

The above images should be repeated mentally over many days and weeks to stabilize the positive experience, to resolve the negative experience, and to lift vagueness from forgotten and inaccessible areas.

EMPATHY: Ask the person(s) working with you, "Please relax and pay attention to the image I am going to read to you. Empathize and experience the image as if it were your own." Then, from the opposite page, read the image written below *picture* aloud and allow sufficient time for concentration and development of empathy. Then say, "Describe what you see." Write the empathy response below. The spaces below can be used by a group, a family, two individuals, or a therapist for recording empathy and re-empathy experience, and expansion of consciousness.

    Empathy 1:

    Empathy 2:

    Empathy 3:

    Empathy 4:

Image: Parents Sniffing

READ the instruction below slowly and allow the image to be formed.

Ep16: *Now set aside this image and look at me. I am sniffing the air here in this room, and you can tell by my facial expression whether I like the air or not. —Now see your parents sniffing the air in the house in the same way. —Do they appear to like or dislike the house atmosphere?*

PICTURE: Write here what is seen in the mind.

STEPS: Concentrate on the above picture in the following stepwise manner and write the experience in each blank space in detail.

1. Picture your parents sniffing the air in the house.

2. Who appears to like the house air more, mother or father?

3. How does the other parent respond to the house air?

4. Concentrate on father sniffing. What are his thoughts?

5. Concentrate on mother sniffing. What are her thoughts?

6. Is the parent who approves of the house air active or passive?

7. Is the parent who disapproves of the house air active or passive?

8. How does the father reconcile his conflict about the house?

9. How does the mother reconcile her conflict about the house?

10. How do you respond to the conflict in the house?

Analysis, Concentration, and Dialogue

READ each response (1–10) on the opposite page. Then select and write below three significant images for concentration: a positive, a negative, and a vague image. Repeat them according to the directions below.

   1. POSITIVE IMAGE: Concentrate for pleasurable release.

   2. NEGATIVE IMAGE: Concentrate for elucidation of the problem.

   3. VAGUE IMAGE: Concentrate for clarity of detail.

The above images should be repeated mentally over many days and weeks to stabilize the positive experience, to resolve the negative experience, and to lift vagueness from forgotten and inaccessible areas.

EMPATHY: Ask the person(s) working with you, "Please relax and pay attention to the image I am going to read to you. Empathize and experience the image as if it were your own." Then, from the opposite page, read the image written below *picture* aloud and allow sufficient time for concentration and development of empathy. Then say, "Describe what you see." Write the empathy response below. The spaces below can be used by a group, a family, two individuals, or a therapist for recording empathy and re-empathy experience, and expansion of consciousness.

   Empathy 1:

   Empathy 2:

   Empathy 3:

   Empathy 4:

Image: Warmth of Parents' Bodies

READ the instruction below slowly and allow the image to be formed.

> Ep17: *Now see your parents standing directly in front of you again. —Do you get a feeling of personal warmth from their bodies? —Whose body gives you a better feeling of personal warmth? —What kind of feeling does the other parent's body give?*

PICTURE: Write here what is seen in the mind.

STEPS: Concentrate on the above picture in the following stepwise manner and write the experience in each blank space in detail.

1. Picture your parents standing directly in front of you.

2. Which parent's body has more personal warmth?

3. How is the other parent's body in comparison?

4. Concentrate on your feelings concerning father's body.

5. Describe how you feel as you see his body.

6. Relax and recall memories as you concentrate on your father's body.

7. Concentrate on your feelings concerning mother's body.

8. Describe how you feel as you see her body.

9. Relax and recall memories as you concentrate on your mother's body.

10. Which parent's body do you wish to know more? Why?

Analysis, Concentration, and Dialogue

READ each response (1–10) on the opposite page. Then select and write below three significant images for concentration: a positive, a negative, and a vague image. Repeat them according to the directions below.

    1. POSITIVE IMAGE: Concentrate for pleasurable release.

    2. NEGATIVE IMAGE: Concentrate for elucidation of the problem.

    3. VAGUE IMAGE: Concentrate for clarity of detail.

The above images should be repeated mentally over many days and weeks to stabilize the positive experience, to resolve the negative experience, and to lift vagueness from forgotten and inaccessible areas.

EMPATHY: Ask the person(s) working with you, "Please relax and pay attention to the image I am going to read to you. Empathize and experience the image as if it were your own." Then, from the opposite page, read the image written below *picture* aloud and allow sufficient time for concentration and development of empathy. Then say, "Describe what you see." Write the empathy response below. The spaces below can be used by a group, a family, two individuals, or a therapist for recording empathy and re-empathy experience, and expansion of consciousness.

    Empathy 1:

    Empathy 2:

    Empathy 3:

    Empathy 4:

Image: Body Acceptance

READ the instruction below slowly and allow the image to be formed.

    Ep18:   *Now look at your parents' skin and concentrate on it for a while. Does it seem to accept you or reject you?—Describe how you feel when you look at their skin.*

PICTURE: Write here what is seen in the mind.

STEPS: Concentrate on the above picture in the following stepwise manner and write the experience in each blank space in detail.

1. Picture your parents standing in front of you again.

2. Concentrate on their skin.

3. Whose skin gives you the feeling of acceptance? To what degree?

4. Whose skin gives you the feeling of rejection? To what degree?

5. Concentrate on your feelings concerning father's skin.

6. Describe how you feel as you experience father's skin.

7. Concentrate on your feelings concerning mother's skin.

8. Describe how you feel as you experience mother's skin.

9. Which parent usually touches you more?

10. Which parent do you usually touch more?

Analysis, Concentration, and Dialogue

READ each response (1–10) on the opposite page. Then select and write below three significant images for concentration: a positive, a negative, and a vague image. Repeat them according to the directions below.

    1. POSITIVE IMAGE: Concentrate for pleasurable release.

    2. NEGATIVE IMAGE: Concentrate for elucidation of the problem.

    3. VAGUE IMAGE: Concentrate for clarity of detail.

The above images should be repeated mentally over many days and weeks to stabilize the positive experience, to resolve the negative experience, and to lift vagueness from forgotten and inaccessible areas.

EMPATHY: Ask the person(s) working with you, "Please relax and pay attention to the image I am going to read to you. Empathize and experience the image as if it were your own." Then, from the opposite page, read the image written below *picture* aloud and allow sufficient time for concentration and development of empathy. Then say, "Describe what you see." Write the empathy response below. The spaces below can be used by a group, a family, two individuals, or a therapist for recording empathy and re-empathy experience, and expansion of consciousness.

    Empathy 1:

    Empathy 2:

    Empathy 3:

    Empathy 4:

218   PSYCHEYE

Image: Health of Skin

READ the instruction below slowly and allow the image to be formed.

Ep19: *Continue looking at your parents' skin. —Does it appear healthy or unhealthy? —Whose skin appears healthier?*

PICTURE: Write here what is seen in the mind.

STEPS: Concentrate on the above picture in the following stepwise manner and write the experience in each blank space in detail.

1. Picture your parents and concentrate on their skin.

2. Whose skin appears healthier?

3. How does the other parent's skin appear?

4. Experience feelings as you concentrate on the healthier skin.

5. Experience feelings as you concentrate on the less healthy skin.

6. What does blemish in father's skin mean to you?

7. What does health in father's skin mean to you?

8. What does blemish in mother's skin mean to you?

9. What does health in mother's skin mean to you?

10. Which parent's skin do you want to see improved in your mind?

Analysis, Concentration, and Dialogue

READ each response (1–10) on the opposite page. Then select and write below three significant images for concentration: a positive, a negative, and a vague image. Repeat them according to the directions below.

    1. POSITIVE IMAGE: Concentrate for pleasurable release.

    2. NEGATIVE IMAGE: Concentrate for elucidation of the problem.

    3. VAGUE IMAGE: Concentrate for clarity of detail.

The above images should be repeated mentally over many days and weeks to stabilize the positive experience, to resolve the negative experience, and to lift vagueness from forgotten and inaccessible areas.

EMPATHY: Ask the person(s) working with you, "Please relax and pay attention to the image I am going to read to you. Empathize and experience the image as if it were your own." Then, from the opposite page, read the image written below *picture* aloud and allow sufficient time for concentration and development of empathy. Then say, "Describe what you see." Write the empathy response below. The spaces below can be used by a group, a family, two individuals, or a therapist for recording empathy and re-empathy experience, and expansion of consciousness.

    Empathy 1:

    Empathy 2:

    Empathy 3:

    Empathy 4:

Image: Arms Giving

READ the instruction below slowly and allow the image to be formed.

    Ep20:   *Now picture your parents giving you something. —Which parent extends the hand more completely for giving? —Show me how your mother extends her arms when she gives. —How does your father extend his arms when he gives?*

PICTURE: Write here what is seen in the mind.

STEPS: Concentrate on the above picture in the following stepwise manner and write the experience in each blank space in detail.

1. Picture your parents giving you something.

2. Which parent extends the hand more completely to give?

3. How does the other parent extend the hand?

4. Concentrate on your father giving to you.

5. As he gives, do you experience pleasant or unpleasant feelings?

6. Concentrate on your mother giving to you.

7. As she gives, do you experience pleasant or unpleasant feelings?

8. What does the parent who does not extend the hand have in the hand?

9. What does the parent who extends the hand have in the hand?

10. Which gift feels more precious to you?

Analysis, Concentration, and Dialogue

READ each response (1–10) on the opposite page. Then select and write below three significant images for concentration: a positive, a negative, and a vague image. Repeat them according to the directions below.

    1. POSITIVE IMAGE: Concentrate for pleasurable release.

    2. NEGATIVE IMAGE: Concentrate for elucidation of the problem.

    3. VAGUE IMAGE: Concentrate for clarity of detail.

The above images should be repeated mentally over many days and weeks to stabilize the positive experience, to resolve the negative experience, and to lift vagueness from forgotten and inaccessible areas.

EMPATHY: Ask the person(s) working with you, "Please relax and pay attention to the image I am going to read to you. Empathize and experience the image as if it were your own." Then, from the opposite page, read the image written below *picture* aloud and allow sufficient time for concentration and development of empathy. Then say, "Describe what you see." Write the empathy response below. The spaces below can be used by a group, a family, two individuals, or a therapist for recording empathy and re-empathy experience, and expansion of consciousness.

    Empathy 1:

    Empathy 2:

    Empathy 3:

    Empathy 4:

Image: Arms Receiving

READ the instruction below slowly and allow the image to be formed.

    Ep21: *Now picture yourself taking something from your parents. —To whom do you extend your arms completely?*

PICTURE: Write here what is seen in the mind.

STEPS: Concentrate on the above picture in the following stepwise manner and write the experience in each blank space in detail.

1. Picture yourself taking something from your parents.

2. To which parent do you extend your hands completely for receiving?

3. How do you extend your hands to the other parent?

4. Relax and recall memories as you extend your hands toward parents.

5. Concentrate on how you take something from your father.

6. Describe what you see.

7. Concentrate on how you take something from your mother.

8. Describe what you see.

9. Wish something from the parent toward whom you do not feel free.

10. Wish something from the parent toward whom you do feel free.

Analysis, Concentration, and Dialogue

READ each response (1–10) on the opposite page. Then select and write below three significant images for concentration: a positive, a negative, and a vague image. Repeat them according to the directions below.

    1. POSITIVE IMAGE: Concentrate for pleasurable release.

    2. NEGATIVE IMAGE: Concentrate for elucidation of the problem.

    3. VAGUE IMAGE: Concentrate for clarity of detail.

The above images should be repeated mentally over many days and weeks to stabilize the positive experience, to resolve the negative experience, and to lift vagueness from forgotten and inaccessible areas.

EMPATHY: Ask the person(s) working with you, "Please relax and pay attention to the image I am going to read to you. Empathize and experience the image as if it were your own." Then, from the opposite page, read the image written below *picture* aloud and allow sufficient time for concentration and development of empathy. Then say, "Describe what you see." Write the empathy response below. The spaces below can be used by a group, a family, two individuals, or a therapist for recording empathy and re-empathy experience, and expansion of consciousness.

    Empathy 1:

    Empathy 2:

    Empathy 3:

    Empathy 4:

Image: Strength of Grasp

READ the instruction below slowly and allow the image to be formed.

Ep22: *Now see that your parents are holding something in their hands. —Tell me which parent grasps more firmly. —How is the grasp of the other parent?*

PICTURE: Write here what is seen in the mind.

STEPS: Concentrate on the above picture in the following stepwise manner and write the experience in each blank space in detail.

1. Picture your parents holding something in their hands.

2. Which parent grasps more firmly? How does the other parent grasp?

3. Concentrate on your father's grasp.

4. Do you experience pleasant or unpleasant feelings?

5. Concentrate on your mother's grasp.

6. Do you experience pleasant or unpleasant feelings?

7. See that the parent who grasps firmly is holding your hand lightly.

8. Concentrate on the picture. How do you feel?

9. See that the parent who grasps lightly is holding your hand firmly.

10. Concentrate on the picture. How do you feel?

Analysis, Concentration, and Dialogue

READ each response (1–10) on the opposite page. Then select and write below three significant images for concentration: a positive, a negative, and a vague image. Repeat them according to the directions below.

    1. POSITIVE IMAGE: Concentrate for pleasurable release.

    2. NEGATIVE IMAGE: Concentrate for elucidation of the problem.

    3. VAGUE IMAGE: Concentrate for clarity of detail.

The above images should be repeated mentally over many days and weeks to stabilize the positive experience, to resolve the negative experience, and to lift vagueness from forgotten and inaccessible areas.

EMPATHY: Ask the person(s) working with you, "Please relax and pay attention to the image I am going to read to you. Empathize and experience the image as if it were your own." Then, from the opposite page, read the image written below *picture* aloud and allow sufficient time for concentration and development of empathy. Then say, "Describe what you see." Write the empathy response below. The spaces below can be used by a group, a family, two individuals, or a therapist for recording empathy and re-empathy experience, and expansion of consciousness.

    Empathy 1:

    Empathy 2:

    Empathy 3:

    Empathy 4:

Image: Swallowing Food

READ the instruction below slowly and allow the image to be formed.

    Ep23:   *Now see your parents eating. —Do they swallow easily? —Who swallows with more ease?*

PICTURE: Write here what is seen in the mind.

STEPS: Concentrate on the above picture in the following stepwise manner and write the experience in each blank space in detail.

1. Picture your parents eating.

2. Which parent swallows with more ease?

3. How does the other parent swallow?

4. Is the image of your father swallowing pleasant or unpleasant?

5. What is your father's attitude toward food in the picture?

6. Relax and recall memories as you concentrate on father swallowing.

7. Is the image of your mother swallowing pleasant or unpleasant?

8. What is your mother's attitude toward food in the picture?

9. Relax and recall memories as you concentrate on mother swallowing.

10. As they swallow, which parent attracts your attention more? Why?

Analysis, Concentration, and Dialogue

READ each response (1–10) on the opposite page. Then select and write below three significant images for concentration: a positive, a negative, and a vague image. Repeat them according to the directions below.

1. POSITIVE IMAGE: Concentrate for pleasurable release.

2. NEGATIVE IMAGE: Concentrate for elucidation of the problem.

3. VAGUE IMAGE: Concentrate for clarity of detail.

The above images should be repeated mentally over many days and weeks to stabilize the positive experience, to resolve the negative experience, and to lift vagueness from forgotten and inaccessible areas.

EMPATHY: Ask the person(s) working with you, "Please relax and pay attention to the image I am going to read to you. Empathize and experience the image as if it were your own." Then, from the opposite page, read the image written below *picture* aloud and allow sufficient time for concentration and development of empathy. Then say, "Describe what you see." Write the empathy response below. The spaces below can be used by a group, a family, two individuals, or a therapist for recording empathy and re-empathy experience, and expansion of consciousness.

Empathy 1:

Empathy 2:

Empathy 3:

Empathy 4:

Image: Drinking Fluid

READ the instruction below slowly and allow the image to be formed.

Ep24: *Now see your parents drinking fluid. —Who drinks faster?*

PICTURE: Write here what is seen in the mind.

STEPS: Concentrate on the above picture in the following stepwise manner and write the experience in each blank space in detail.

1. Picture your parents drinking fluid.

2. Which parent drinks faster?

3. How does the other parent drink in comparison?

4. Is the image of your father drinking pleasant or unpleasant?

5. What is your father's attitude toward the drink in the picture?

6. What is your father drinking? Look at it closely.

7. Is the image of your mother drinking pleasant or unpleasant?

8. What is your mother's attitude toward the drink in the picture?

9. What is your mother drinking? Look at it closely.

10. As they drink, which parent attracts your attention more? Why?

Analysis, Concentration, and Dialogue

READ each response (1–10) on the opposite page. Then select and write below three significant images for concentration: a positive, a negative, and a vague image. Repeat them according to the directions below.

    1. POSITIVE IMAGE: Concentrate for pleasurable release.

    2. NEGATIVE IMAGE: Concentrate for elucidation of the problem.

    3. VAGUE IMAGE: Concentrate for clarity of detail.

The above images should be repeated mentally over many days and weeks to stabilize the positive experience, to resolve the negative experience, and to lift vagueness from forgotten and inaccessible areas.

EMPATHY: Ask the person(s) working with you, "Please relax and pay attention to the image I am going to read to you. Empathize and experience the image as if it were your own." Then, from the opposite page, read the image written below *picture* aloud and allow sufficient time for concentration and development of empathy. Then say, "Describe what you see." Write the empathy response below. The spaces below can be used by a group, a family, two individuals, or a therapist for recording empathy and re-empathy experience, and expansion of consciousness.

    Empathy 1:

    Empathy 2:

    Empathy 3:

    Empathy 4:

Image: Jaw Pressure

READ the instruction below slowly and allow the image to be formed.

Ep25: *Now see your parents chewing something. —Describe how they chew. —Do they chew with pressure? —Who chews with more pressure?*

PICTURE: Write here what is seen in the mind.

STEPS: Concentrate on the above picture in the following stepwise manner and write the experience in each blank space in detail.

1. Picture your parents chewing something.

2. Which parent chews with more pressure?

3. How does the other parent chew in comparison?

4. Is the image of your father chewing pleasant or unpleasant?

5. What is your father's attitude toward what he is chewing?

6. What is your father chewing in the picture?

7. Is the image of your mother chewing pleasant or unpleasant?

8. What is your mother's attitude toward what she is chewing?

9. What is your mother chewing in the picture?

10. As they chew, which parent attracts your attention more? Why?

Analysis, Concentration, and Dialogue

READ each response (1–10) on the opposite page. Then select and write below three significant images for concentration: a positive, a negative, and a vague image. Repeat them according to the directions below.

    1. POSITIVE IMAGE: Concentrate for pleasurable release.

    2. NEGATIVE IMAGE: Concentrate for elucidation of the problem.

    3. VAGUE IMAGE: Concentrate for clarity of detail.

The above images should be repeated mentally over many days and weeks to stabilize the positive experience, to resolve the negative experience, and to lift vagueness from forgotten and inaccessible areas.

EMPATHY: Ask the person(s) working with you, "Please relax and pay attention to the image I am going to read to you. Empathize and experience the image as if it were your own." Then, from the opposite page, read the image written below *picture* aloud and allow sufficient time for concentration and development of empathy. Then say, "Describe what you see." Write the empathy response below. The spaces below can be used by a group, a family, two individuals, or a therapist for recording empathy and re-empathy experience, and expansion of consciousness.

    Empathy 1:

    Empathy 2:

    Empathy 3:

    Empathy 4:

Image: Parents' Brains

READ the instruction below slowly and allow the image to be formed.

Ep26: Now look at me. Imagine that my upper skull has been surgically removed and that you can see my brain. You can touch my visible brain with your finger and feel the temperature there. —Now picture your parents in a similar way. —Touch their brains alternately with your finger. You will similarly get a feeling of temperature there. —Describe the temperature of each parent's brain. Is it cold, warm or hot?

PICTURE: Write here what is seen in the mind.

STEPS: Concentrate on the above picture in the following stepwise manner and write the experience in each blank space in detail.

1. Picture your parents' visible brains.

2. Touch each parent's brain and feel the temperature there.

3. Now, touch your father's brain. Describe the temperature.

4. Is touching your father's brain pleasant or unpleasant?

5. Now, touch your mother's brain. Describe the temperature.

6. Is touching your mother's brain pleasant or unpleasant?

7. What does hot temperature of a brain mean to you?

8. What does cold temperature of a brain mean to you?

9. What does neutral temperature of a brain mean to you?

10. Which parent's brain do you tend to avoid touching?

Analysis, Concentration, and Dialogue

READ each response (1–10) on the opposite page. Then select and write below three significant images for concentration: a positive, a negative, and a vague image. Repeat them according to the directions below.

    1. POSITIVE IMAGE: Concentrate for pleasurable release.

    2. NEGATIVE IMAGE: Concentrate for elucidation of the problem.

    3. VAGUE IMAGE: Concentrate for clarity of detail.

The above images should be repeated mentally over many days and weeks to stabilize the positive experience, to resolve the negative experience, and to lift vagueness from forgotten and inaccessible areas.

EMPATHY: Ask the person(s) working with you, "Please relax and pay attention to the image I am going to read to you. Empathize and experience the image as if it were your own." Then, from the opposite page, read the image written below *picture* aloud and allow sufficient time for concentration and development of empathy. Then say, "Describe what you see." Write the empathy response below. The spaces below can be used by a group, a family, two individuals, or a therapist for recording empathy and re-empathy experience, and expansion of consciousness.

    Empathy 1:

    Empathy 2:

    Empathy 3:

    Empathy 4:

Image: Brain Efficiency

READ the instruction below slowly and allow the image to be formed.

Ep27: *Look at your parents' exposed brains again. —Imagine them as thinking machines, and describe how they look. —How do you feel about their efficiency as thinking machines? —Whose brain looks more efficient?*

PICTURE: Write here what is seen in the mind.

STEPS: Concentrate on the above picture in the following stepwise manner and write the experience in each blank space in detail.

1. Picture your parents' exposed brains again.

2. Imagine their brains as thinking machines.

3. Which parent's brain appears more efficient?

4. How is the other parent's brain in comparison?

5. Concentrate on how your father's brain looks.

6. Describe what your father's brain signifies to you.

7. Concentrate on how your mother's brain looks.

8. Describe what your mother's brain signifies to you.

9. Picture a defect or blemish in a brain. What does it look like?

10. Picture a perfect brain. What does it look like?

Analysis, Concentration, and Dialogue

READ each response (1–10) on the opposite page. Then select and write below three significant images for concentration: a positive, a negative, and a vague image. Repeat them according to the directions below.

   1. *POSITIVE IMAGE:* Concentrate for pleasurable release.

   2. *NEGATIVE IMAGE:* Concentrate for elucidation of the problem.

   3. *VAGUE IMAGE:* Concentrate for clarity of detail.

The above images should be repeated mentally over many days and weeks to stabilize the positive experience, to resolve the negative experience, and to lift vagueness from forgotten and inaccessible areas.

EMPATHY: Ask the person(s) working with you, "Please relax and pay attention to the image I am going to read to you. Empathize and experience the image as if it were your own." Then, from the opposite page, read the image written below *picture* aloud and allow sufficient time for concentration and development of empathy. Then say, "Describe what you see." Write the empathy response below. The spaces below can be used by a group, a family, two individuals, or a therapist for recording empathy and re-empathy experience, and expansion of consciousness.

   Empathy 1:

   Empathy 2:

   Empathy 3:

   Empathy 4:

Image: Parents' Heartbeats

READ the instruction below slowly and allow the image to be formed.

> Ep28: *Now see your parents' complete images standing in front of you again. —Imagine that a window has been carved in each chest and that you can see their hearts beating there. —See the hearts beating, and describe how each parent's heart beats. —Is there any sign of anxiety in the heartbeats?*

PICTURE: Write here what is seen in the mind.

STEPS: Concentrate on the above picture in the following stepwise manner and write the experience in each blank space in detail.

1. Picture your parents' complete images standing in front of you.

2. Imagine a window in each parent's chest and see the hearts beating.

3. See father's heart beating. Describe its beat and its appearance.

4. Is there any sign of anxiety in father's heartbeats?

5. Imagine a picture of someone in father's heart. Who do you see?

6. See mother's heart beating. Describe its beat and its appearance.

7. Is there any sign of anxiety in mother's heartbeats?

8. Imagine a picture of someone in mother's heart. Who do you see?

9. In what way do you wish your father's heart to appear different?

10. In what way do you wish your mother's heart to appear different?

Analysis, Concentration, and Dialogue

READ each response (1–10) on the opposite page. Then select and write below three significant images for concentration: a positive, a negative, and a vague image. Repeat them according to the directions below.

    1. POSITIVE IMAGE: Concentrate for pleasurable release.

    2. NEGATIVE IMAGE: Concentrate for elucidation of the problem.

    3. VAGUE IMAGE: Concentrate for clarity of detail.

The above images should be repeated mentally over many days and weeks to stabilize the positive experience, to resolve the negative experience, and to lift vagueness from forgotten and inaccessible areas.

EMPATHY: Ask the person(s) working with you, "Please relax and pay attention to the image I am going to read to you. Empathize and experience the image as if it were your own." Then, from the opposite page, read the image written below *picture* aloud and allow sufficient time for concentration and development of empathy. Then say, "Describe what you see." Write the empathy response below. The spaces below can be used by a group, a family, two individuals, or a therapist for recording empathy and re-empathy experience, and expansion of consciousness.

    Empathy 1:

    Empathy 2:

    Empathy 3:

    Empathy 4:

Image: Parents' Intestines

READ the instruction below slowly and allow the image to be formed.

Ep29: *Now look at your parents' intestines. —Do they appear healthy or unhealthy? —Whose intestines appear healthier?*

PICTURE: Write here what is seen in the mind.

STEPS: Concentrate on the above picture in the following stepwise manner and write the experience in each blank space in detail.

1. Picture your parents' intestines.

2. Which parent's intestines appear healthier?

3. How do the other parent's intestines appear?

4. Is the image of your father's intestines pleasant or unpleasant?

5. Does concentration on father's intestines remind you of anything?

6. Is the image of your mother's intestines pleasant or unpleasant?

7. Does concentration on mother's intestines remind you of anything?

8. In your view, what causes healthy intestines?

9. In your view, what causes unhealthy intestines?

10. Picture perfectly healthy intestines. What do they look like?

Analysis, Concentration, and Dialogue

READ each response (1–10) on the opposite page. Then select and write below three significant images for concentration: a positive, a negative, and a vague image. Repeat them according to the directions below.

1. POSITIVE IMAGE: Concentrate for pleasurable release.

2. NEGATIVE IMAGE: Concentrate for elucidation of the problem.

3. VAGUE IMAGE: Concentrate for clarity of detail.

The above images should be repeated mentally over many days and weeks to stabilize the positive experience, to resolve the negative experience, and to lift vagueness from forgotten and inaccessible areas.

EMPATHY: Ask the person(s) working with you, "Please relax and pay attention to the image I am going to read to you. Empathize and experience the image as if it were your own." Then, from the opposite page, read the image written below *picture* aloud and allow sufficient time for concentration and development of empathy. Then say, "Describe what you see." Write the empathy response below. The spaces below can be used by a group, a family, two individuals, or a therapist for recording empathy and re-empathy experience, and expansion of consciousness.

Empathy 1:

Empathy 2:

Empathy 3:

Empathy 4:

Image: Parents' Genitals

READ the instruction below slowly and allow the image to be formed.

> Ep30: *Now see your parents' genitals. —Touch the genitals of each parent and describe the feelings of temperature there. —Describe how each parent reacts to the touch and any feelings you have while seeing this image. —Are there any memories associated with this image?*

PICTURE: Write here what is seen in the mind.

STEPS: Concentrate on the above picture in the following stepwise manner and write the experience in each blank space in detail.

1. Picture your parents' genitals.

2. Touch each parent's genitals and feel the temperature there.

3. Describe the temperature and appearance of father's genitals.

4. How does your father react to you touching his genitals?

5. Does touching his genitals remind you of anything?

6. Now, describe the temperature and appearance of mother's genitals.

7. How does your mother react to you touching her genitals?

8. Does touching her genitals remind you of anything?

9. In your opinion, how did your mother influence your sexual life?

10. In your opinion, how did your father influence your sexual life?

Analysis, Concentration, and Dialogue

READ each response (1–10) on the opposite page. Then select and write below three significant images for concentration: a positive, a negative, and a vague image. Repeat them according to the directions below.

    1. POSITIVE IMAGE: Concentrate for pleasurable release.

    2. NEGATIVE IMAGE: Concentrate for elucidation of the problem.

    3. VAGUE IMAGE: Concentrate for clarity of detail.

The above images should be repeated mentally over many days and weeks to stabilize the positive experience, to resolve the negative experience, and to lift vagueness from forgotten and inaccessible areas.

EMPATHY: Ask the person(s) working with you, "Please relax and pay attention to the image I am going to read to you. Empathize and experience the image as if it were your own." Then, from the opposite page, read the image written below *picture* aloud and allow sufficient time for concentration and development of empathy. Then say, "Describe what you see." Write the empathy response below. The spaces below can be used by a group, a family, two individuals, or a therapist for recording empathy and re-empathy experience, and expansion of consciousness.

    Empathy 1:

    Empathy 2:

    Empathy 3:

    Empathy 4:

6 ⁊ Positive Group: A Group Therapy Technique Against Mass Imagery

A forest tribe, a settled commercial community, and a mass society share something in common: the practice of image making to structure and maintain their respective concepts of society. This practice is systematically observed by the contemporary mass society as the ultimate in societal control, in order to formulate living styles along pre-decided lines.

In a mass society where the picture-making activity of the mass media controls all picture-making activity, the control may in certain areas generate false notions, needs, and concepts in consciousness, damaging severely the gift of Nature and the fundamental ability to survive as a functioning biological organism. The mass-image society constantly bombards consciousness with arbitrary picture-making slogans and visual images which invade thought in so subtle a way that they are hardly noticeable. These images print out publicity advertisements in our minds for products, services, current issues, and social orientations.

In this contemporary era of mere negative motion and fast change, the presence of something permanent in the mind may be considered a definite psychological advantage. As the first image-makers of our lives, parents do represent an imposition upon original and native consciousness, but they borrow this authority from a legitimate biological foundation, the function of child rearing. Although not free from contamination by the mass-image makers, parents' images may be conducive to the recovery of biological awareness and, in this particular sense, health-provoking.

The individual, born free and then molded by publicity-contaminated parents, lives generally at a quasi-mechanical level, minimally experiencing his original nature. Where are the images of his original nature stored? They appear to be buried under the manufactured notions and the associated experiences of isolation, anger, rebellion, anxiety, and depression resulting from an imposition upon his original self, initiated by mass imagery. The eidetic images of parents serve as the prime medium of search beyond mass-hypnosis for those fundamental modes of experience which represent everyone's first and true knowledge. These images bring the original capacity for positive experience out of oblivion and into the world split apart by contemporary isolation.

Out of the ongoing momentum of parental images a vast potential for personal knowledge of truth can be envisioned. Such a process in a systematic setting is most useful in restoring a proper biological orientation. Concentration on the parental imagery evokes biological structures in the individual from sources which originate entirely from truth. Original and uncontaminated biological information is elicited from parental images by internal concentration, revealing primary endowment, and a subsequent blemish, an injury or a limitation imposed by the mass picture-making process. The true biological feelings and their associated pictures are unlocked from suppression and made available through imagery projection. Consciousness is thus able to generate a wholesome picture of life complete in all respects and unaffected by the current fixations, conflicts, crises, and reactions which emerge from a negative and unbiological life style imposed by arbitrary structuring.

Imagery experience as a mental process seems to function best when conflict is not imposed arbitrarily on the participating images. The conclusion is that there is no unnecessary conflict possible if the ideas truly evolve on their own and they are responded to in a natural biological manner. As in mental imagery, hostility between the group members (except when it is transitory and playful) is not natural to the group process. If it appears in a fixed manner, it disrupts the group and tears apart the biological functions of the group. Many group therapy approaches erroneously use group hostility as a technique, constantly throwing the mental mechanisms of the group members into a state of conflict and disruption. In our experiments we have noted that when group members intercommunicate without resorting to deliberate hostility, a deep empathic process is initiated among the group members, with interplay of gratifications. Free of the necessity to display aggression, the group members gradually enter into a pleasurable experience of the group activity, generating a pleasant experience of knowing, sharing, and comprehending psychological states. Supported by this favorable activity, the individual enters into a state of group security.

The process of imagization in the mind reminds one of what naturally happens in a herd of animals. The animals in a herd do not learn by attacking each other or negating each other's behavior over a period of time, but by experiencing their biological capacity to interact and respond meaningfully and spontaneously to an occurrence. The capacity to interact meaningfully exists because the herd is a unified mass of activity and behaves as one biological body. Messages are transferred not by role observation and conscious imitation but through a truly spontaneous biological group process. Interactive events in the herd are like events in the body which transcend the limbs; messages communicated by one part are transmitted to the other parts and to the general collective function through a central biological unity. Biological centrality is inherent to the process of image formation, image progression, between two individuals, among many individuals, and among groups.

The eidetic process in a group setting is thus useful in restoring the proper biological orientation to the corrupted areas of biological group functioning. Such a positive group process evokes positive imagery structures in each individual from sources which originate entirely within. Uncontaminated biological information emerges from within the group through the help of parental images, which evidence original endowment and any blemish or deviation imposed by the mass opinion-making agency. As the original biological needs and their associated tendencies are freed from suppression and realized through collective projection and empathy, the group is finally able to generate a wholesome and complete view of life unaffected by the current mass value system and its attendant conflicts, crises, and reactions.

Since each civilization generates from a typified pair of parents, each civilization's typified beliefs play a part in the consciousness of the ensuing generations. Complete knowledge is, therefore, realization of this complex structure in movement. The essence of understanding lies in understanding this social process. One does not seek a single propagandized image as the final solution of an issue, but moves over many generations of images, experiencing each in turn and developing the varied features of the collective experience. The process of recovery of this collective experience can be engaging. Each image generates the feeling of finality; yet it is not final, since other images gradually develop and take its place. As the edges of each assumed experience become fuzzy, a new, sharper experience appears on the horizon. This continuous generation and catalysis provides a breakdown of information to enhance experience and facilitates birth of a new vision in a civilization.

Just as the individual hides his personal thoughts, being ashamed of them, he may hide his societal images. The group process of empathy is the process of eliciting parental images which have parented the current nature of experience in a particular civilization. The psychological struggle within a severely obstructed society represents this specific struggle and the feelings of shame or trauma which attend it. When the experience is generated forthrightly, without subterfuge, it generates a new mode of social awareness. During the exchange of imagery information, many old doors are sealed and many new ones are opened. As various levels of group experience are achieved, new insights into human functioning and human potential are experienced. One comes to understand that such group activity involving an open experience of mental processes reveals profound sources of ideation not elicited by any known process of analysis. The individual breathing in the context of group ideation breaks his self-limiting boundaries and bursts forth into a new, universal experience.

The positive group, to achieve this goal, functions as a leaderless group or a moderated group in which the group moderator participates in the imagery process as a regular member. A therapist guiding such a group is expected to limit his supervisory role or use a co-therapist as a moderator who participates democratically in the process. The main thrust of the group is in the direction of a leaderless, democratic experience at the psychological level, uncovering the biological ideas where the mass-image society has generated corrupt ideas. The group, by its own picture-making ability, uncovers the original concepts lying suppressed or dormant under mass-hypnosis. The group exploits the vast inner possibilities and exposes the individuals to the generation of a new basis of percepts and concepts for an appropriate understanding of the true biological life. Experiments have revealed that any rational or academic understanding of human relationships turns out to be far poorer than what the individual arrives at through his own resources during such group activity.

Exposure to the biological imagery is generated through empathic imagery exercises involving feelingful duplication or replication of the imagery of other individuals in a group setting. During this duplication of mental imagery in which parents are seen behaving naturally or unnaturally, important information on human interaction is revealed. The awareness of appropriate relationships is generated in the form of mental images containing an original ethos of proper human response and expression.

When a person empathizes into another person's image, he learns about the basis of mental life. By exchanging, at the interactive level, emotional information which reaches beyond conscious orientations, the two persons take inside new perceptual modes. In this state of duplicating the experience, the two know their own respective states of feeling. The experience releases universal knowledge about Man, its particulars, its universals, and its dialectics, in the interactive flow of feelingful consciousness.

The process of visualization of another person's image represents a feelingful entry into unknown vistas of emotional life at critical instants of involvement. In the words of an empathy participant, "Empathy is not merely an image experience; it is a total feeling, a shoulder-to-shoulder, eye-to-eye, heart-to-heart and toe-to-toe feeling of another person's life at a specific instant." In such a complete projection into an object of experience through an empathy image, the object and the person envelop each other. The true knowledge regarding complicated experiential structures emerges from the "what" and "how" of this imagery.

In psychotherapy, an individual who has had a traumatic past does not easily reenact his painful experiences. All common forms of conscious recall, including dramatization techniques, fail, because the ego tends to reenact the experience from a "safe," "conscious" standpoint. However, as our experiments reveal, empathy is an "unselfish" and "uncontaminated" original ability which bridges the emotional gap between two persons by creating an experiential environment in which they can share perceptions. The process breaks down barriers of narcissism. Through taking inside another person's perceptions, one is automatically led out of one's ego-centered perceptions. The narcissistic capsule, otherwise pressurized and defended through self-centered thought, comes into contact with a catalytic counterprocess, and the individual sees the beginnings of his own original experience in the other person's image. This experiential communion through the images breaks isolation, enabling the person to yield to new ideas.

When an individual reproduces the experience of the other person, he duplicates the image as a present experience. This he can express better and more readily than his own past experience, to which he is tied. As each person proceeds to empathize deeply, elaborating the image experience, deepening the feelings, knowing the pain and suffering, an oceanic movement of optimum feeling develops in which spontaneous emotions are surfaced in an atmosphere of total mental contact and emotional unity. The resistant part of the person is carried along until he relaxes and comes into contact with his own true self. When he observes that the participants genuinely experience mental events rather than merely intellectualize, interpret, criticize, or blame, it helps him break his own isolation from his biological foundation and enables him to join others in an integrative experience of life.

POSITIVE GROUP

The positive empathy group is formed essentially as a leaderless group for the exploration of consciousness. The group meets at each other's homes or a convenient place, such as a school or club facility, or a clinic if working under the guidance of a trained therapist. Since the group needs someone to integrate its business activity, a rotating leadership is recommended so that each member of the group becomes a leader in turn. If the group meets at the members' houses, the host that week should be the moderator. The members should not meet more than twice in succession at one house, and the moderator should be called the "host," or the "leader." Light snacks and beverages should be served to create a friendly atmosphere. The host participates in the images with the rest of the group. When the group meets under the guidance of a therapist, the therapist may or may not use a co-therapist or a moderator, but he should guide the group with democratic leadership. In the following pages the term "moderator" will be used for the person responsible for the direction of the group.

FIRST SESSION

The positive group should consist of at least three and not more than fifteen members. (Two interested individuals can also use this format as "Consciousness Friends.") Age, cultural background, education, and sex of the participant do not matter since the aim of the imagery process is empathic learning about others. The composition of the group can be diversified, according to the group's ability to handle the differences. The group participants sit in a circle facing each other, in sufficient proximity for a feelingful interchange.

At the start of the positive group, the moderator brings the rules of imagery projection (given under the section, "The Picture," in this chapter) to the attention of the members, who are asked to study them at home. During the first session, the moderator reads to the participants the "Positive Group: Introductory Model" below. This model provides some basic idea of the imagery work and introduces the first instruction (Ep1) of the Eidetic Parents Test. The model can also be used to introduce a new member into an already functioning group.

Positive Group: Introductory Model

In this session, we are going to do some interesting work involving images. As I read the instructions, please pay attention to what I say and form the images in your mind accordingly.

> *Picture your parents in the house where you lived most of the time with them, the house which gives you the feeling of a home. —Where do you see them? —What are they doing? —How do you feel when you see the images? —Are there any memories connected with this picture?*

WRITE what you see in the IMAGE in the empty space below or on a separate sheet of paper or on a 3 x 5 card.

A Group of People were asked to picture their parents along the above line and Bobby, who was one of the group, saw the following image:

> *I see my mother clearly in the house and she is working. My father is vaguely visible. When I try to see my father clearly, I see him going to work. He is in the process of leaving. I feel lonely and anxious. He is always leaving the house for work. He is never home.*

EMPATHY: Now close your eyes and put yourself in the place of Bobby. Experience this image as if it were your own. Write what you see in the image in the empty space below or on a sheet of paper or on a 3 x 5 card.

DID YOU DUPLICATE Bobby's experience? This is called EMPATHY, a complete and living experience of another person's image as if it were your own image. EMPATHY is an image experience in which you put yourself totally in the place of the other person. It is an experience of the other, for the other's sake.

DEEPENING EMPATHY: Now empathize deeply into Bobby's image, so that you feel all the details of the image.
> If you experience pain in the image, allow yourself to experience the pain.
> If you feel sympathetic in the image, allow yourself to feel the sympathy.
> If any other emotion, such as irritation or anger, is present, experience that emotion.
> If you tend to act in the image, let it happen. Experience what you tend to do in the image.

DISCUSSION: So far, we have three images: your own first image, Bobby's image, and your empathy into Bobby's image. We now can have an interesting discussion about what happened in the family in these three images and what created problems in the house. The discussion can create many spontaneous solutions by analyzing images in a common setting. We can arrive at a true biological understanding of positive interactions in a family.

Empathy Responses to Bobby's Image

Bobby being the first individual to respond to the main test instruction in the form of an image, his response is treated as the first response in which empathies are experienced by other members. The above instructions created the development of imagery along the following lines.

> *Bobby's Image:* I see my mother clearly in the house and she is working. My father is vaguely visible. When I try to see my father clearly, I see him going to work. He is in the process of leaving. I feel lonely and anxious. He is always leaving the house for work. He is never home.
>
> *Allan's Empathy:* I see my mother in the house and she is preparing things for father, his breakfast. I see my father in a bad mood. He is kicking things around in the house, getting ready to go. I want to get out of his way.
>
> *Pete's Empathy:* I see my mother in the kitchen. I cannot see my father at all. He had already gone to work before I got up. He comes home very late, after I am asleep. When I try to see my father, I see him working somewhere, and it is a vague image.
>
> *Carol's Empathy:* I see my father going in the image and he is not paying any attention to me and he is too busy with the idea of the work. He does not even notice me. I feel I am not as important as his work.
>
> *Tommy's Empathy:* When I see my mother in the image, I hear her voice first and she is yelling. When I see my father, I am afraid to see him clearly. There is something there which keeps me from seeing the image, like fear. I am afraid of him. Now I experience anger toward him. He is going to work. I do not relate to this image. Work doesn't appear to be important; it is his presence which frightens me.

SECOND SESSION

During the second meeting, the group moderator administers the full Eidetic Parents Test (EPT) to the participants. Each participant records his own responses in the blank spaces provided in the chapter entitled the "Eidetic Parents Test," or on sheets of paper or on 3 x 5 cards. The moderator administers the EPT to the group along the following lines.

The moderator reads out the EPT instructions (there are 30 instructions, in total) slowly and clearly to the group. During the reading of each instruction, the members of the group allow an image to form in their minds and record each response separately. The image responses to all 30 instructions should be recorded during this session, which may take one to a few hours. Following this, the recorded image responses are ready for self-analytic empathy work. These basic records should be brought to all subsequent meetings.

THIRD AND SUBSEQUENT SESSIONS

After the image responses to the instructions have been recorded in the suggested form, the empathy work starts from Ep1. The moderator requests one of the participants, called here "A," to read his image response to Ep1, called the *Primary Image,* slowly and clearly to the group. All the other participants silently listen and each visualizes "A"'s image in his mind as if it were his own image. The participants keep their eyes open or closed, as preferred.

Visualization

Each member sees and experiences his own personal parents in the role of "A"'s parents in the image. If a person cannot experience his own parents in that situation, he "adopts" "A"'s parents and allows the visual process to develop from that view. This latter variation in which one's own personal parents' images are replaced by someone else's parents' images is called *Adoption of Parents.*

> *Example:* An individual who was trying to empathize into Bobby's image could not see his own parents in the situation in which Bobby saw his parents. This individual's father's behavior was different because his father worked from an office at home and was always present around the house. This individual was instructed to see Bobby's own parents and experience himself as their son and form the image along this line. He was then able to see the father absent in the image in the style of Bobby's projection. This is an example of adoption of parents. Another individual did not have to do this, since he saw his parents easily behaving in the image in the style of Bobby's image.

Duplication

A proper empathy is complete duplication of "A"'s image, with feelings. One does not criticize, analyze, interpret, or evaluate the image, but feels it as if the experience were happening right now. In this spirit, the participant uses only the present tense to communicate and says "I see" and "I feel," rather than "I saw" and "I felt."

> *Example:* An individual empathizing into Bobby's image said: "I saw Bobby's image . . ." He was told, "No. See Bobby's image as your own and describe it as you are experiencing it right now. Talk about the image as your own and not as Bobby's image."

Pain and Sympathy

During empathy, one allows oneself to feel all the emotions present in the picture, such as pain, grief, sympathy, etc. If emotions are absent, one develops them in the image by relaxation and repeated concentration. As the emotions develop slowly, detailed experience of them is allowed to come through.

> *Example:* An individual saw Bobby's image but did not experience the emotions. He was asked to relax and concentrate on Bobby's image again. In a few minutes he suddenly experienced an image response with accompanying emotion. This emotion involved an extreme experience of anger. He felt furious with the father in the image. He said, "I do not respond by experiencing pain and isolation in the image, but anger and the desire to break the wall of isolation between me and my father."

Action and Solution

If an event tends to develop in the image spontaneously in a direction which provides some kind of action in the image, let it happen. If a solution tends to emerge out of this action, allow the solution to take place. Since the problems in the images require solutions, actions and solutions in the images tend to emerge naturally. This happens most often in the case of an activity-oriented individual who usually deals with any problem with activity or an attempt at solution. On the other hand, passive individuals and those overly blocked do not show activity in the image and solutions do not come through. However, some minor progress in the events of imagery helps in the positive progression of experience.

> *Example:* An individual responding to Bobby's image felt completely isolated in the image. However, he saw himself in the image occasionally looking at the father, who was ready to go. This occasional looking at the father was an activity with positive implications that he wanted a relation-

ship with the father. Another individual, instead of seeing himself looking at the father, saw that he clung to the father. Another hid father's briefcase so that father could not find it. Another individual went outside and let the air out of father's car tires, which made father helpless and exasperated. These images gave a feeling of relief and humor to the group. The obstructed individuals in the group laughed over the events and enjoyed the releaseful activity as it developed. They even wanted to concentrate on this image as a basis of a new line of empathy experience, which is called *Re-empathy*.

Recording of Empathy

After forming empathy along the suggested lines, each participant writes down his own empathy image clearly. All members do this simultaneously.

Communication of Empathy

After recording of images, the stage is set for communication of empathy. The moderator asks "A" to read out his primary image. Next, the moderator asks "B" to read out his empathy response to "A"'s primary. If "B" has not formed the empathy image, the moderator proceeds without any critical comments on "B" to the next participant, "C." The group silently listens to each empathy image and attempts to experience it by deep empathy. This second-level empathy is called *Re-empathy*. By this time the following levels of experience have been established:

Level I: Primary images
Level II: Empathy images
Level III: Re-empathy images

Empathy Dialogue

This final phase of the group empathy process depends upon the previous empathy images for its material. The procedure reminds one of the Greek dialogues, in which concepts of life are evolved out of a flowing experience rather than abstractions. All the participants, having shared the first two visualizations, enter into re-empathy and the dialogue associated with it contributes meaningful ideas based on the current flow of the imagization process. Here is an example of the development of ideas through such a dialogue.

Example: Bobby, in response to Ep1, had said that the image of his father going to work provoked anxiety in him, since father was always leaving the house for work.

Allan contributed the idea of father being in a bad mood in the morning due to work anxiety, and kicking things around in the house. Pete never knew his father, and had only a vague image of him working somewhere. Carol felt that father did not even know that she lived in the house, and Tommy did not even want him in the house. Others reported a total submission to isolation or furious anger against it to the point of invention of tricks against the father. One of the participants during the discussion said, "I see my father going and I feel that the work is taking my father away from me. He gives more attention to work than to me. Why doesn't he know that I am more important than the work? Why doesn't he know that I need *him,* and not the money?" As the participants reported their images, they felt surprised by the flow of emotions which elucidated their experiences in detail. They felt gratified by the variety of responses, and felt that their experience was not a mere idiosyncratic flow of projections. In fact, it contained roots of relationships in the family within the context of effective living.

Later, dialogue fully developed around the work theme, that work was, in fact, an important event in the family, and that Man's attitude to work finally involved the question, "How does work restore or take away human dignity?" This ensuing empathy dialogue was helpful in developing life concepts from within the group resources again. An experiential philosophy emerged out of the flesh and blood of living people when they collectively saw and felt this basic situation of life. This new philosophy did not develop out of cold reasoning, but out of a contemplative contact with the work problems of current life. The group asked these fundamental questions to develop imagery and empathy exercises on them:

"What was the work life of the early man thousands of years ago?"
"When did human civilization invent work?"
"Was the first work of man pleasurable?"
"How did work volume gradually increase for the human father?"
"Has more work increased anxiety or pleasure?"
"Is the contemporary father not only an absent but also an alienated father?"
"What does the emotion of 'loss' mean when father spends long hours at work?"
"What is the happiness like when he returns from work in the evening?"

At this phase of imagery projection and discussion, the group decided to form images, to visualize father in the above situations. For instance, an entirely new line of imagery developed when the group saw father returning home in the evening. The participants reported a variety of images connected with the return of the father in the evening. Most images revealed pleasant, buoyant feelings emerging from his return. Empathic exchange of these buoyant images led to an experience of collective release in which the individual negative experiences associated with father were resolved. Those who had reported initial negative feelings about the father's return learned new concepts about the relationship between parents. They found that the anxiety connected with father's return was not based on facts but on purely conjectured feelings that he did not like the children. This theme was found connected with the father's inability to play with children and the fact that he always returned home tense and anxious, a state induced by stressful conditions at work. The group members freely visualized and held group discussions dealing with these problematic images of father. Group empathy revealed answers to the group members which they had never thought of before. The members tried to relate to the questions not intellectually but by developing the imagery process, which surfaced the answers spontaneously along with an associated deep emotional awareness.

As the many individuals in the group proceeded along the path of many images, experiential processes were released constantly, culminating in a rich surge of imagistic communication. The final awareness was experienced in the form of a speechful silence among the group members. Despite ongoing dialogue and discussion, a feeling of rest enveloped the group and immersed each participant in a deep feeling of silence. This pleasurable condition of silence developed because the group had proceeded with complete adherence to empathy and steps of communication had been performed without undue hurry. The successful culmination of the group experience was represented in the spirit of silence, that everything had been successfully communicated. In most groups this silence matures near the last half hour of the group process, during which one witnesses a restful resurgence of ideation and a psychical nearness among the participants which unites them in a gratifying experience of social expression and harmony. It is important for the group to experience this phenomenon of speechful silence since it develops deep confidence in the human potential for restful communication. In short, speechful silence is the final goal of the group and the group process should be carefully directed to achieve it.

The above was a description of a theme involving work, its problematic relationship with father's absence and the emotions and crises connected with his absence. It should be clear that the group process reveals first a store of imagery of the negative nature connected with the theme; as the imagery procedure develops the stages of crisis, and surfaces the interaction during these phases, the biological foundation involving a positive relationship with the father is uncovered. The whole gamut of imagery—how the theme originated and how it was related to the current problems of the individual—becomes the process of knowing the nature of conflict and the procedures for therapeutic resolution of the situation.

It should be obvious to the reader that the positive group does not always develop the same theme every time (here, work theme) but any theme which becomes surfaced through primary projection of the Eidetic Parents Test imagery. The participants may bring about a theme, for instance, connected with the negative behavior of the mother in the house, or the parents' attitudes to a warm physical relationship, and to reason, feeling, and sexuality. The theme develops out of a painful critical image brought in by one participant. After other participants empathize into this specific image, the details of the theme start developing and the total theme starts taking shape. After empathy by so many individuals, the theme finally develops into a rich store of relevant imagery involving ideas of conflict, diversity of feelings, and various solutions which are projected into it. The group should pick up various dimensions of the theme and develop the related imagery toward experiential resolution.

For the Sake of the Other Person, or a New Reality

Finally, it is important to remember that (a) while empathy is a personal experience in a group setting, it is essentially an experience for the sake of the other person, and that (b) all assembled have accepted and understood the benefits of such experience. The principle should be kept in view all the time and the moderator may conduct himself in a relevant way in order to guide one particular person at a time or the whole group in the direction of systematically dealing with the experience. Empathy is a very precise procedure which should follow the feeling of democracy rather than authoritarian leadership. The pressure of individual emotions should be handled in a helpful manner, remembering that participants who have never communicated with others and participants who were always criticized and thereby learned to keep a distance from others, will profit from the empathy experience because the process is devoid of personal criticism.

The group empathy process aims at the creation of a new reality for the individual. This reality is gradually born out of the empathic experience as it crisscrosses the group, and as the individuals lose their old perceptions and develop new ones in their place. This birth of the new reality is not merely an ordinary change in a few areas, but a change in the total outlook. The individual comes to understand the true nature of his perceptions and how they can be kept buried, stagnant, or blocked. He learns to be totally available by offering an open consciousness. Unless the individual experiences some of this new reality, he has not broken his previous modes of behavior which imprison him in an ineffective life style.

The Picture

Because the birth of the new reality takes place out of the images which are concentrated upon by the group members, a special orientation toward the picture experience must be practiced by the group. The group must treat each picture with openness and a certain feeling of "sanctity" and "mental care." It also must faithfully follow certain rules while dealing with the picture, as a casual attitude toward the picture can block or terminate the experience of growth. The group must recognize each picture as having special attributes and follow specific rules for effective empathy work on images, such as these.

1. Always "see" an image, rather than merely think or imagine about it in a casual way.
2. Concentrate on the image for at least 5 to 10 seconds before you report it.
3. Describe what you see visually and report on the feelings.
4. While describing the image, use the present tense, as if it were happening here and now, like in a movie. Say, "I see" and "I feel," rather than "I saw" and "I felt."
5. See the image and do not derive too many meanings from one image at one time; if you try to derive too many meanings, you will end up brooding over old meanings you already know.
6. After the first person communicates his image, the empathy procedure requires that this image be seen by the other participants without evaluation or criticism. Each participant should duplicate the image in his mind, in silence.
7. When an individual does not want to participate at a certain time, he should not be forced to do so. The next participant should be asked to communicate his image, and, following this, the former participant should be asked if he is now ready to report the image.
8. Some individuals show fear or shame concerning images, treating them as if they are more real than reality. The image should not be treated as secret or a personal belief, but as an internal mental description which no one should hide or suppress. One should proceed with total rejection of personalism concerning it.
9. True empathy is, foremost, a communication of your own personal image. You see the image and report it without altering it in any way, due to shame, fear, or apprehension. In a sense, the group represents a crowd or a mob, and the individual fears disclosure. The empathy group, however, is neither a crowd nor a mob; it is a helpful and positive group.
10. When a participant shows resistance to participation or communica-

tion, he should be encouraged but should not be forced. He may be asked about the difficulty, and the group may offer helpful suggestions.

11. When a participant shows fear of a traumatic image, he should be helped to see an earlier image, one which he once was able to project without too much stress or reaction. The group may join in to empathize in this earlier image.

12. The group may treat a traumatic image through massive concentration. All members of the group simultaneously and collectively concentrate on the negative image of the individual, pulling the individual out of isolation. During massive concentration all members of the group empathize into the negative image silently, and then each, in turn, describes the details of the image to the individual. Through this, the traumatized individual comes to know how various responses to his problem image contain many variations and solutions.

13. Each massive concentration is developed and communicated to the traumatized participant in the following manner. The empathizer first describes the primary image, as he sees it. After this, he experiences the image in a manner that he lives its traumatic aspect deeply. Then he involves the most traumatic aspect and deepens that, suffering the experience in his own consciousness to the point that he develops the painful experience to an optimum level. At the peak point he allows the experience to move toward a solution, which emerges spontaneously at the end of these profound emotional experiences. The empathizer describes the solution in a feelingful style as it emerges in his mind. The traumatized participant and the group members listen to all the details attentively. The rest of the participants also experience and describe their empathies in the same manner. Thus, in the group, many solutions emerge, and these solutions are personal to each individual who has empathized, and are not necessarily true or ultimate. The participant who originally projected the problem image gives his views on each solution, chooses the one which is most helpful to him, and projects it in his mind. The group participates in his new image, treating it as a new primary.

14. If an obstructed individual shows extreme sensitivity to his negative images because he never experienced gratifying aspects of life, a massive concentration on positive images may be attempted by the group. For this purpose nature images, such as grass, water, the breeze, lakes, and mountains, are most useful. Positive images of parents from the Eidetic Parents Test, assembled in list form, may also provide pleasurable experience.

15. Some individuals avoid pain; others become addicted to it and show insensitivity at the mental level. Pain is a normal human experience and, therefore, becoming aware of pain is important. The group should concentrate on a list of negative images from the EPT to increase awareness of the nature of pain and its role in human life. This approach to the understanding of painful experiences will also provide an experiential basis for tolerance of stress in life.
16. The group should differentiate between negative and positive images, but to concentrate, as a rule, only on negative images or only on positive images would bias the experience and would not involve the potential of the individual in a more natural manner. Therefore, it would be more helpful to move from one image to another in the sequence of the EPT, concentrating on each response in turn, without special regard to whether it is positive or negative.
17. While experiencing images and empathizing into them, the traumatized individual may show an absence of understanding regarding an experience. This is called the *C-I-G* or *Consciousness-Imagery Gap*, i.e., a gap between one's conscious view of the images and emotional awareness of their real meaning through a group process. This gap should be bridged slowly by other individuals empathically providing an emotional access to the new emotion and meanings for the individual. Just the attempt by the group to relate to the image is helpful to the individual, since it shows concern and thus overcomes the basic lack of concern he has experienced from others in his life, it being one of the basic problems which created the cause for the C-I-G in him. The individual suffering from obstruction comes to know that he is receiving the needed interest and concern in the area of his problem and, therefore, he bridges his gaps.
18. A cold intellectual approach to meaning-deriving may show itself as an unemotional approach to experience. Instead of promoting the experience and waiting until it stands on its own emotional ground, the rational individual hurriedly interprets it as he wishes and rips it apart. He should be instructed to put his reasoning aside and empathize into the images instead.
19. An individual who uses rough and assaultive language (e.g., "damn it," or "what the hell is that?") to suppress another person's experience in the group should be asked to improve his language and use empathic idiom instead. Assaultive language, although it is popularly presented as forthrightness, does not generate empathy and should be minimized. The group members should communicate with "Integrative Language" which fosters the elucidation of experience. They should avoid mugging each other verbally.
20. Aggression is copiously expressed at the imagery level when dealing

with an obstruction within the empathic experience. For instance, a suppressed individual who may be afraid of responding to a threatening person in the image may feel strengthened when the group joins in and each member releases aggression against the negative person in the image. During this empathic encounter, the group releases a valid store of aggressive energy at the collective level.

A REPORT

Following is an interesting, brief report from a Positive Group working as a leaderless therapy group which describes how it was formed, how it actually started off, gradually stabilized itself on its own, and learned to handle the experiential process in a self-educational manner.

> We had a choice to meet under a trained therapist or entirely on our own, along the lines of a Positive Group, and we chose the latter, just to see how it would work out. We took up this project to know whether self-education could work in the area of psychotherapy, i.e., whether we could learn on our own if we knew we had the resources.
> We first went through the preliminaries of providing instructional material to the members. During our first meeting at "A"'s home, we introduced the "Positive Group: Introductory Model" and discussed these instructions. We developed a pretty good idea of what we were going to do.
> At our second meeting, one of the members came a couple of minutes late to "A"'s house. After brief chitchat and socialization, we started off. We administered the whole test [Eidetic Parents Test] the very first time and wrote down our responses on 3 x 5 cards, which we had brought with us.
> At our next meeting we were supposed to empathize, but we didn't. Instead, we told about our own images without experiencing the other person's images. It was not right, but it was okay. At the next session we started with empathy. We seemed to be going along pretty good with the images. We were amazed that in the empathy we seemed to get a lot of the same feelings through these images. We came up with some interesting points.
> During our next session we developed some self-leadership. A strong inclination to talk about things, but not to get into them in the sense of empathy, emerged. Most of the time we would talk about each other's images and say, "Okay, that's the way it is for you, but that's not the way it is for me." We wouldn't put ourselves into each other's images. When

this happened, it almost seemed like it turned into a competition thing, like, "Who's got the best image?" We decided to discipline ourselves a little by reading the rules again and sticking to them.

At the next meeting we did better than we had ever done before. There were some problem areas. "C" was angry and obstructive, but with some guidance from the rules, we dealt with it.

We have finally come to understand that it is nice to contribute as well as help. We have a certain format to follow, a kind of aim. Every one of us has developed a sheet of self-guidance, because we feel our meetings have to follow a clear line of interaction and not deteriorate into a social group. We do try to follow the "host," but we also show independence. We always rotate the leadership. Usually we meet twice at a house and then move on to the next house on the list. The "host" serves light refreshment. It is not costly, as the costs are rotated. We have come to know a lot about each other and we try to accommodate each other's shortcomings and needs. For instance, "B" and "D" show a need for a conversational period before the work starts; it seems like the preliminary chitchat really benefits them. As a consequence of these accommodations, the experiences are deeper and more profuse than before. We have developed skills for handling situations both of the procedural and emotional nature. Shouldering the responsibility of management and experience simultaneously is challenging, but beneficial at the same time.

New Member

It is common to see that a new member joins when a group is already functioning very well and has gone way ahead in the ability to manage mental experience. A new member is, therefore, naturally treated as an intruder by some group members. However, experience has revealed that the group can learn something very valuable when a new member joins the group. The opportunity involves the discipline of presenting something which one has already learned, without problems or stage fright. The presentation of the technique and education of the new member in the group process discloses how much the members have learned, and where learning is still marked by insecurity, fear, or lack of clarity regarding concepts. Older members should assume the responsibility of introducing the new member to the group and seeing him through the preliminary learning.

The induction of a new member is thus a new opportunity to learn, and no hostility should be expressed toward the entry of a new member, nor should he be considered a hindrance. The group should voluntarily stop the forward activity of the group and experience some imagery steps with the new member in a slow, demonstrative fashion. This will teach old members caring intercommunication, patience, and stability, since it will involve some work which may be bothersome and repetitive to the group members.

The new member, in the beginning of induction in the group, should study the imagery rules on his own, after he is introduced to the group process in a separate session by a volunteer who enacts the empathy atmosphere by reading the "Positive Group: Introductory Model" to him. During a second separate session the volunteer also administers the Eidetic Parents Test, and the new member records his responses, to arrive at the basic records for the empathy work with the group.

Group empathy exploits the vast potential of human interaction and exposes the individual to an extensive generation of percepts and concepts which spontaneously develop and surface an appropriate understanding of the true biological potential. Obviously, any artificially induced imagery exercises or institutionalized development of concepts will be limited in scope and effectiveness, and the understanding of human relationships will be poorer.

The table of imagery projections provided below gives a view of the progressively larger count of images with progressively larger groups. A carefully structured group can spend months exploring these experiential images that result in a spontaneous education. A sample group of six participants (A, B, C, D, E, F), responding to an eidetic instruction, experiences empathy and re-empathy pictures according to the following table, a progressively growing store of picture experience.

Table of Empathy Pictures

Primaries: (A group of six responding to an eidetic instruction)

A, B, C, D, E, F
Total Number of Pictures = 6

Empathies: (Pictures of A are empathized into by participants B, C, D, E, F. Next, pictures of B are empathized into, and so on.)

AB, AC, AD, AE, AF
BA, BC, BD, BE, BF
CA, CB, CD, CE, CF
DA, DB, DC, DE, DF
EA, EB, EC, ED, EF
FA, FB, FC, FD, FE
Total Number of Pictures = 30

Re-empathies: (Empathy of B into A's primary picture, i.e., AB, is re-empathized into by participants A, C, D, E, F. Next, AC is empathized into, and so on.)

ABA,	ABC,	ABD,	ABE,	ABF
ACA,	ACB,	ACD,	ACE,	ACF
ADA,	ADB,	ADD,	ADE,	ADF
AEA,	AEB,	AEC,	AED,	AEF
AFA,	AFB	AFC,	AFD,	AFE
BAB,	BAC,	BAD,	BAE,	BAF
BCA,	BCB,	BCD,	BCE,	BCF
BDA,	BDB,	BDC,	BDE,	BDF
BEA,	BEB,	BEC,	BED,	BEF
BFA,	BFB,	BFC,	BFD,	BFE
CAB,	CAC,	CAD,	CAE,	CAF
CBA,	CBC,	CBD,	CBE,	CBF
CDA,	CDB,	CDC,	CDE,	CDF
CEA,	CEB,	CEC,	CED,	CEF
CFA,	CFB,	CFC,	CFD,	CFE
DAB,	DAC,	DAD,	DAE,	DAF
DBA,	DBC,	DBD,	DBE,	DBF
DCA,	DCB,	DCD,	DCE,	DCF
DEA,	DEB,	DEC,	DED,	DEF
DFA,	DFB,	DFC,	DFD,	DFE
EAB,	EAC,	EAD,	EAE,	EAF
EBA,	EBC,	EBD,	EBE,	EBF
ECA,	ECB,	ECD,	ECE,	ECF
EDA,	EDB,	EDC,	EDE,	EDF
EFA,	EFB,	EFC,	EFD,	EFE
FAB,	FAC,	FAD,	FAE,	FAF
FBA,	FBC,	FBD,	FBE,	FBF
FCA,	FCB,	FCD,	FCE,	FCF
FDA,	FDB,	FDC,	FDE,	FDF
FEA,	.FEB,	FEC,	FED,	FEF

Total Number of Pictures = 150

Series of Pictures Involving the Following Projections

Primaries	=	6
Empathies	=	30
Re-empathies	=	150
Total Pictures	=	186

The total of pictures regarding one eidetic test item or instruction equals 186; considering that there are 30 test items, the final sum of pictures equals a staggering 5,580. That this total geometrically grows with more participants suggests such a scope for selection of images that the group should select only the most problematic pictures out of each individual's Eidetic Parents Test. When a group is expected to function over a short period of time, careful selection should be made at the very beginning, i.e., during the administration of the Eidetic Parents Test, which takes place at the second meeting of the group. The group should concentrate on the most problematic pictures, emphasizing the flow of pictures as they develop, and concentrate also on other pictures which evolve along the way. This flexibility between test-induced pictures and other spontaneous pictures should be a part of the group process and should not be given up in any way.

In the case of group usage of other imagery schedules given in this book, the same rules apply without any change. If long-term self-educational work is visualized, other sections of this book may be freely used following the group principles.

The chapter entitled "Orientation Exercises" is recommended for short-term group education using only one EPT instruction (Ep1). It opens up the group on a variety of imagery fronts from the very beginning and keeps the process lively and challenging. The short-term group should terminate following exposure to a pleasurable projection of Nature Images.

7 ∞ More on Adjustment

What is the true nature of emotional disturbance? It is resistance to self-learning and education about the behavior of mind. When an individual wants to find out how symptoms develop and he reads a textbook analysis of neurosis, he finds the descriptions incomprehensible and the symptoms as formidable states of mind frightening to him. However, much of the confusion and fear concerning mental symptoms arises out of an abstract treatment of the subject of neurosis, which cares more for terms than feelingful description of mental states and how they can be experientially managed and what causes obstruction in their management.

An individual who is able to deal with mental states in a self-analytic and self-educational manner should not be kept from further knowledge of symptom formation in the general area of mental illness. The need for further enlightenment in seeking a frame of reference which tells how exactly his own neurosis relates to the emotional issues which other people face represents a genuine thirst for knowledge. An individual who wants to understand how another person develops a symptom different from his own, such as an hysterical symptom or an obsessional neurosis, is not asking to know something which is incomprehensible or outside his domain.

How exactly is a neurosis formed? It is formed when a natural experience is subjected to authoritarian change and is kept from total recall. In this process, memory is encouraged to function independent of the experience, inducing an unnatural need for corruption of information. While the experience is still fresh, the individual has total recall; the visual images, emotional reactions, and meaning of the original event are all available to consciousness. Soon, due to authoritarian corruption, he starts recalling just the minimum, the visual picture is changed around, and the emotions are dropped out and only a vague idea of the original event is left behind. Eventually, a twisted picture with a new meaning emerges, and this is subjected to further generalization, corruption, and misrepresentation. After layers of confusion have been generated, it is not easy for the mind to know appropriately, and make decisions correctly, which worsens the ability to respond to a new situation in a fruitful manner. Healing means restoring the original details of life events and mind's capacity to respond and function without corruption, confusion, or misrepresentation.

When the person actively progresses his experience through the eidetic exercises, a new process of encounter occurs in the mind. At the critical point where the problem lies, the original event is brought into focus and understood. In the process, the person comes to know his natural life in the situation where it was corrupted by pressure, confusion, or trauma. He rebuilds the original perspective all over again on the foundations of Nature.

In this light, neurosis is not at all difficult to understand. Clearly, one needs to study what light eidetics throw on the relationship between natural structures and mental illness in general. A study program can help the individual in understanding the general structure of neurosis and psychosis, viewed from the eidetic standpoint. This can provide a context to the specific information presented in the book. The present chapter serves this purpose of guiding the interested individual as well as the professional in the direction of further information on application of eidetics.

The essence of the eidetic approach presented in this work has specific applications. The reader is instructed to acquaint himself thoroughly in all its facets and learn its application in a practical manner. A wider application of the eidetic process in the various areas not covered in this work have been described in the earlier books. The interested reader who wants to further educate himself about application of the eidetic in other areas of mental disturbance should use the reference guide to these works which is presented below. For reference to specific readings on concepts and procedures, the notation used is: the topic for study, the name of the book, and the page number. Each book is briefly referred to by an initial as follows:

Basic Concepts in Eidetic Psychotherapy: **B**
Eidetic Parents Test and Analysis: **E**

A Guide for Further Study

History of the Eidetic Theory and Method, **E:** 11–29; **B:**19–51
The Nature of Words and their Limitation as a Vehicle of Experience, **B:** 24, 47–51, 57–65
Visual Experience and its Expressive Functions in the Psyche, **B:** 69–77, 81–89
Pure Perception and Images of the Self, **B:** 209–221
How One Gets Visually Fixated on Negative Memories, **B:** 105–117, 122–130
Fearful Remoteness from Important Experiences, **B:** 33–34, 98–99, 134–141

Neurotic Equilibrium of Memories, **E:** 24, 163–164
The Nature of the Individual's Autonomy, **B:** 34–40
Is Identity Merely What You Think You Are, **B:** 33–40, 209–221; **E:** 26, 128, 172–178, 200–205
The Undifferentiated Unity of Experience in the Eidetic, **B:** 229–230
How Images, Words, and Wishes Are Found Mixed in the General Experience, **B:** 225–231, 246–248
Defense Against Experience of Images and Repression, **B:** 47–51; **E:** 22, 26, 29, 39–44, 49–50, 159, 160, 162–163, 174, 177–178
On the ISM Structure, **B:** 30–32, 84–87, 96; **E:** 18
On Personality Multiples, **B:** 32, 93–102, 133–144
Emanation Behavior of Images Leaping out of Images, **B:** 95–98, 134–137
Magical Behavior of Images, **B:** 32, 47, 147–181
Structures Composed of Mythology, **B:** 231–245, 248–249, 395–434
Parallel Projection into Objects and People, **B:** 100–102
Bipolarity, How Images Oppose Each Other, **B:** 32, 36–40, 88–89, 121–130
Simultaneous Appearance of Opposites, **B:** 36–40
The Nature and Behavior of Parental Images, **B:** 185–206, 231–249, 395–434
Mutilated Images of Parents, **E:** 50, 161–162
Specific Behavior of Mother Image, **B:** 194–206, 231–245, 257–391; **E:** 24–25, 124–126, 163, 166, 168, 176–177
Specific Behavior of Father Image, **B:** 195–206, 231–245, 357–391; **E:** 24–25, 165–166, 176–179
Age Projection Test, **B:** 137–140, 149–150, 245–247, 253–261
Eidetic Parents Test, **B:** 262–288; **E:** 34–50, 51–111, 230–241
How to Give Brief Eidetic Parents Test, **E:** 152–156
Making a List of Positive and Negative Images of Parents, **E:** 168–169, 190–194
Nature of Identification with Negative Aspects of Parents, **E:** 172–179, 200–205
Nature of Conflict, and How to Study It, **E:** 17–27, 129–133
Activating the Mind through Eidetics, **E:** 114–133
How to Create Internal-to-Internal Causation in Mental Events, **E:** 17–24, 133–150
How Developmental Dynamics Are Revealed through Eidetics, **E:** 158–178
EPT Instructions with Images of Natural Parents (Psychosomatic Column), **E:** 52–110
How to Explore Parental Images during the EPT (Exploratory Column), **E:** 53–111
How to Interpret the Parental Images Appearing in the EPT (Interpretive Column), **E:** 53–111
Analytic Guide Involving the Following Aspects of Eidetic Response
    Primary Response to Instructions, **E:** 114, 158–183
    Primary Picture with Feelings, **E:** 115
    Associated Memories, **E:** 115

Experiential Interpretation, **E:** 116
Deepening of Primary Response, **E:** 116–118
Resistance to Picture Experience, **E:** 118–120
Overt Behavior, **E:** 120, 161, 163
Lack of Awareness, **E:** 120–121
Interaction between Parents, **E:** 121–123, 163–165, 184–186
Interaction with Father, **E:** 123–129, 165–166, 186–188
Interaction with Mother, **E:** 124–126, 166–168, 188–190
Reaction to Interactions, **E:** 126
Empathy in Interactions, **E:** 127, 172–179, 200–205
Conscious Views, **E:** 129
C-I-G (Consciousness-Imagery Gap) as Scope for Mental Change, **E:** 129–130, 170–172, 194–200
Reaction to C-I-G as Groundwork for Mental Change, **E:** 25, 26, 130–133, 170–172, 194–200
The Eidetic Treament Method for Psychosomatic, Hysterical, and Psychoneurotic Symptoms with Representative Case Histories
    A Case of Post-Accident Trauma and Mental Fatigue, **B:** 106–111, 123–125
    A Case of Hysterical Pain at the Back of the Head, **B:** 329–331
    A Case of Neuralgic Pain at the Side of the Neck, **B:** 293–309
    A Case of Dizziness and Fear of Being Alone, **B:** 311–319
    A Case of Menstrual Pain, **B:** 341–342
    A Case of Bad Eyes, Blepharitis, **B:** 350–351
    A Case of Duodenal Pain, **B:** 352
    A Case of Ulceration and Swelling, **B:**345
    A Case of Dysentery, **B:** 343–344
    A Case of Chronic Constipation, **B:** 346–347
    A Case of Ulcerative Colitis, **B:** 340
    A Case of Recurrent Common Cold, **B:** 348–349
    A Case of Asthma, **B:** 339
    A Case of Mild Depressions and Insomnia, **B:** 112–116
    A Case of Loss of Speech, **B:** 321–327
    A Case of Compulsive Weeping, **B:** 333–335
    A Case of Muscular Cramps, **B:** 137–139
    A Case of Severe Jealousy, **B:** 149
    A Case of Somnambulism, **B:** 149
    A Case of Phobias, **B:** 133–137, 395–405
    A Case of Sexualized Fear of Father, **B:** 357–391, 432–434
    A Case of Hysterical Psychosis (Menstrual Hysteria), **B:** 353–354
Eidetic Treatment Methods for Healing Disturbed Functions in the General Area of Psychoses and Personality Dysfunction
    Treating Ego Functioning in Schizophrenia, **E:** 148–150, 139–146
    Treating Thought, Feeling, and Memory, **E:** 21–22, 139–144

Treating Obsessive-Compulsive Reactions, **E:** 146–147
Treating Hysterical and Phobic Reactions, **E:** 49, 147–148, 160–163; **B:** 253–261
Treating Anxiety and Depression, **E:** 137–139
Treating Drive for Acting Out, **E:** 134–135
Treating Relationship with Others, **E:** 134–137
Treating Personality and Life Patterns, **E:** 145–146
Treating Marital and Family Problems, **E:** 206–241

Bibliography

Ahsen, A. *Eidetic Psychotherapy: A Short Introduction.* New York: Brandon House, 1965.

Ahsen, A. *Basic Concepts in Eidetic Psychotherapy.* New York: Brandon House, 1968.

Ahsen, A. *Eidetic Parents Test and Analysis.* New York: Brandon House, 1972.

Ahsen, A. Eidetics: An overview. *Journal of Mental Imagery,* Spring, 1977, in press.

Ahsen, A. Idein: The real meaning of ideomotor. Paper presented at the Eidetic Analysis Institute, Yonkers, New York, 1975.

Ahsen, A. Anna O. — Patient or therapist? An eidetic view. In V. Franks and V. Burtle (Eds.), *Women in Therapy,* Brunner/Mazel, New York, 1974.

Ahsen, A. Eidetics: A visual psychology. Invited Address, American Psychological Association, 81st Annual Convention, Montreal, Canada, 1973.

Ahsen, A. & Lazarus, A. A. Eidetics: An internal behavior approach. In A. A. Lazarus (Ed.), *Clinical Behavior Therapy,* Brunner/Mazel, New York, 1972.

Ahsen, A. The nature and behavior of pure eidetics. Doctoral dissertation, University of the Panjab, 1970.

Ahsen, A. Eidetic images of parents, their relationship with symptoms and character formation. Paper presented at The Psychological Society, Rawalpindi, 1964.

Ahsen, A. Eidetic images: A study of imagery steps for the evocation of mental structures. Paper with data presented at The Psychological Society, Rawalpindi, 1962.

Ahsen, A. Experimental study of the eidetic mana in dress, costume, and disassociable body organs, such as shirts, hats, nails, teeth, involving 31 subjects. Presented at Government College Psychological Society, Lahore, 1959.

Ahsen, A. Eidetic images of parents: Fifty basic experiments of repeatable relationships between parental images and body feelings; Summary and data. Paper presented at The Psychological Society, Rawalpindi, 1959.

Ahsen, A. Urethral anxiety and mental expression: Psychological influence of micturition muscles over facial and abdominal muscles and other ideomotor muscular patterns. Paper presented at The Psychological Society, Rawalpindi, 1958.

Ahsen, A. An experimental study of free association, dream imagery, and yogic-concentration imagery of Shiva. Paper presented at Government College Psychological Society, Lahore, 1956.

Ahsen, A. An examination of the concept of death instinct. M. A. Diss., University of the Panjab, 1954.

Ahsen, A. Experiences from the thumb: A study of spontaneous phantasy correlate during nail etching on paper. Paper presented at Government College Psychological Society, Lahore, 1953.

Ahsen, A. An experimental study of mental resistance to falling objects. Paper presented at the Annual Meeting of the Pakistan Science Conference, Lahore, 1952.

Ahsen, A. Simultaneous contradiction: Study of a basic psychological phantasy in metaphysics. Paper presented at the Philosophical Society, Government College, Lahore, 1950.

Allport, G. W. Eidetic imagery. *Brit. J. Psychol.*, 1924, *15*, 99–110.

Anderson, L. M. Personality characteristics of parents of neurotic, aggressive, and normal preadolescent boys. *J. Consult. Clin.Psychol.*, 1969, *33*, 575–581.

Anderson, R. E. Where's Dad? Paternal deprivation and delinquency. *Arch. Gen. Psychiat.*, 1968, *18*, 641–649.

Andry, R. G. Paternal and maternal roles in delinquency. In *Deprivation of Maternal Care.* Public Health Paper No. 14. Geneva: World Health Organization, 1962, 31–43.

Antrobus, J. S., Antrobus, J. S. & Singer, J. L. Eye movements accompanying daydreaming, visual imagery and thought suppression. *J. Abnorm. Soc. Psychol.*, 1964, *69*, 244–252.

Arnheim, R. *Visual Thinking.* Berkeley: University of California Press, 1971.

Barber, T. A. Hypnotically hallucinated colours and their negative after images. *Amer. J. Psychol.*, 1964, *77*, 313–318.

Barratt, P. E. Use of the EEG in the study of imagery. *Brit. J. Psychol.*, 1956, *47*, 101–114.

Berry, W. The fight of colours in the after-image of a bright light. *Psychol. Bull.*, 1922, *19*, 307–337.

Betts, G. H. *The Distribution and Functions of Mental Imagery.* New York: Columbia University Teacher's College, 1909.

Biller, H. B. Father-absence and the personality development of the male child. *Dev. Psychol.*, 1970, *2*, 181–201.

Biller, H. B. & Weiss, S. The father-daughter relationship and the personality development of the female. *J. Genet. Psychol.*, 1970, *114*, 79–93.
Bowlby, J. *Attachment and Loss—vol. I, Attachment*. New York: Basic Books, 1969.
Bowlby, J. *Attachment and Loss—vol. II, Separation Anxiety and Anger*. New York: Basic Books, 1973.
Brill, N. Q. & Liston, E. H., Jr. Parental loss in adults with emotional disorders. *Arch. Gen. Psychiat.*, 1966, *14*, 307–314.
Brownfield, C. A. *Isolation: Clinical and Experimental Approaches*. New York: Alfred A. Knopf, 1965.
Bugelski, B. R. Words and things and images. *Amer. Psychol.*, 1970, *25*, 1002–1012.

Costello, C. G. The control of visual imagery in mental disorder. *J. Ment. Sci.*, 1957, *103*, 840–849.

Day, R. H. On interocular transfer and the central origin of visual after–effects. *Amer. J. Psychol.*, 1958, *71*, 784–790.
Dolan, A. T. Introduction. In A. Ahsen, *Eidetic Parents Test and Analysis*, Brandon House, New York, 1972.
Dolan, A. T. & Sheikh, A. A. Short-term treatment of phobia through eidetic imagery. Paper presented at the Eidetic Analysis Institute, Yonkers, New York, 1975, in press.
Dolan, A. T. & Sheikh, A. A. Eidetic therapy: Ahsen-Penfield psychotherapy-process model. *J. Contemp. Psychother.*, in press.
Doob, L. W. Exploring eidetic imagery among the Kamba of Central Kenya. *J. Soc. Psychol.*, 1965, *67*, 3–22.
Doob, L. W. Eidetic imagery: A cross-cultural will-o'-the-wisp? *J. Psychol.*, 1966, *63*, 13–34.
Doob, L. W. Correlates of eidetic imagery in Africa. *J. Psychol.*, 1970, *76*, 223–230.

Fisher, S. Body image boundaries and hallucinations. In L. J. West (Ed.), *Hallucinations*, Grune & Stratton, New York, 1962.
Freedman. S. J., Grunebaum, H. V., Stare, F. A. & Greenblatt, M. Imagery in sensory deprivation. In L. J. West (Ed.), *Hallucinations*, Grune & Stratton, New York, 1962.
Freides, D. & Hayden, S. P. Monocular testing: A methodological note on eidetic imagery. *Percept. Mot. Skills*, 1966, *23*, 88.
Freud, S. *Collected Papers*. International Psycho-Analytical Library. London: Hogarth Press and Institute of Psycho-Analysis, 1925.

Gazzaniga, M. S. The split brain in man. In T. J. Teyler (Ed.), *Altered States of Awareness*, W. H. Freeman & Co., San Francisco, 1972. (See also M. Pines' article, "We are left-brained or right-brained," in *The New York Times Magazine*, Sept. 9, 1973.)

Goldin, P. C. A review of children's reports of parent behaviors. *Psychol. Bull.*, 1969, *71*, 222–236.

Golla, F. L., Hutton, E. L. & Walter, W. G. The objective study of mental imagery I. Physiological concomitants. *J. Ment. Sci.*, 1943, *89*, 216–223.

Haber, R. N. & Haber, R. B. Eidetic imagery I: Frequency. *Percept. Mot. Skills*, 1964, *19*, 131–138.

Hanawalt, N. G. Recurrent images: New instances and a summary of the older ones. *Amer. J. Psychol.*, 1954, *67*, 170–174.

Harris, C. S. & Haber, R. N. Selective attention and coding in visual perception. *J. Exp. Psychol.*, 1963, *65*, 328–333.

Hetherington, E. M. & Frankie, G. Effects of parental dominance, warmth, and conflict on imitation in children. *J. Pers. Soc. Psychol.*, 1967, *6*, 119–125.

Holt, R. R. Imagery: The return of the ostracized. *Amer. Psychol.*, 1964, *19*, 254–264.

Holt, R. R. & Goldberger, L. *Personological Correlates of Reactions to Perceptual Isolation.* WADC Tech. Rep. 59-753. Wright-Patterson A. F. B., Ohio, 1959.

Horowitz, M. J. The imagery of visual hallucinations. *J. Nerv. Ment. Dis.*, 1964, *138*, 513–523.

Jaensch, E. R. *Eidetic Imagery.* Trans. by Oscar Oeser. New York: Harcourt Brace & Co., 1930.

Jordan, S. The assertive person: Assertiveness training through group eidetics. American Group Psychotherapy Association Meeting, San Francisco, 1977, in press.

Kamiya, J. Posterior alpha wave characteristics of eidetic children. *Psychophysiology*, 1974, *11*, 603–606.

Khaldun, Ibn. *The Muqaddimah.* Trans. by Franz Rosenthal. New York: Bollingen Foundation, 1967.

Kirlian, Semyon & Valentina. "Pictures of an unknown aura," article by S. Aaronson in *The Sciences.* New York: The New York Academy of Sciences, January/February, 1974, 15–22.

Klüver, H. Studies on the eidetic type and on eidetic imagery. *Psychol. Bull.*, 1928, *25*, 69–104.

Klüver, H. The eidetic child. In C. Murchison (Ed.), *A Handbook of Child Psychology*, Clark University Press, Worcester, 1931.

Klüver, H. Eidetic phenomena. *Psychol. Bull.*, 1932, *29*, 181–203.

Kubie, L. S. Discussion on papers by Drs. Cobb and Penfield, *A. M. A. Arch. Neurol. Psychiat.*, 1952, *67*, 191–195.

Kubzansky, P. E. Creativity, imagery and sensory deprivation. *Acta Psychol.*, 1961, *19*, 507–508.

Lazarus, A. A. *Multimodal Behavior Therapy.* New York: Springer Publishing Co., 1976.

Leuner, H. The interpretation of visual hallucinations. In *Psychopathology and Pictorial Expression,* Sandoz, 1963.

Luce, R. A. The new eidetic psychotherapy. Paper presented at the Ethical Society, Philadelphia, 1968.

Müller, M. *Natural Religion.* The Gifford Lectures delivered before the University of Glasgow in 1888, London, 1889.

Nash, J. The father in contemporary culture and current psychological literature. *Child Dev.,* 1965, *36,* 261–297.

Paivio, A. On the functional significance of imagery. *Psychol. Bull.,* 1970, *73,* 385–392.

Panagiotou, N. & Sheikh, A. A. Eidetic psychotherapy: Introduction and evaluation. *Int. J. Soc. Psychiat.,* 1974, *20,* 231–241.

Panagiotou, N. & Sheikh, A. A. The image and the unconscious. *Int. J. Soc. Psychiat.,* in press.

Pavlov, I. P. *Conditioned Reflexes and Psychiatry.* Trans. and ed. by E. Horsley Gantt. New York: International Publishers Co., 1941.

Penfield, W. Memory mechanisms. *A. M. A. Arch. Neurol. Psychiat.,* 1952, *67,* 178–191.

Penfield, W. The interpretive cortex. *Science,* 1959, *129,* 1719–1725.

Penfield, W. The brain's record of auditory and visual experience—a final summary and discussion. *Brain,* 1963, *86,* 595–696.

Piaget, J. *Play, Dreams and Imitation in Childhood.* New York: W. W. Norton & Co., 1962.

Piaget, J. *The Origins of Intelligence in Children.* New York: W. W. Norton & Co., 1963.

Pinard, W. J. Spontaneous imagery: Its nature, therapeutic value, and effect on personality structure. *Boston University Graduate Journal,* 1957, *5,* 150–153.

Pritchard, R. M., Heron, W. & Hebb, D. O. Visual perception approached by the method of stablized images. *Canad. J. Psychol.,* 1960, *14,* 67–77.

Purdy, D. M. Eidetic imagery and plasticity of perception. *J. Gen. Psychol.,* 1936, *15,* 437.

Radhakrishnan, S. (Ed.) *The Principal Upanishads.* London: George Allen & Unwin Ltd., 1953.

Reiff, K. & Sheerer, M. *Memory and Hypnotic Age Regression.* New York: International Universities Press, 1959.

Ribot, T. A. *The Psychology of Emotion* (2nd ed.). London: Scott, 1911.

Richardson, A. The place of subjective experience in contemporary psychology. *Brit. J. Psychol.,* 1965, *56,* 223–232.

Richardson, A. *Mental Imagery.* New York: Springer, 1969.

Robson, K. S. The role of eye-to-eye contact in maternal-infant attachment. *J. Child Psychol. Psychiat.,* 1967, *8,* 13.

Rogatus, Bro. Eidetic ability in boys of various nationalities. M. A. Diss., Catholic University, 1933.
Rosenthal, M. S., Ni, E., Finkelstein, M. & Berkwits, G. K. Father-child relationships and children's problems. *Arch. Gen. Psychiat.*, 1962, 7, 360-373.

Sarmousakis, G. Eidetic analysis: A comparison with other imagery techniques. Paper presented at Eidetic Analysis Institute, Yonkers, New York, 1970.
Sebeok, T. A. (Ed.) *Myth: A Symposium.* Bloomington: Indiana University Press, 1968.
Sheehan, P. W. A shortened form of Betts' Questionnaire Upon Mental Imagery. *J. Clin Psychol.*, 1967, 23, 386-389.
Sheehan, P. W. (Ed.) *The Function and Nature of Imagery.* New York: Academic Press, 1972.
Sheikh, A. A. & Panagiotou, N. Use of mental imagery in psychotherapy: A critical review. *Percept. Mot. Skills*, 1975, 41, 555-585.
Sheikh, A. A. Eidetic psychotherapy. In J. L. Singer & K. Pope (Eds.), *The Power of Human Imagination,* Plenum Publishing Corp., New York, 1977, in press.
Sheikh, A. A. Treatment of insomnia through eidetic imagery: A new technique. *Psychol. Reports*, in press.
Sheikh, A. A. Left-right in the brain: Hemispheric projection of eidetic parents among college students. Unpublished manuscript, Marquette University, 1975.
Siipola, E. M. & Hayden, S. D. Exploring eidetic imagery among the retarded. *Percept. Mot. Skills*, 1965, 21, 275-286.
Simpson, H. M., Paivio, A. & Rogers, T. B., Occipital alpha activity of high and low visual imagers during problem solving. *Psychon. Sci.*, 1967, 8, 49-50.
Singer, J. L. & Antrobus, J. S. Eye movements during fantasies. *Arch. Gen. Psychiat.*, 1965, 12, 71-76.
Singer, J. L. *Imagery and Daydream Methods in Psychotherapy and Behavior Modification.* New York: Academic Press, 1974.
Straus, M. & Brown, B. W. *Family Measurement Techniques* (2nd ed.). Abstract: Eidetic Parents Test by Akhter Ahsen. Minneapolis: University of Minnesota Press, 1977, in press.
Sumner, F. C. & Watts, F. P. Rivalry between uniocular negative after-images and the vision of the other eye. *Amer. J. Psychol.*, 1936, 48, 109-116.

Tasch, R. J. Interpersonal perceptions of fathers and mothers. *J. Genet. Psychol.*, 1955, 87, 59-65.

Urbantschitsch, V. *Ueber subjektive optische Anschauungsbilder.* Leipzig und Wein: Deuticke, 1907.

Wolpe, J. *The Practice of Behavior Therapy.* New York: Pergamon Press, 1969.

Yuille, J. C. & Paivio, A. Latency of imaginal and verbal mediators as a function of stimulus and response concreteness–imagery. *J. Exp. Psychol.*, 1967, 75, 540–544.

Zuckerman, M. Perceptual isolation as a stress situation. *Arch. Gen. Psychiat.*, 1964, *11,* 255–276.

Index

Ahsen, Akhter, eidetic method, 15–43
  idein, root meaning of idea, 26–27, 31–33
  undifferentiated unity of mental levels, 29–32
  psychofeedback, 95–98
  phenomenology, 16, 34
  dialectics, 16, 30, 36–41
  psychoanalysis, 19, 24, 25, 37, 40
  behaviorism, 7, 24–25, 34, 36–40
  synthesis of schools, 24–25
  self-education and psychotherapy, 5–8, 34, 39–40, 115–116, 138
Allport, G., 30
Analysis, levels and forms of
  basic analysis levels, 141–142
  orientation exercises, 153–179
  therapy process model, 118–137
  individual or personal analysis, 139–142
  consciousness friends, 142–144
  family and marriage counseling, 144–145
  group therapy, 145–146, 242–262
  a map of investigations, 114–115
  therapist's self-analytic model, 116–118
Analysis of parental ground
  mother images
    mother's symptoms, 156, 158
    maternal ground, 133–134
    deep interaction with, 107–112, 134–136
    inversion process, 61
    early image, 170
    early anger and pity associated with the mother image, 61–62
    images of depressed mother, 62–63
    quarrelling images of parents, 63–65
    mother: communication image, 65–67
    positive mother, 170, 171, 174
  father images
    father's symptoms, 157, 159
    deep interaction with, 107–112, 134–137
    double-faced emotions concerning father, 67
    lifting image, 172
    father: communication image, 67–68
    positive father, 68–69, 172–173, 174
    father in the evening, 69–70
    eidetic parents test: positive images of father, 70–71
    father: work image, 71–73
    father: humor image, 73–74
    father: man-monkey, 74
    helping father in his problem, 75–78
    resolution of identifications, 78, 106–107
Arnheim, R., 34, 47
Artist, 31, 38–39

Avoidance, 158–159
Attachment, feelings of, 104–105
Attention, passive, 132
  see Fixed attention

Basic analysis levels, 141–142
Betts, G. H., 47
Biofeedback, 45, 95–98
Biolatency, 51–53
Bipolarity, 25, 93–95
Body images of parents, 188, 190, 192, 194, 214, 216, 218, 224, 226, 230, 238, 240
Body experience, 148, 164, 166
Bogen, Joseph, 53
Bowlby, John, 58–60
Brain images of parents, 232, 234
Brain waves, and eidetic images, 84, 50–51, 56
Bugelski, B. R., 46

Catharsis, 164
Censorship, 18–19
  see C-I-G
C-I-G (consciousness-imagery gap), 33, 130–133, 257
  image gap, 131
  somatic gap, 131
  meaning gap, 132
Cognition, 34, 45–46, 51, 56, 77–78
Communication image of parents, 202, 204
Concentration, nature of, 18, 19, 44–46, 56–57, 83–84, 256
Conflict with parents, 21–22, 79–81
Confusion, 120
Consciousness friends, 142–144
Criteria for imagery distinctions, 28–30

Daydreams, 19, 31, 47
Defense, 18–19
  see C-I-G
Dialectics, 16, 30, 36–41
Dissociation, see C-I-G
Doob, L. W., 47
Double consciousness, 125
Dreams, 19, 25, 47, 132

Drinking image of parents, 228
Duplication of images, 250

Early consciousness, 57–60
Eating image of parents, 226, 228, 230, 238
Economic image of parents, 220, 222, 226, 228, 230, 238
Ego, 35–37, 80–81, 87–92
Eidetics
  definition and method, 14, 15–43, 44–57
  biolatency, 51–53
  stored, 16
  latent, 29–31
  ISM (image-somatic response-meaning), 17, 20–21, 30, 33
  personality multiples, 87–89, 125, 129–130
  emanation images, 89–91
  left-right hemispheric images, 53–56, 79, 184
  bipolarity, 25, 93–95
  C-I-G (consciousness-imagery gap), 33, 130–133, 257
  magical behavior of images, 92–93, 125–126
  experiments on experience, 86–111, 169
  levels of imagery, 141–142
  training in visualization, 116, 147–150, 177–179
  psychofeedback, 95–98
  psychosomatics, 26–28, 33–34
  empathy, 163, 231–241, 242–262
  negative images, 25, 35, 164–165, 168–169, 256–257
  negative-positive alternation, 95–98, 168–169, 257
  positive images, 25, 32, 35, 166–167, 170–177, 257
  nature images, 166, 174–176, 243–246
  longevity, 32, 26–33
  further reading on, 263–267
  can you see an eidetic?, 177–179
Eidetic parents test, 21–24, 160–163, 180–241

house image, 182, 212
left-right image, 184
separation or union image, 186
strength image, 188, 190, 192, 194, 224, 230
eye image, 196, 198, 200
observation image, 196, 198
voice image, 202, 204, 206
communication image, 202, 204
hearing image, 208, 210
understanding image, 210
intelligence image, 232, 234
giving and receiving image, 220, 222
economic image, 220, 222, 226, 228, 230, 238
warmth image, 214, 216, 218
love image, 236, 240
Eidetic tests
eidetic parents test, 21–24, 160–163, 180–241
age projection test (or symptom oscillation test), 100–102
Emanation images, 89–91
Empathy, 163, 231–241, 242–262
Experiments on experience, 86–111, 169
Eye as sun, 44
Eye image of parents, 196, 198, 200
Eye, third mental, 44

Family and marriage counseling, 144–145
Fantasy, 16, 23, 47, 69, 71–73, 125–127
Father images, see Analysis of parental ground
First consciousness, 57–58
Fixed attention, 17–19, 44–46, 57–58, 82–83, 94
Fixed views, 87, 113–114
Forgetting, repression, and unconscious, 47, 103–104
Free association, 19, 25, 47, 56
Freud, Sigmund, 16, 36, 40, 52
Frozen identity, 113–114

Gaps in consciousness, see C-I-G
Gazzaniga, Michael, 53–56

Giving and receiving image of parents, 220, 222
Gottheil, E., 31
Grandparents and other figures, 102, 131, 141, 182
Group therapy, 145–146, 242–262
introductory model, 247–248
first and subsequent sessions, 246–248, 249
picture, rules for concentration, 255–258

Haber, R. N., 271
Hallucination, 47
Heart image of parents, 236
Hearing image of parents, 208, 210
Hemispheric images, 53–55, 79, 184
Henning, H., 31
Homework for the patient, 25, 164–165
House, 182, 212
Humor, 73–75
Hypnagogic images, 19
Hypnosis, 47

Idea, 26–27
Idein, root meaning of idea, 26–27, 31–33
Identifications, resolution of, 78–81, 106–107, 113–114
Identity, 77–78, 84–86, 87–92, 98, 113–114, 137, 140
Ideoglandular, 26
Ideomotor, 26
Ideovascular, 26
Illusion, reality and, 46
Image experience, 16–18, 164–169
Imagination, 29, 47, 62, 91
Individual or personal analysis, 139–142
Initiative, 65–67
Inner assertiveness, 65
Internal causation, 20
Intelligence image of parents, 232, 234
Interpretation, 16, 119–128, 147, 257
Investigations, a map of, 114–115
Inversion process, 61
ISM (image-somatic response-meaning), 17, 20–21, 30, 33

Jaensch, E. R., 31
Jung, C. G., 24, 52
Justice and wisdom, 164

Kamiya, J., 47
Kirlian photography, 48–49, 51–53, 56

Laing, R. D., 40
Latent eidetics, 29–31
Lazarus, Arnold A., 7, 25
Left-right hemispheric images, 53–55, 79, 184
Light, experiential theory, 17–19, 44, 83
Longevity, 32, 26–33
Loss, feelings of, 105–106
Love image of parents, 236, 240

Magical behavior of images, 92–93, 125–126
Marburg school of psychology, 30–31
Marriage and family counseling, 144–145
Mass-image society, 242–246
Maternal ground, 133–134
Memory image, 30–31, 34, 57, 86–87
Mind-body unity, 33
  see Idein
  see ISM
Mother images, see Analysis of parental ground
Mutilation of images, 119

Nature images, 166, 174–176, 243–246
Negative images, 25, 35, 164–165, 168–169, 256–257
Negative-positive alternation technique, 95–98, 168–169, 257
Neurotic projection, 107
New member, introduction in group, 259–260

Objects, mental, 63, 71, 91–93, 127, 171, 173, 178–179
Orientation exercises, for individual analysis, 153–177
  group application of, 262

Pain and sympathy, 250
Paivio, A., 46
Parallel projection, 91–92
Parental ground, 142
Parental quarrel images, 63–65
Parents, relationship with
  eidetic parents, 21–22, 98, 182–240
  attachment to, 104
  imitation of, 105, 158–159
  reaction to, 105, 158–159
  avoidance, 158–159
  loss concerning, 105
  identification with, 106
  deep interaction with images of, 107–112, 134–137
  eidetic parents test interaction with parental images, 134–137
  adoption of parents in group therapy, 249
  see Analysis, levels and forms of
  see Orientation exercises
  see Analysis of parental ground
  see Group therapy
Parents as social issues, 242–246
Parents, conflict with, 21–22, 79–81
Past images, 84–87
Pavlov, I. P., 8, 36–40
Penfield, Wilder, 8, 49–51, 56
Personality multiples, 87–89, 125, 129–130
Phenomenology, 16, 34
Piaget, Jean, 57–58, 59–60
Picture, rules for concentration, 255–258
Positive group, 145–146, 242–262
Positive images, 25, 32, 35, 166–167, 170–177, 257
Preliminary exercises on images, 146–150
Problematic experience, reenacting, 119–128
Professional's analytic guide, 146
Psychical autonomy, 168–169
Psycheye, 44–81
Psychofeedback, 95–98
Psychosomatics, 26–28, 33–34
  see ISM
  see C-I-G

Resistance, 34
Ribot, T. A., 47
Richardson, A., 47

Self-Doubt, 102–103
Self-education and psychotherapy, 5–8, 34, 39–40, 115–116, 138
Semantics, 38–40
Separation or union image of parents, 186
Sheehan, P. W., 46
Sheikh, Anees A., 7
Sibling, 102, 131, 141, 144, 174, 182
Silence, speechful, 253
Situation elements, 164
Social object, picture as, 145, 244–245
Solution and action in images, 164–165, 250–251
Sperry, Roger, 53
Strength image of parents, 188, 190, 192, 194, 224, 230
Sympathy, 250
Symptoms: parallels to parental problems, 99–100, 154–159
  preparing list of, 107–109, 154–159
  experiencing in parents, 109–112, 156–157
  integration of information on, 114–115, 154–159
Symptoms in parents, 109–112, 156–157
Synthesis of schools, 24–25

Target recollection, 119–128
Therapist's self-analytic model, 116–118
Therapy process model, 118–137
Training in projection of images, 86–112, 116, 147–150, 168–169, 177–179

Understanding image of parents, 210
Undifferentiated unity of mental levels, 29–32
Unconscious, forgetting, repression and, 47, 103–104
  see Resistance, 34
  see C-I-G
Union or separation image of parents, 186
Upanishads, 48

Vague images, 131, 146, 161, 163, 182–241
Visualization, 249, 255–258
Vogel, Philip, 53
Voice image of parents, 202, 204, 206

Warmth image of parents, 214, 216, 218
Wolpe, Joseph, 7, 25
Words, 31, 38–40, 51–52
Work, 69, 71–78, 133, 247–253

Yuille, J. C., 46

Notes

Notes

Notes

Notes

Notes

Basic Concepts in

EIDETIC PSYCHOTHERAPY

Akhter Ahsen, Ph.D.

We are currently seeing a tremendous explosion of interest in imagery and eidetics. This fascinating book is for the inquisitive reader who wants to further educate himself about the eidetic and its special application in various neuroses and psychophysiological disturbances, such as phobias, depressions, compulsions, mental fatigue, and ulcerative colitis. This important work explores the negative nature of conscious mental control and the corruptions it imposes on the expressive functions of the psyche, causing a variety of mental distortions.

The process of eidetic treatment through release of specific images which cure disturbances is presented in this book in a rich dialogue form. The result is a lively, instructive and experiential study of the conflict process in movement. The format of the book is most useful to the student-therapist who wants to learn the intricacies of treatment in an eidetic setting. To study how exactly the neurotic process works and maintains itself, this book, with its vivid scenarios of activated imagery dialogue, is a must. Recommended especially for the wealth of knowledge and experience it reflects. The most stimulating and valuable volume you may have seen in recent years.

It deserves a wide and enthusiastic audience, and will reward the careful reader many times over.

—Ralph A. Luce, M.D.

Clothbound: 434 pages
Direct Order Special Price: $12.95
Regular Price: $17.50

BRANDON HOUSE, INC.

For orders write to P.O. Box 240
Bronx, New York 10471

Eidetic Parents Test and Analysis

A Practical Guide to Systematic and Comprehensive Analysis
Akhter Ahsen, Ph.D.

This widely acclaimed work is a goldmine of information on the meaning of specific eidetics. While working with the Eidetic Parents Test, the person may often ask the question, "What is the meaning of a particular image?" This book is a brilliant guide to the various levels of meanings, and explores them in all their minute details. For example, read below these interpretations of the first three items of the test.

> Ep1: If a parent is absent or extremely vague in the image, it indicates prolonged physical absence of the parent or an hostile relationship with that parent. A highly displaced and fantastic location of a parent suggests an underlying theme which can be surfaced by directly asking the subject about its possible significance.
>
> Ep2: Pronounced rigidity of the left-right positions indicates inflexibility in the parental relationship. Pronounced flexibility of the positions signifies a weak relationship with the parents, emotional isolation, or extreme fear of relating to the parents. Such problems result in a conscious ability to manipulate the figures at will.
>
> Ep3: A cold space around a parent indicates a cold parent; a warm space, a warm parent. Strength and vibration in the space indicate strength and vibration in the parent. Overly vague or dark images indicate withdrawal of the parent or withdrawal from the parent; shooting lights indicate extreme aggression.

The inquiring reader searching for specific levels and meanings of special images will find this book extremely rewarding.

> *The amount of practical imagery that can be revealed through the method described is . . . unmatched in the clinical literature. The book represents a methodological advance.* —The American Journal of Psychiatry

Clothbound: 256 pages
Direct Order Special Price: $12.95
Regular Price: $17.50

BRANDON HOUSE, INC.

For orders write to P.O. Box 240
Bronx, New York 10471